275

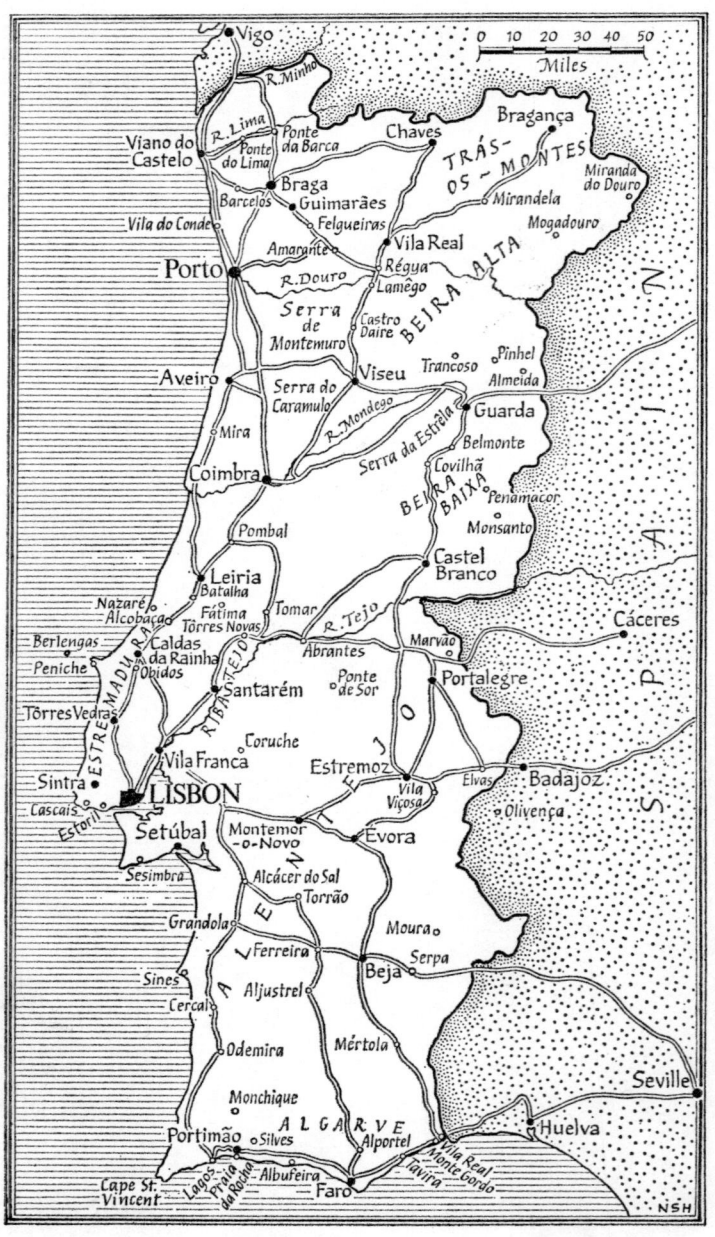

PORTUGAL

Henry Myhill

FABER AND FABER
3 Queen Square
London

First published in 1972
by Faber & Faber Limited
3 Queen Square London WC1
Printed in Great Britain by
Latimer Trend & Co Ltd Plymouth

ISBN 0 571 09640 9

© *1972 by Henry Myhill*

To PETER CRAWLEY
to whose unexpected invitation to write
a book about Portugal I owe one of the
happiest years of my life

CONTENTS

ILLUSTRATIONS

☙

13

FOREWORD AND
ACKNOWLEDGEMENTS

ɕ֍_ ⸾Ꙭ

'But surely there's no room for yet another book about Portugal?'

That was my own reaction, too, when the idea was first put to me. But the seed, once planted, grew.

'Write a book on Portugal'. The task lies in some comfortable median position on the line joining the schoolboy told to write an essay on his holidays, and the astronaut ordered to explore some new quarter of the moon. Previously, whenever I had wanted to learn more about another country, I had found that the best means was a university course organised there for foreigners. So I signed on for the *Curso Anual de Língua e Cultura Portuguesas* at Lisbon University.

This automatically gave me all sorts of facilities: a base in the capital, free medical and dental treatment, free entry to all Portuguese museums and monuments, the best university restaurant in Europe at which to eat, and to meet people from all over Portugal, and the opportunity to join some of them in excursions to supplement the many journeys I made in my motor caravan. Above all, it allowed me to attend some of the most interesting lectures I have ever enjoyed. I have endeavoured to incorporate in this book the little I retained out of the many good things placed before me; and my first acknowledgement is to those wise men at whose feet I was privileged to sit: Dr. Pina Martins, and Professors Lindley Cintra, Prado Coelho, Borges de Macedo, Pais da Silva, Pereira Neto, and Délio Santos.

A young neighbour of many years ago married a scion of one of Oporto's great port-shipping families. To them, Amyas and

15

Gillian Symington, I owe special treatment at Vila Nova de Gaia, and an introduction to Messrs. Sandemans' most hospitable factor up at Régua, Senhor José Pinto de Gouvêa. To the photographic department of the Direcção Geral do Turismo in Lisbon I owe all the photographs reproduced in this book. And to the Director of its Casa de Portugal in London I owe a most helpful letter of introduction.

A NOTE ON NAMES AND
PRONUNCIATION

Portuguese surnames, and many Christian names too, cannot be anglicised. Nor do we feel that they should be. Vasco da Gama sounds entirely appropriate.

This is not the case with some royal personages. It is only after some months in Portugal that the comic image conjured up by Dom Diniz fades into the statesmanlike figure of King Dennis, or that the unpredictable madcap O infante Dom Henrique merges into Prince Henry the Navigator.

Others, on the contrary, sound equally ridiculous in their English form. Emmanuel could never have presided over the flowering of Manueline architecture. After considerable hesitation, therefore, and consciously exposing myself to the charge of inconsistency, I have transcribed Diniz as Dennis, João as John, Duarte as Edward, Henrique as Henry (leaving Afonso Henriques untouched), Sebastião as Sebastian, Catarina as Catherine, Felipe as Philip, and José as Joseph.

Amongst commoners Camões has well earned his anglicisation as Camoens.

Having found that the constant appearance of São, Santo and Santa in the text puzzled and distracted me when first I was reading about Portugal, I have shortened all these forms to S.

All place-names are in their Portuguese form except for the time-hallowed Lisbon, Oporto, Tagus and Cape St. Vincent.

My publishers have suggested a note about the pronunciation of Portuguese. It is very far from being phonetic. Only practice enables one to recognise all the words whose final syllable almost disappears when spoken. Initial reactions to the numerous nasal sounds, *ão*, *ães*, *ões*, tend to be unfavourable. But with further familiarity comes an affection for the quaint final *o*, sounding like 'oo', for the variety of soft, caressing *s*s, and for the unique melancholy of a long diphthong like the *eir* of *feira* or *brasileiro*.

This melancholy, one of the caressing *s*s, and a disappearing final syllable are all exemplified in *saudade*, perhaps the most Portuguese word in the language. I found I had written this entire book, and used the word several times, without ever explaining its meaning. For it is so much a part of the very soil and soul of Portugal, that for anyone who has once been there an explanation seems superfluous. If I define it as a profound yet gentle sentiment of melancholic longing, I shall at least have given the reader a starting point from which to build up his own personal *saudade* for Portugal.

INTRODUCTION

Cabeça de Europa

1066 is the first date learned by every English schoolboy. Millions of other people around the world know it too, and believe it to be of great significance.

In 1066 a bastard called William, Duke of Normandy, won a victory near the Sussex town of Hastings. Later he built there an abbey called Battle, to commemorate the engagement by which England lost her independence.

Many books have been written explaining the importance of this event. It is said to have given England stronger government but also parliamentary democracy; to have made her part of Europe but also to have given her the institutions of a nation-state; to have brought in the feudal system but also a king strong enough to control his barons.

Many of its supposed results are contradictory. Most needed several centuries to ripen. And they were significant for the history of England rather than for that of the world.

Three hundred and nineteen years later a far more momentous battle took place. It set in motion a chain of events which in just over a century changed the face of the earth. Many of its consequences are with us still. But for every hundred people who know 1066 perhaps two know 1385.

In 1385 a bastard called John, Master of the Knights of Avis, won a victory near the Portuguese village of Aljubarrota. Later he built there an abbey called Battle, to commemorate the engagement by which Portugal retained her independence.

It was not his ambition, but popular choice which made John King of Portugal when the death of his legitimate stepbrother threatened her with absorption by Castile, her powerful neighbour. The victory was therefore a national victory. And it led to an upsurge of national consciousness and creative endeavour such as England experienced after the victory over the Armada, or Periclean Athens after the victory over the Persians.

Portugal is only a small country, as the Portuguese themselves are always telling you. It is in fact almost exactly the same size as the truncated Hungary which has emerged from the losing side in two world wars.

Try drawing a map of Hungary from memory, and see how little it corresponds to the shape it is meant to represent. Try even pointing to where Hungary ought to be on an outline map of Europe: the chances are that you will be several hundred miles off target.

It is easy enough to draw a rough map of Portugal, however. A long narrow rectangle. You have probably even remembered to indicate the estuary of the River Tagus, two-thirds of the way down, and the sharp point of Cape St. Vincent at the bottom left-hand corner. These things are almost built into the pattern of our minds. And if I were to ask whether you can indicate Portugal on an outline map of Europe you would feel offended. It is as obvious as Italy or Britain, and a good deal more obvious than France or Germany.

> '*Eis aqui, quase cume da cabeça*
> *De Europa toda, o Reino Lusitano,*
> *Onde a terra se acaba e o mar começa*'

> 'Behold here, almost the apex of the head
> Of all Europe, the Lusitanian Kingdom,
> Where the land ends and the sea begins'

wrote Camoens, the greatest Portuguese poet. If we agree with him that the Iberian peninsula looks like the head of Europe, we can continue the parallel by describing Portugal as the face.

There is more to this parallel than the literal shape on the map. Portugal is not simply the most advanced point of Europe. In the impetus generated by Aljubarrota she led Europe's advance into the modern world. No less an authority than Arnold Toynbee regards the invention of the caravel—the heavy ocean-going ship which could 'tack' and therefore sail against even a contrary wind—as the earliest of those great technical discoveries which allowed Europe to dominate the world for five centuries.

By means of this first technological breakthrough it was Portuguese ships which first struck out beyond the ancient limits of the narrow seas. They discovered and settled the uninhabited Atlantic islands of Madeira, the Azores, and Cabo Verde. Reaching West Africa they were rewarded with the gold of Guinea. And six years after Columbus discovered a New World of whose existence the Portuguese may already have been secretly aware, Vasco da Gama reached India.

For the next hundred years the face of Europe thus unexpectedly revealed to the East was the face of Portugal. It is important to remember how long ago this was in time, and how extensive in space. Many decades before the Pilgrim Fathers left Plymouth the ancestors of the de Sousas and da Silvas, who still play such a leading part in Ceylon's political life, were already living in the island they called Taprobana. The language which has left so much of its vocabulary in modern Malay was already being spoken in Malacca. Portuguese motifs were already being worked into their designs by the carpet makers of Persia.

Visitors to that treasure house on the Tagus, Lisbon's Museum of Ancient Art, sometimes miss a fascinating exhibit. In one of its remoter galleries stand two Japanese screens. Though executed with the simplicity which is the supreme skill of Japanese painters, they deserve a few minutes' study. For they depict visiting Portuguese merchants.

Observe first their ships. These have carried them either from Macao, a mere thousand or so miles away, or perhaps from the distant viceregal capital of Gôa on the farther coast of India. Though they are big enough to withstand these immense voyages, the artist has succeeded in indicating that the caravels did not carry large crews. For they needed room for all the provisions required at sea, and room too for merchandise.

Some of this merchandise has been unloaded on the beach with the help of some figures of darker skin than either the Portuguese merchants or their Japanese customers. These no doubt are Indians, already members of the Portuguese community in this early stage of that gigantic process of 'assimilation' which today incorporates a hundred and ten million people of all races, spread over five continents.

But although the screens represent only an early stage in that long process, they were painted at the high water mark of the maritime expansion which made the process possible. It was 1542 before the Portuguese reached Japan, and they date from a few decades later still. The clothes these merchants wear are not the heavy, square-cut draperies in which Vasco da Gama and his men arrived at Calicut in 1498. They are the trim doublet and hose of late Elizabethan times. Worn as here, in black, they remind us of two personalities of that period who are often represented in the same sober fashion: Philip II of Spain, and his enemy William the Silent who led the Dutch revolt against him.

That they should thus remind us is ironic. For these two men symbolise the forces which ended Portugal's golden century in the East.

For when young King Sebastian, and with him much of Portuguese manhood, was defeated and killed in Morocco in 1578, his nearest living relative after his aged celibate uncle was his great Spanish neighbour. Thus, nearly two hundred years after Aljubarrota, Philip II at last succeeded in uniting the crowns of Castile and Portugal.

It was never more than a personal union. But in those days of personal rule it meant that Portugal had to follow the same foreign policy as that of Philip's other dominions.

This meant that she had to go to war with England, her ally even before some of the famous English longbowmen had helped to win Aljubarrota. Without the Portuguese fleet Philip could never have mounted the Spanish Armada.

Naturally she had also to close her ports to the rebellious Dutch. The merchants of Holland, thus prevented from acquiring orien-

tal goods at Lisbon, decided to collect them directly. In the years
which followed they captured many of Portugal's dependencies,
from Curaçao where a Portuguese dialect is still spoken, to the
vast archipelago long known as the Dutch East Indies, where
half of Timor still remains Portuguese.

They tried to take even more, occupying Angola in Africa and
the northern parts of Brazil. But Portugal, restored to independence under the Bragança dynasty in 1640, reconquered these two
territories, and saved dominions elsewhere by a renewed alliance
with England.

In Japan, too, the Dutch succeeded the Portuguese, being for
two centuries the only outsiders allowed to trade there. The
citizens of both nations probably looked very much alike to the
Japanese, who on arrival in Europe have as much difficulty in
recognising individual faces as westerners on a first visit to the
Far East. The features of all the Portuguese reproduced on the
two screens are identical: the same bright eyes, sharp nose, and
bristling moustache under the same Guy Fawkes hat. Observe
that face as carefully as if it were your own. It is the face of
Europe.

Portugal then can claim to be the face of Europe by her shape
on the map, and by the fact that in her person Europe first made
direct contact with Africa south of the Sahara, with India, and
with the Far East. She is the face of Europe in yet another, and
still more essential sense.

Perhaps the cardinal characteristic of European culture in every
age has been its polarity: Roman and barbarian; Empire and
Papacy; Reformation and Counter-Reformation; Romantic and
Classical. Quarrels have often been violent, but fertilisations between the two opposites have always been fruitful. I use the
word 'fertilisation' deliberately, for there has been an almost
sexual relationship between an aggressive, thrusting, 'male'
north and a passive, creative 'female' south; between the out-
going Atlantic which has carried European civilisation to all the
other five continents, and the womb-like Mediterranean where it
was born.

Most European nations belong unequivocally to one pole or the other. The British, the Germans and the Scandinavians are as uncompromisingly Atlantic as the Greeks and Italians are entirely Mediterranean. Of the two lands with coast lines on both, France has succeeded better than Spain in harnessing their two cultures to the service of a common nationality. But only one country manages by its very position to create a unity out of their duality.

It may at first seem surprising that one of Portugal's greatest modern geographers, Orlando Ribeiro, has chosen to write of his own country under the title *Portugal: o Mediterrâneo e o Atlântico*. For, of course, it has no Mediterranean coast. Half of Andalusia separates the Straits of Gibraltar from the mouth of the Guadiana where Portugal begins.

Yet much of Portugal is essentially Mediterranean: in climate, in vegetation, and in way of life. The Algarve alone amongst Atlantic coasts competes with the Rivieras and the Costas for the retired of Northern Europe. The Serra da Arrábida, a mere fifteen miles south of Lisbon, steeply sloping to 'waters serene as those of an inland sea', is covered by 'the rarest survival of a primitive Mediterranean flora', where the visitor recognises rosemary, juniper, members of the cistus family, and many other friends from Provence. Among the cork oaks and pinewoods of the Alentejo he often feels himself in an undiscovered corner of Catalonia. 'Portugal is Mediterranean by nature, Atlantic by position,' declared another of her geographers.

That is perhaps going too far. There is nothing Mediterranean about the breakers which burst against the Cabo da Roca, Europe's most westerly point, or on the long beaches to the north of Oporto. There is an un-Mediterranean greenness about spring in the Minho, and a bitter edge to winter in Trás-os-Montes such as Mistral or Tramontano at their worst cannot bring.

The truth is that Portugal combines both worlds. The Minho has been likened to Ireland. But it is an Ireland with vines and oranges. The *terras frias* or cold lands of the Trás-os-Montes plateau drop suddenly to the *terras quentes* or hot lands of the Douro tributaries, where olives and almonds rise above the grapes which owe to the intensity of the sun the high sugar content which gives to port its sweetness and its strength. The golden beaches of the Algarve, on the other hand, are washed by vaster tides than those of any inland sea.

But it is in the capital that the two contrasts achieve the most perfect marriage. If Portugal is the face of Europe, then surely her eye is Lisbon.

I

THE CITY OF ULYSSES

1. UNDER POMBAL

Even when Lisbon is approached from the Atlantic, the first comparisons that come to mind are always with Mediterranean lands.

The tower of Belém, an ornamental but real fortress guarding the mouth of the Tagus, sparkles in a sun inimaginable in any northern sea. The lagoon-like expanse into which the estuary broadens upstream from this narrow mouth brings a reminder of Venice, even in the misty quality of the light which often hides the details of its farther shores. And to take one of the ferries from those farther shores is to be reminded, like thousands of earlier visitors, of the arrival at St. Mark's Square.

The vast Praça do Comércio, open to the river, has an older name still often in use, a name which evokes an older Lisbon: the Terreiro do Paço. *Paço* means palace, for Portuguese often contracts its ancestral Latin out of recognition: the ancestor in this instance is *palacium*.

Here until 1755 stood a building which was far more than a mere royal residence. It was Buckingham Palace, Whitehall and Somerset House thrown into one, with Chatham Dockyard at the back door. Of all that perished in the great earthquake of that year, it is the 'Somerset House' section of the palace which we most regret. For in that vanished tower lay the royal archives, with all the documents relating to the voyages of discovery and the settlements overseas. There, in an even richer mine than that provided by its Spanish equivalent, the Casa de las Indias at Seville,

27

modern historians could have dug for solutions to the many mysteries which still surround the Lusitanian heroic age.

The earthquake determined the city's present pattern. Everything built on the low-lying band of soft soil running north from the palace was destroyed by the tremors themselves, by the tidal wave which swept up it an hour later, and by the subsequent fires. Here, therefore, everything had to be rebuilt. The slate had been wiped even cleaner than the City of London's after the Great Fire, and the powerful Marquis of Pombal was able to give his architects planning powers Sir Christopher Wren would have envied.

To them we owe the government buildings which now surround the Praça do Comércio, painted now a water green which happily blends with the verdigris of the equestrian statue of Joseph I in the centre, the king whom Pombal served. Of a piece with them are the three parallel streets—Aurea, Prata and Augusta—which link the Praça do Comércio to Lisbon's second main square, the Rossio. Like the thoroughfares which run parallel with and at right-angles to them, they are narrow, and seem canyon-like although but a few storeys high. The name given to this commercial heart of Lisbon, the Baixas, which simply refers to its low-lying position, always sounds peculiarly appropriate.

Its restrained and functional architecture is due partly to the need to rebuild economically, with identical, almost pre-fabricated windows, and indeed only four types of house; and partly to the austere philosophy behind Pombal's benevolent despotism. The neo-Classical thus arrived half a century earlier than might have been expected in Portugal, where fashions tend to arrive late and to survive after their disappearance elsewhere. For this reason Rococo, which has left such unforgettable monuments in the north of the country, was hardly given the chance to develop in Lisbon itself.

Hardly ever known by its official name of Praça Dom Pedro V, the Rossio was the pulse of Lisbon even before the earthquake, although it then had a less regular shape than the rectangle it forms today. On the one side of this rectangle issue the parallel streets leading to the Praça do Comércio, with at one corner the excellent bookshop of the *Diario de Noticias*, one of the capital's leading dailies, whose status as an opinion-maker in Portugal was in the last century on a level with that of *The Times* in England.

Opposite stands the National Theatre, built in the 1840s on the initiative of Almeida Garrett, the greatest writer of Portugal's Romantic Movement, a Lusitanian Malraux, who fought in the liberal army and later took ministerial office.

Down one of the longer sides a more recent, and posthumously a more famous writer, Fernando Pessoa, used to sit writing for hours in the café of the Irmãos Unidos. Later a famous portrait was hung there showing this figure of the twenties seated, pen poised, his face a mask behind which might lurk any one of the 'heteronyms' or different personalities under which he wrote. And when in 1969 the café was closed to make way for a shop, the portrait was sold for the highest price recorded in the Lisbon art market.

The disappearance of the Irmãos Unidos has left only the terrace of the Suíça, alongside, for the newly-arrived visitor to sit and survey the Rossio's crowded scene: the flower-sellers on the central pavement of those black and white mosaics which are a feature of every city of the Portuguese world, and the crowds emerging from the underground railway—Lisbon's swiftest and most inexpensive form of transport. It is unfortunate that the routes of this scrupulously clean system serve the newer residential districts rather than the older quarters which the visitor will most wish to explore.

One corner of the Rossio leads into another square, that of the Restauradores who restored independence by shaking off Spanish domination in 1640. Here the visitor's attention is likely to be drawn neither by the extravaganza of the two-level railway station near the entrance, nor by the tourist information office in its elegant late eighteenth-century palace, and the twenty-four-hour Post Office which faces it, useful though all three will subsequently prove. The most riveting prospect is the magnificent ten-lane avenue which takes birth here.

If the Terreiro do Paço has been compared to the Piazza San Marco, the Avenida da Liberdade has with greater justice been likened to the Champs-Elysées. But again there are significant

differences. Though some of its buildings are every bit as luxuri-
ous as those of the French avenue, their quality is in general more
uneven. Its wide, tree-shaded pavements run like long islands
surrounded by lanes of traffic, with only one or two of the open-
air cafés which are the pride of Paris. But beyond the 'star' of
intersecting roads to which, like the Champs-Elysées, the Avenida
da Liberdade slopes gently upwards, it is Lisbon which triumphs.

For beyond the Arc de Triomphe lie merely more wealthy streets.
But the giant effigy of the Marquis of Pombal, high on a column
around which circulates the densest concentration of traffic in
Portugal, is backed by a steeply-rising park, whose wide paths
continue the Avenida da Liberdade right up to the horizon.

On one side of this park lies the Estufa Fria, or 'cold hot-house',
best described as a palm court to beat all palm courts. For me it
exemplifies an admirable Portuguese trait: the ability to conjure
up an atmosphere of past luxury at a minimum of expense. The
impressive sacred staircases of Lamêgo and of Bom Jesus at Braga
demand a minimum of upkeep. The countless employees tending
the vast gardens of Monserrate prove to be the trainees of the
State School of Forestry. And here, too, there is an illusion of the
Amazon or the Moluccas, a hint of orchids of immeasurable rarity,
in a hothouse without heat.

The view down the Avenida da Liberdade from the top of the
park (opened by and named after Britain's Edward VII) is even
better than the view up from its other end in the Restauradores
Square. Here the backcloth is the Tagus itself, while the frame is
the hills which hem in the low-lying land ravaged by the tremors
of 1755.

From the river to the Rossio, as we have seen, this is Pombal's
city, and symbolically his statue at the head of the Avenida presides, too, over the nineteenth- and twentieth-century extension
of the town plan laid down by him. These wide boulevards, bearing names like Alexandre Herculano or Sidónio Pais, which mean
little to the new arrival but which celebrate the greatest figures of
Portuguese literature and history, have indeed a Latin regularity.
But they are not specifically Mediterranean: they could belong
anywhere. We must climb those enclosing hills before we can

recover something of the older, pre-1755 Lisbon, or of its essential Mediterranean flavour.

2. BENEATH THE CASTLE

According to one of those legends which local patriots delight in inventing, Olisipo, the name by which Lisbon first emerged into history, is derived from Ulysses, credited by mythology as the first Mediterranean mariner to navigate the outer ocean. Any credence we might have given to the legend is destroyed by a further embroidery which takes him up the Tagus to seduce the daughter of a Lusitanian chieftain, who in committing suicide at his departure gave her name to Scalabis—the modern Santarém. But the legend often points towards a truth. Whether or not Ulysses ever visited Lisbon, Mediterranean men sailed and settled these as no other Atlantic shores.

The Phoenicians certainly knew them, even if we regard as far-fetched the claims that Peniche, Nazaré, and fishing villages even farther north show traces of Phoenician blood in their present-day inhabitants.

Under Rome, it fell to the most Mediterranean of all the Italian peoples to romanise the conquered Lusitanians. Language itself is here the clue. For although it is hazardous to guess exactly how long Portuguese has existed as a separate language, or how deep the differences which separated it from its neighbours in the remote past, some of these seem to go right back to the earliest times when Latin was spoken in these parts.

Very curious these differences are, too: just those which confound the traveller familiar with Spain who imagines that his Castilian will provide him with a ready passport beyond the Guadiana. There is that strange *o* or *a* standing by itself which proves to be the definite article. There is the letter written as *o* but pronounced as any other language would pronounce a *u*. Most idiosyncratic of all, there is that frightening, but in fact extraordinarily supple construction called the personal infinitive. What made them develop here and nowhere else in the Latin world?

Nowhere else—except in southern Italy, Sicily, and parts of Sardinia, where the same constructions are found in medieval documents, and still survive in local dialects. If this is not enough to prove a connexion, there are place-names, and even family names on tombs of the Roman period, to argue for a movement of colonists from these areas to the far west of Iberia.

But Portugal received her most recent Mediterranean immigrants from the southern shores of the inland sea. The older Lisbon we are about to visit is the city not so much of Ulysses as of Sinbad. Climbing only a few yards above the straight lines and right-angles of the Baixas we can soon lose our way in a very different kind of street plan: that of the north African 'kasbah'.

It is true that the modern Alfama, as this district is called, has inherited only its name and its street plan from the days when Lisbon was a Moslem city. Few buildings in London or Paris survive from the year 1147, when it was captured by Portugal's first king, Afonso Henriques, aided by groups of Crusaders travelling from northern Europe to Palestine by sea. And in Lisbon's case the inevitable replacements and rebuildings have been speeded on by the earthquakes which strike the city approximately every two hundred years. (That of the mid-eighteenth century had been preceded by one in the mid-sixteenth century, and that by one in 1344. Another is due any day.) But whereas the Baixas were destroyed in 1755, Alfama, because it is rooted on a rocky hillside, was merely shaken.

Paradoxically, indeed, one suspects that the need to rebuild the Baixas may have reprieved some older corners of the city. The tortuous narrow streets of medieval Europe were not so very different from the tortuous narrow streets of medieval north Africa. But medieval Rome was swept away by Mussolini. Medieval Paris was profoundly altered by Haussmann. Even medieval London was transformed by Wren. The Portuguese, even in the twentieth century, are just as capable of levelling a medieval quarter which gets in their way, as we shall see when we visit Coimbra. And in the eighteenth, with Brazil the world's greatest gold producer, they would have had the money to do so. Had there not been the necessity to rebuild elsewhere, who can

1. Lisbon: street in Alfama

2. Lisbon: the Tower of Belém

3. Lisbon: the façade of the Jerónimos

say that they might not have invented a need to rebuild Alfama?

The hill on which it straggles held the nucleus of the original city, before it spilled out over the Baixas and scaled the farther heights. Of this original city Alfama was only one quarter, and by no means the oldest. Clambering up the hill from the direction of the Rossio, for example, we shall pass through a less well-known district called the Mouraria, its equally Moorish origins indicated by its very name. And, like the knights of Afonso Henriques probing round the battlements which rise high above the narrow streets, we shall at last find an entrance to the Castle of St. George. Martin Moniz, one of those knights, placed his body within the closing gate, and in thus sacrificing his life opened a passage for his companions.

For us entry is easier—and it is free. The little plateau, defended by fortifications which are not only of medieval and Arab, but of Visigothic and even Roman construction, has been converted into a park for the people of the city which it dominates. Within the walls of the ruined inner fortress—though one can still walk along its battlements—ducks, swans, and even flamingos enjoy a series of artificial ponds. On the wide airy belvedere outside, white peacocks spread their tails alongside the visitor gazing out over the Tagus, and trying to recognise the various landmarks on the skyline.

It was not only for this view of the modern city that I used to take up to the Castle all my friends passing through Lisbon. For within a vaulted chamber, which alone remains of the royal palace which preceded King Manuel's on the Terreiro do Paço, lies a large-scale model of what Lisbon looked like on the eve of 1st November 1755. Here the task of recognition is not so easy. Only by consulting the key can we make out the irregular open space which was then the Rossio. Even on the hills many new monuments have arisen during the intervening two centuries, while the older ones seem often to have changed in appearance. The very building we are in was obviously bigger, and the nearby fortress was more than a mere shell.

For the tremors did not spare these hills, though their granite showed greater resistance. Leaving the castle by another gate, past a statue of Afonso Henriques pointedly presented by the city of Oporto (rubbing in the truth that it was Portuguese while Lisbon was still in Moslem hands), we pass a street of houses before leaving the outer line of defences. In the earliest days castle and city were almost one, and we find again and again, as at Bragança, Monsaraz, and Vila Viçosa, whole townships nestling within castle walls.

Continuing in the same clockwise direction that we climbed up to the castle, we shall come upon the *miradouro* of S. Luzia, one of the loveliest of the many belvederes which Lisbon at once merits and provides. Descending onwards we shall reach the Cathedral, built immediately after the reconquest of 1147, in a Romanesque style which owed much to the connexions with France established by Afonso Henrique's father, Henry of Burgundy. Not one of the country's seven Romanesque cathedrals has retained as much of its original fabric as, for example, the contemporary Norman cathedral of Durham. But Lisbon's seismic history has provided special excuses for restoration.

For the Sé (a relatively easy word to learn, which can be useful when trying to locate cathedrals) was badly damaged in the earthquake of 1344, and much of the Gothic reconstruction which then took place was itself destroyed in 1755. We can count ourselves lucky that the carved main doorway still survives and that the dark interior retains an essentially Romanesque atmosphere.

Although I do not suggest that the visitor should linger too long in this well-worn and rather unimpressive building, I shall devote another page to it in order to introduce two themes which will often recur as we travel round the country.

The first is its comparative insignificance. In what English city is it ever necessary to ask the way to the cathedral, whose spire or towers are visible from far away? Admittedly, medieval English dioceses were huge, with correspondingly high prestige expenditure on their mother churches. But there does seem to have been a tendency in Portugal for the secular church to get the second best. The really magnificent buildings were for the Orders: the Orders of Chivalry which played so prominent a part in the reconquest—and were appropriately rewarded in the resettlement—and the monastic Orders of both sexes, which undoubtedly made a particular appeal to the Portuguese temperament.

The second theme is the Baroque in Portuguese art. Sacheverell Sitwell, who revealed southern Baroque to the English-speaking world, also contributed *Portugal and Madeira* to the Batsford series 'Countries of Europe'. He transports his reader to a lush world of gilt convolutions and writhing mermen, and on arrival in Portugal the reader is rarely disappointed. Even in the remotest deserted convent he is liable to come across crumbling Joanine carving (from John V, whose munificent reign, fed by Brazilian gold, filled the first half of the eighteenth century). Visiting Belém or Tomar he may wonder if the relationship of Manueline to Gothic did not prefigure that of Baroque to Renaissance; whether there is not, indeed, a Baroque quality in the very soul of a country whose motorists' national plaques often bear a 'P' twisted and curved almost beyond recognition.

Yet there is little strictly Baroque architecture in Portugal, and much of what there is—as with other styles—is late. The earthquake which prematurely brought in the neo-Classical also destroyed much of the legacy of that personification of the Baroque, John V, who had died only five years earlier. But even his legacy was mainly in painting, sculpture, and above all in the decorative arts. It is these rather than their architecture which give to so many monuments the Baroque flavour which so appealed to Sitwell.

So it is with the Sé. I once attended a concert there of Baroque music sponsored by John V's twentieth-century successor in munificent patronage, the Calouste Gulbenkian Foundation. I wondered why this Romanesque building should have been chosen for the music of a culture in some ways even farther removed from that of the twelfth century than from that of our own. Surely there was something akin to sacrilege in exposing these stones from the age of Faith to the music composed for the *castrati* of a rarefied court by Domenico Scarlatti (who, like his son, undertook commissions for the Portuguese Royal Choir during his long years at Madrid)?

But as the first notes came from the organ I noticed its magnificent carved case. Then as the music poured forth the whole interior of the Cathedral, helped by those clever light effects at which the Portuguese excel, underwent a sea-change. Forgetting the Gothic ambulatory, with its stern granite tombs, my eye was drawn towards the open sacristy, furnished in eighteenth-century sculpted wood from Brazil, and to the *presépio* or Crib of the same period, whose scores of figures were carved by Machado de Castro with the same devotion to detail and Baroque love of movement that he gave to the statue of King Joseph in the Terreiro do Paço.

Above all I found myself gazing at the high altar,* which by its very position symbolises the achievement by John V of his greatest ambition. This was the elevation of the see of Lisbon to a Patriarchate, so that the Archbishop-Patriarch, like the Pope himself, could say mass facing (instead of with his back to) the congregation.†

In the Introduction I described John of Avis, the victor of Aljubarrota, as being raised to the throne by 'popular choice'. That choice took the form of an armed revolution at the very centre of Lisbon, which in 1383 was in the Limoeiro between the Sé and S. Luzia. Interesting comparisons can be made between this revolution and our own Peasants' Revolt of only two years earlier. But we know much more about it, because it has been described in detail in the *Crónica de D. João I* by Fernão Lopes, the first major prose-writer in Portuguese, and one of the earliest true historians in modern European literature. Thanks to Fernão Lopes we can still feel the atmosphere of the crowded streets as the quisling archbishop was thrown from the cathedral tower, and still see riding in the Tagus the ship prepared by John of Avis for his flight to England should the plot fail.

In this same heart of the old city was born, two centuries earlier still, in 1195, the *lisboeta* who is better known than any other Portuguese throughout the world at large. Indeed few of the

---

* *Altar-mor. Mor* derives from the Latin *major*. Again Portuguese has achieved the ultimate in contraction.

† A new generation of Catholics is growing up, of course, who have almost forgotten that this was once the prerogative of Popes and Patriarchs.

millions who pray to St. Anthony of Padua realise that he is Portuguese at all. But this particular prophet receives full honour in his own country, too. His feast on June 13th is the occasion of great processions, and opposite the Sé a small neo-Classical church bearing his dedication marks the site of his birthplace.

The Sé is the natural starting point for a detailed exploration of Alfama, though detailed exploration is really what it least demands. For one is searching not for specific monuments, of which there are few, but rather for an intangible savour. So wander at will, to the left, to the right, up a staircase here, down a cul-de-sac there. You will never be able to retrace your steps exactly, nor will you want to. In many places the authorities seem to have mounted a tidying-up operation, and here the pastel-shaded house-fronts and the newly-painted wrought-iron brackets of the gas-lamps might almost fit into Chelsea, recalling the centuries immediately after the reconquest when Alfama was the elegant, aristocratic suburb of the city above.

A few steps down from such a quiet, cleaned-up backwater will run a noisy, narrow street which is still what it was made into by the working and fisher-folk who took over the district in the fourteenth century. A kaleidoscope of laundry dries from the upper windows and balconies. At street level, faces we half recognise from Nuno Gonçalves, extras ready-made for a crowd-scene of Fernão Lopes, move in and out of the tiny grocers' shops and the swing-door taverns, while the *varinhas*—Lisbon's fish-wives—call their wares.

Then a street with a name like Judiaria will remind us that here lay the ghetto of Lisbon's powerful Jewish community.

Some of the roads run down towards the waterfront, to the pyramid-studded façade of the sixteenth-century Casa dos Bicos, and to the station of S. Apolónia, terminus of the lines from the north and the centre. A mile beyond, and to the north of the railway line, lies the church of Madre de Deus, with even finer Baroque furnishings than the Sé itself. But to conserve our energies we should proceed at a higher level. For our destination is the huge square church of gleaming white which reappears wherever a street is straight, or there is a gap between the crowded houses.

S. Vicente de Fora was built at the end of the sixteenth century by Felipe Terzi, an Italian architect appointed Master of Works for the Kingdom of Portugal by Philip II, whose dominions included half of Italy. It is modelled on that of the Jesuits at Rome, and is one of the first European churches where towers reappear after the Middle Ages. Within the rich interior a guide will take visitors to the Pantheon installed in the former monastic refectory. Here lie all the sovereigns of the Bragança dynasty, including the last, Manuel II, whom a British warship carried into exile in 1910, and whose body was brought back for burial by another British warship twenty-two years later.

S. Vicente marks the end of Alfama. Beyond it, under an arch, lies a welcome open space, the Campo Santa Clara. Here every Tuesday and Saturday is held the Feira da Ladra, a large second-hand market. I particularly enjoy the selection of Army surplus stores, which show interesting differences from our own, notably in the greater use of leather, of excellent quality.

Below the Campo S. Clara stands S. Engrácia, one of Portugal's rare Baroque churches. Its date, 1682, gives us a clue to this rarity. For the years from the declaration of independence from Spain in 1640 until the discovery of Brazilian gold in 1697 were years of war and economic crisis, when the value of Portugal's imports often exceeded that of her exports by as much as 400 per cent. Today S. Engrácia is also a Pantheon, but not for royalty. Here amongst others lie Almeida Garrett, Teófilo Braga, poet and first President of the Republic, and Marshal Carmona, also President of the Republic which he had helped to renew.

Higher still—indeed as high as the Castle itself, though on a different hill—stands the vast church of Graça, restored at the beginning of this century. And higher still is the tiny chapel of Nossa Senhora do Monte, where a woman will unlock a door revealing the stone chair of S. Gens, a bishop of Lisbon said to have been martyred, untypically, by the tolerant Arabs.

S. Gens must have an affinity with hills. The *pousada* a few miles before the frontier on the road to Seville stands on a hill crowned by a chapel bearing his dedication. And here in Lisbon this hill gives us the best opportunity to survey the new suburbs of the north without actually visiting them.

The main artery almost directly below, the Avenida Almirante Reis, runs out towards the airport less than three miles away—does any other capital have its airport so close?—and joins up with the first completed section of the motorway to Oporto. A rich district of new avenues lies between this and another artery, the Avenida da República. The Campo Pequeno square with its ugly red brick bullring breaks this last avenue shortly before it runs on north through a park, the Campo Grande.

From Nossa Senhora do Monte we can even distinguish some of the buildings which have made a veritable campus of the ridge beyond the Campo Grande. It is the corner of Lisbon where I spent most time myself, living in my motor caravan in a park full of flowering shrubs. This park lay between the Faculty of Letters, where I was attending the Course for Foreigners, and the University Restaurant, where twice a day I enjoyed a three-course meal (four choices of main dish), with wine included, for 12p. For further reading I had the National Library close at hand. When I needed a stamp I had only to walk across to the vast new teaching hospital of S. Maria, with its own post office.

There, in the city where influences from Atlantic and Mediterranean blend to give one of the mildest winter climates in Europe, I was equally comfortable, equally free of catarrh, in February as in May. Why did you return to Ithaca, o Ulysses?

3. AROUND THE ESTRÊLA

The view from Nossa Senhora do Monte is broken to the west by the heights which hem in the Baixas on the opposite side to the Castle. Clear against the skyline stands the neo-Classical silhouette of the huge basilica of the Estrêla, the work of Mateus Vicente who also showed himself, at Queluz, a master of the Rococo. He had also worked at Mafra, from which he has copied the cupola. It takes a long time to reach, not only because there is so much to see on the way, but also because the hills which make up so much of Lisbon's surface are nowhere steeper or closer together. From the very busiest part of town, indeed, ingenious arrangements have been devised to save us a climb: a tramcar adjusted to the gradient by having one end deeper than the other; and an extraordinary steel lift. We are not the least surprised to learn that it was designed by Eiffel (of the Tower).

This lift deposits us on a level with the ruined, roofless church of the Carmo, an eloquent witness of the great earthquake, which houses the poorly displayed collection of the Portuguese Archaeological Association, with some medieval tombs of interest. We can rejoice that no attempt was made at rebuilding, for the church was erected by John of Avis's commander at Aljubarrota, Nuno Alvares Pereira. Even at that early stage in his career he was noted for piety. After he died in 1431 in the convent adjoining this church, where he had taken his vows as a Carmelite brother eight years earlier, he became known to history as the Holy Constable.

The streets running north from the Largo (square) do Carmo lead to another square, where the church of S. Roque—another by Felipe Terzi—survived the earthquake with the loss of nothing more than its façade. This was fortunate, for it has the richest interior in Lisbon. Every side-chapel has things of interest, sixteenth-century *azulejos* (glazed tiles) or seventeenth-century paintings, but it is the chapel of St. John the Baptist, last on the left before the high altar, before which we should linger longest. This masterpiece of marbles and precious stones was created at Rome by artists commissioned by John V. And in the museum alongside (it can be reached either from the street or directly from the nave) are magnificent Baroque ecclesiastical jewellery and plate commanded from Italy by the same prodigal monarch.

S. Roque is nothing other than the chapel of the Misericordia. This is better translated as almshouse than as workhouse: the word means pity freely given, without Protestant overtones of retribution or of getting value for money. We shall find one in the smallest of Portuguese towns, always with a chapel in proportion to its size.

The Rua da Misericordia runs down to the Praça Luis de Camões, presided over by a statue of the one-eyed poetic genius

whose work not only crowned Portuguese literature, but con-
secrated it, just before the loss of independence made such a
consecration vital. Hearing of King Sebastian's defeat at Alcázar-
Quibir, he declared himself glad to die with his country. But he
had himself ensured the immortality of both.

We could have reached here more directly by climbing up the
steep, broad and fashionable Rua Garrett, familiarly known as the
Chiado. It has three pleasantly decorated churches of the 1780s,
and some of the best known of the teashops which have so much
more important a role in Portugal than in other parts of the Latin
world. Like English teashops, Portuguese teashops have no
chairs and tables out of doors on the pavement. Though tea is
drunk less than coffee, and on nowhere near the English scale, it
has an established place at all levels of Portuguese society. The
word for tea, *chá*, has exactly the same origin as the British 'cup o'
char'. It is one of many reminders of our common imperial past
in the Indian subcontinent.

Continuing the Rua da Misericordia, the Rua do Alecrim runs
at right angles to the Chiado but just as steeply, reaching the Tagus
at Cais do Sodré, terminus of the railway line to Estoril and
Cascais, near where the covered market is as colourful and entertaining as it is useful. With the continuation of the Rua da Misericordia in the other direction, this serves as a main artery up from
the river to one of the city's subsidiary centres, a busy oblong
square called the Rato.

This artery follows the ridge between the Baixas and the next
valley—to reach the Estrêla involves yet another descent and
climb. On its way it changes its name yet another three times.

From its first metamorphosis, it emerges as the Rua S. Pedro de
Alcântara on which is the Lisbon limb of the Port Wine Institute,
a palace of 1747 almost opposite another delightful *miradouro*. It
has a bar where every variety of port can be sampled. Do not
complain if your drink is a little more expensive than you antici-
pated: a glance at any grocery will reveal that port is by no means
cheap, even in the bottle, in its country of origin. The road is continued by the Rua Dom Pedro V, which has several antique
dealers, and a curious shop specialising in artefacts of cork. These

seem to make a particular appeal to Americans, to judge by the number of transatlantic honorary citizenships and life-memberships—all framed in cork—which the proprietor displays in his window. Finally, as the Rua da Escola Politécnica, the road runs past one entrance to the green oasis of the Botanic Gardens. They offer a convenient descent towards the middle reaches of the Avenida da Liberdade.

This road with five different names eventually ends in the Rato, from which radiate eight other streets. One goes down towards the column bearing the Marquis of Pombal. Others run up towards the new suburbs to the north. Another bisects the little quarter of Amoreiras under the shadow of the aqueduct of Aguas Livres—the only wholly utilitarian monument of that big spender, John V. The narrow Rua de S. Bento drops towards the well-placed Parliament buildings of the National Assembly, past the last tavern in Lisbon to serve wine kept and cooled by the age-old process of deep burial. Finally the Avenida Pedro Alvares Cabral leads gently up to the Gardens of the Estrêla, beyond which lies the great basilica itself.

In this part of the city, more than any other, one is liable to hear English voices and to see GB number plates. The British Council, whose library has a fine collection of English books about Portugal, is in a side-street between the Ruas da Escola Politécnica and S. Bento. The Anglican church of St. George lies just opposite the Garden of the Estrêla. Its beautiful tree-shaded cemetery shelters the tomb of Henry Fielding, whose 'Voyage to Lisbon' of 1754, undertaken for his health, was his last journey and his last work. The members of many non-Anglican Protestant communities who lie here include such unexpected figures as Admiral Horthy, Regent of Hungary from 1920 to 1945. Half an hour's walk amongst the graves is a lesson in Anglo-Portuguese relations over the past two centuries, telling of fortunes made in years of peace, and of lives lost in a dozen wars.

The present protagonists in those relations have their headquarters just round the corner, at the British Club. This also contains the office of the British Chamber of Commerce, which I personally found more helpful and more efficient than many other

Anglo-Portuguese institutions. The British Hospital, too, is a stone's throw away.

The British Embassy, along with most other diplomatic missions, lies in the district called Lapa, between the Estrêla and the river. An enclave within this quainter Kensington, however, is Madragoa, smaller and more strictly delimited than Alfama, but with an even greater proportion of fishing folk in its population.

Madragoa, like Alfama, has produced some notable singers of *fado*, that unique manifestation of Lisbon folk-culture. Like many other things in the city, it was probably imported, adopted and transformed. For its origins we should probably look to Brazil rather than to Africa. For although the word *fado* cannot be traced in Portugal before 1833, it was used in Brazil as early as 1819.

Two events probably assisted its migration. One was the liberation of the black slaves in Portugal in 1761. Many of these established themselves in Alfama, bringing a musical style and tradition eminently sympathetic to such an innovation.

The other was the return of the court to Lisbon in 1822 after fifteen years in Rio de Janeiro.

My personal feeling is that *fado* owes a great deal more than is generally allowed to the soil of Portugal. I shall never forget the shock I had when first I caught sight, on the sleeve of an LP, of the profile of its greatest practitioner, Amalia Rodrigues. I had expected someone dark, perhaps with almost negroid features. To my surprise she looked Aryan enough to have arrived with the Suevi.

Every visitor should spend one evening in a *fado*-house. He will enjoy quite a reasonable meal, as well as an extraordinary musical and emotional experience. Lacking the aesthetic sense and the musical education to describe it myself, I shall quote some remarks about *fado* by Rodney Gallop, in *Portugal, a Book of Folk Ways*:

'It is emotional, passionate, erotic, sensuous, one might say meretricious, and yet, like some rustic courtesan, fundamentally simple and unpretentious. Perhaps this is because these qualities, however irreconcilable to the Anglo-Saxon way of thinking, are nevertheless reconciled in the Portuguese temperament, or at least in one aspect of it.'

4. MUSEUMS: BELÉM

Like any capital city, Lisbon has museums of every kind: public and private, general and specialist. There is a concentration of them at Belém, to which we shall presently proceed down the river. Of those nearer the centre, four in particular should not be missed.

The Calouste Gulbenkian Museum, on the Avenida de Berna (underground station Praça de Espanha), is private and general. It is described in the 'Tailpiece' to Chapter 7.

The Overseas Ethnography Museum in the Rua Portas de S. Antão, behind the twenty-four-hour Post Office, is private but specialist. It belongs to that cosiest of clubs, the Lisbon Geographical Society. Many of its display cases are grouped around the society's principal lecture-room, a magnificent survival from the *Belle Epoque* in red plush and gleaming brasswork.

The guide may have to be reminded to show you, between the ivories from Goa and the carvings from Guinea, the folding camp chair in use by Livingstone when he died. It is not his Protestantism which makes this Scottish missionary a less than popular figure here. It is his explorations, which in making possible British Central Africa (with its bitter fruits) destroyed the dream of Serpa Pinto and others of linking Angola with Mozambique across 'Rhodesia'.

An interesting room is devoted to souvenirs of Admiral Gago Coutinho, a sypathetic and many-sided figure who was co-pilot on the first aeroplane to cross the South Atlantic to Brazil in 1922.

The Military Museum, near the S. Apolónia station, comes under the authority of the War Ministry instead of the Ministry of Education. It can be recommended to anyone who wants to know more about little-known corners of Portuguese history (such as her participation, in both Europe and Africa, in the First World

War), and to anyone who enjoys uniforms, old guns, or the flavour of battles long ago.

Some of the battles were not so long ago. Before visiting this museum I had never realised that certain Portuguese officers lost their lives in heroic circumstances during the 'bloodless' Indian invasion of Goa, Diu and Damão in 1961.

Even in the Introduction we had reason to refer to the Museum of Ancient Art. Standing on the Street of the Green Windows, it is generally referred to—even by those experts who know most about its contents—as 'Janelas Verdes'. Although not quite as vast as it seems on first acquaintance, two or more shorter visits will invariably bring more pleasure and profit than one mammoth tour.

'Ancient' is used in opposition to 'Contemporary' (which has its own museum elsewhere), and includes everything up to the mid-nineteenth century. It also includes, as we might expect in an ancient land with a wealthy and cultivated court, works by leading artists from elsewhere in Europe: Dürer, Van Dyck, Ribeira, Tiepolo, Fragonard and Romney, to mention but a few.

And because Portugal has for over five hundred years been at the centre of an overseas empire spreading to all parts of the globe, it contains many precious things from other continents. These are most interesting of all when, like the Japanese screens we described showing Portuguese merchants, they illustrate the unexpected interaction of Portuguese with exotic cultures. Another example of this is *Chine decommarde*, porcelain specially produced during the seventeenth and eighteenth centuries in China with Portuguese motifs for the Portuguese market.

Naturally, too, certain works take the individual fancy. Thus I was fascinated by a miniature of 1720 by the Italian A. Castrioto, showing John V taking chocolate in the house of the Duke of Lafões.

But inevitably what we most wish to see in Portugal is work by Portuguese artists. In painting at least the 'Janelas Verdes' faithfully reflects the national achievement.

This runs parallel to the national experience. The appearance of an artistic genius just as the voyages of discovery broke through to profitability was followed by a busy century of production. But the loss of independence drew talent away to the court in Madrid (and the parents of Velázquez, incidentally, from Oporto to Seville). The gloom in the few and dark canvases of the seventeenth century reflected the bankruptcy of the early Restoration. Then the steadily increasing prosperity of the eighteenth century was crowned by the great figure of Sequeira.

The life of Domingos António Sequeira (1768–1837) has curious parallels with that of his Spanish contemporary Goya. Both painted Wellington during the Peninsular War. Both spent their later years abroad. And both entered a final phase—in Goya's case under the influence of madness, in Sequeira's under that of religion—which carried them almost to the threshold of Romanticism.

It is as superb portraitists that both are best remembered. Even a hurried visitor should allow himself enough time to enjoy the room devoted to Sequeira's portraits; they include charming ones of the artist's own children, and nowhere else will he find so complete a collection of the artist's work.

The work of Josefa de Ayala, on the other hand, may be studied as easily at Obidos, as that of her contemporaries of the seventeenth century at Evora. And several schools of the prolific sixteenth century are even better represented in their provincial centres at Coimbra or Viseu. But for one artist we can come only to the Janelas Verdes, over which his greatest work presides.

The 'Panels of Nuno Gonçalves', however, are given none of the theatrical treatment of soft lights and black velvet screens reserved for Rembrandt's 'Night Watch' at the Mauritshuis, or for Velázquez's 'Las Meninas' at the Prado. Such is not the Portuguese way.

Here, in any case, it would be technically and aesthetically inappropriate. Technically because these are six individual panels, each crowded with portraits requiring separate attention. Aesthetically because these portraits are of the *lisboetas* we have just left outside, behind bank counters in the Rua Aurea, drinking in Alfama, or directing traffic in the Rossio. Even the attendant who hovers discreetly on the look-out for vandalism may bear an uncanny resemblance to one of these portraits—all of which he will willingly identify. It would be wrong to place any barrier between us and these our contemporaries, even if they are wearing the fashions of the Wars of the Roses.

We know little of the life of Nuno Gonçalves. Nor is the purpose of these panels—for long neglected—absolutely certain. They are often called the Triptych of St. Vincent, after the central character of the two middle panels. But the absence of the usual attributes of this patron of Lisbon: crows and martyr's palm, makes even this unsure.

The fact that his face is not all idealized saintliness, but is clearly a living portrait of *someone*, has led to conjectures that he may be the Infante Santo, the 'holy prince', brother of Henry the Navigator, who died in captivity in Morocco. It also enables us to conclude that this artist, who in portraiture transcended the Flemings from whom he had learned so much, could never divorce himself from the living models whose features he so faithfully interpreted. Here are the Portuguese of every estate, complete right up to the 'double cheeks' of several of the nobles and burgesses, which today, five centuries later, is still a common Portuguese characteristic.

Two figures in the 'Panel of the Knights' may be the Duke of Bragança and his son, ancestors of the kings of the last Portuguese dynasty. A figure kneeling before 'St. Vincent' on only one knee (which in itself proves his exalted category) may be King Afonso V. The child behind him may be his son, the future John II, who promoted the later voyages of discovery.

But the one identification of which we can be almost certain is that of the figure just behind this child, a sallow, square-faced man with a large black hat. Only one other portrait of him exists, in a manuscript of the Paris Bibliothèque Nationale. But the presence there of that same hat, and a sufficient likeness in the features, enable us to identify him as John II's great-uncle, Afonso V's uncle, the Infante Santo's brother, the initiator of those voyages of discovery: Prince Henry the Navigator.

That same large hat and those same genial features form the most advanced point of a marble prow, crowded with figures, which juts out over the Tagus three miles downstream from the Janelas Verdes. This Monument to the Discoveries was erected in 1960, on the five-hundredth anniversary of Prince Henry's death.

Its site is appropriate. For although most of the early voyages started from Lagos and Sagres in the Algarve, it was from here, Belém, that there set forth the major expeditions to India and Brazil which those earlier voyages had made possible.

These expeditions sailed under John II's nephew and successor, Manuel 'the Fortunate', who came down here to provide a royal send-off at their departure, and a royal welcome at their return.

Belém was indeed the focal point of the age. Here the returning sailors stepped from their spice-laden ships on to the dear soil for which two years in the East had only heightened their so Lusitanian longing. Here the nobility from their palaces in this then fashionable suburb mingled on the quays with the merchants of Lisbon. And here, where a Christianity of still crusading fervour was infused with the exotic currents from a thousand alien shores, there arose a monastery which has preserved in stone that moment of Manueline glory.

First impressions of the long white mass of the Jerónimos, suddenly unrolling into view as road, rail, or river carry us west along the Tagus, are not at all of Manueline intricacy and luxuriance. They are rather of a monument which adds the patina of the Parthenon to the location of Hampton Court. This impression is aided by the Ethnological Museum of the last century, which continues the façade of the church, obscuring the west doorway in the process. But this, and the lofty south doorway, outside which the Cardinal-Patriarch blesses the cod-fishing fleets in a moving ceremony each spring, can be properly appreciated only from a closer view.

We can then make the acquaintance of two men whom we shall be meeting many times again. The sculptor of the west doorway, with its portraits of the founder, King Manuel, and his Queen, is Nicolas Chantarène. He was first and greatest of a whole school of French artists who came to Portugal in the sixteenth century, already imbued with the spirit of the Renaissance.

4. Lisbon from the air. The rebuilt, Pombaline city occupies the lower ground between the older quarters on the hills

5. Seventeenth-century Japanese screen portraying the arrival of Portuguese (*Museum of Ancient Art, Lisbon*)

The south doorway, on the other hand, is like the church as a whole the design of Boytac, one of the initiators of Manueline. We shall not find here his trade mark of spiral pillars. But the shafts which support the interior are nevertheless of rich and unusual decoration, looking down on the modern tombs of Vasco da Gama and Camoens, and on the contemporary tombs of the last two kings of the House of Avis: Sebastian and the Cardinal-King Henry.

Though we have already suggested that Manueline may reflect some innate Baroque tendency in the Portuguese soul, it owes to its discipline a power lacked by Baroque itself. Manueline decoration, though exuberant, is concentrated, and leaves vast spaces uncovered. Both the doorways outside, and the pillars within command our attention because of their isolation amid seas of empty stone.

Cloisters, however, receive from this, as from other styles, a special treatment. The cloister of the Jerónimos—entered by a passage beyond the west door—is two-storeyed. Its stone lacework is therefore even more overpowering than in other Manueline cloisters at Batalha and Tomar. This is Gothic which has undergone a sea-change after being dipped 'full fathom five' in the tropic seas.

Other things brought back from those seas can be seen in the Overseas Agricultural Museum and Gardens, opposite the east end of the Jerónimos. To anyone pressed for time I would recommend this rather than the poorly-displayed Ethnological Museum at the other end. But he should slip inside the latter to see the giant prehistoric statues of Lusitanian warriors. It was they who stood ready to welcome the legions who first tried to storm the hill-forts of the north.

More essential visiting than either, however, is the beautifully arranged museum of Popular Art near the Monument to the Discoveries. Costumes, handwoven textiles, agricultural and fishing implements, cooking and cleaning utensils are displayed province by province. Photographs illustrate these provinces' everyday life. Vast murals interpret their essential characteristics. Although everything seems to have been included, the museum

D

is small and uncrowded; and selection must have been as ruthless as it was brilliant.

During the spring a 'fair' is held alongside. Products similar to the exhibits can be purchased there at most reasonable prices. Aran-style knitwear is one of the bargains. Dishes from a dozen 'regional kitchens' can be enjoyed at an open-air restaurant.

Yet another museum at Belém illustrates life in the past at the other end of the social scale. This is the famous Coach museum, in the riding school of a royal palace which is now the official home of the President of the Republic. It is an excellent example of that admirable Portuguese trait to which I have already drawn attention when writing of the Estufa Fria: the ability to conjure up vanished grandeur at minimal cost.

The vehicles, from Philip II's to those of the later Braganças, inevitably reach their Baroque culmination in those of John V, with their gilded siren outriders. Most were collecting dust and dry rot when in the 1890's Queen Marie-Amélia suggested that they could be grouped to form a collection of public interest.

High on the hill behind stands the early nineteenth-century Palace of Ajuda, to visit which requires special permission. Its rooms and furnishings recall the last century of Bragança rule: hindsight lends them the same doomed enchantment it gives the lawns of the Petit Trianon. The Ajuda Library is one of the country's most important collections of documents and manuscripts.

Down beside the Tagus again, we finish our visit to Lisbon where we began, at the point where Ulysses himself, had he come here, would surely have landed. The Tower of Belém is still an island—just. But for some time after it was built in 1515 it stood at a fair distance from the shore. This can be seen in Felipe Lobo's painting of Belém in the seventeenth century, in the Janelas Verdes.

Francisco de Arruda, one of two brothers who were both architects of King Manuel, drew his inspiration less from the East than from the traditional enemies against whose attacks the Tower was built. For he had worked on the fortresses occupied by the Portuguese during the later fifteenth century on the Moroccan coast.

While there he had almost certainly travelled to that golden city beneath the snow-covered Atlas, Marrakesh. When the Almohad sultans ruled from the Sahara to the Sierra Morena they built both the landmark of Seville, the Giralda, and the landmark of Marrakesh, the Koutoubia.

It was with a certain excitement that I drew up beside the Tower of Belém with my mother and aunt, whose ship bearing them from Casablanca to London had docked for twelve hours at Lisbon. I was not disappointed. Pointing to the curious turrets jutting out from amongst the emblazoned Crosses of the Order of Christ, my aunt exclaimed:

'But those are just like that big mosque where we've been staying for the last two months, at Marrakesh!'

TAILPIECE: A CIDADE E O CAMPO

Describing Lisbon as the 'eye' of Portugal was not an inexact metaphor.

Through Lisbon, by sea and air, rail and radio, Portugal communicates with the outside world. At Lisbon, now as in the time of King Manuel, disembark the exotic products and people of her far-flung overseas provinces. In her cafés the successors of Camoens and Fernando Pessoa ponder the masterpieces of the late twentieth century. Like London or Paris it gives foreigners their first view of the country, and natives their first view of the outside world.

Like those cities, too, it is large in relation to the country it serves and lives on. It always has been. In the Age of the Discoveries about one-tenth of the Portuguese population of a mere million lived in the capital. Today it still holds about one-tenth of the present population of nine million.

Oporto, second city and 'capital of the north', is well under half this size, and itself has an immense lead over Setúbal with rather more than 50,000, Braga with 40,000, and Coimbra and Évora with around 35,000 each. The other provincial capitals are but country towns. Eighty per cent of the population is still rural.

To find a third Portuguese city with a six-figure population one must go overseas, to Luanda or Lourenço Marques.

At under a million inhabitants Lisbon is nevertheless well down the league of capitals, and even the list of 'big cities of the world'. This may be one of the reasons why it is more easily comprehended, and less of a world to itself, than some of those other cities. The foreigner who never leaves London or Paris has a very unrepresentative idea of Britain or of France. But the foreigner who unwisely never leaves Lisbon can still carry away a true, if inadequate, impression of Portugal.

This is partly for the very reason that the whole country is represented here: officially in institutes and ministries and museums; unofficially in the makeup of the people themselves. In recent years Portugal has experienced that internal emigration which always accompanies the first stages of industrialisation. Lisbon, both as capital and as centre of the more important of the two industrial zones, has naturally received the lion's share of the incoming countrymen. To manufacturing suburbs to the north, and upstream by the Tagus, and to shanty towns which against the authorities' wishes have grown up near the heart of the city, come the landless labourers displaced by mechanisation from the vast estates of the Alentejo, and the peasants who have given up the losing battle to farm their uneconomic holdings in the Beiras.

Their rustic accents, the baskets full of crusty brown *pão de centeio* and of dark wine from distant *adegas*, with which they arrive after visits 'home' at the S. Apolónia station, renew the rural flavour of a city which was never truly urban.

This penetration of the city by the country is a further reason why Lisbon succeeds in epitomising Portugal as a whole. Not only is the countryside near: it is often within sight. From the Castle or the Estrêla the gentle hills of Estremadura rise behind the still exploratory antennae of the new avenues. And from the steep streets of Alfama or Lapa meadows fringe the horizon which lies beyond the sparkling Tagus in the foreground.

It is within earshot, too. On the fourth floor of your luxury hotel you will be woken not by the first sounds of a city preparing for work, nor even by the untimely farewells of all-night revellers, but by the crowing of cocks. For every concierge or tenement dweller keeps his own chickens, and even grows his own lettuce, so much the favourite vegetable of the Lisbon-born that he is familiarly known by its name: *alfacinha*.

Though this city has a soul, and a flavour quite its own, it has been quite content to borrow the constituents of that flavour. Even the *varinhas* who hawk the fish, often regarded as the most typical of all *alfacinhas*, are said to have originated from Ovar on the coast far to the north. *Fado* itself was probably imported from Brazil. The most self-conscious of *lisboetas* has one foot in the country. Cesario Verde, son of an ironmonger, so identified himself with the city that his poems celebrating different aspects of nineteenth-century Lisbon at different hours of the day are strewn with the possessive 'my' and 'our'. Yet he excelled equally in bucolic themes, inspired by long stays on a family smallholding where the *auto-estrada* still runs through open country towards Estoril.

For if even Lisbon itself retains a country flavour, its hinterland remains profoundly rural in a way that the sophisticated, suburbanised Home Counties and Ile de France have long since ceased to be. It is this hinterland which now invites us—with the promise of yet more repose than that offered by Kent or Surrey, by the forests of Rambouillet or of Fontainebleau—to its exploration.

2

WITHIN THE LINES OF
TÔRRES VEDRAS

֍

Many of those who have learned the date 1066, but to whom
1385 means nothing, have learned also a name with a proud place
alike in the history of Britain and of Portugal: the Lines of Tôrres
Vedras. These were a series of positions fortified by Wellington
from the Atlantic, through the small town of that name, to the
Tagus south of Vila Franca de Xira, just where it begins to swell
into the wide 'straw sea' which so effectively protects Lisbon to
the east.

It was into this redoubt, limited by the Tagus, the Atlantic, and
his fortifications, that in the autumn of 1810 Wellington deliberately led his armies, fresh from their strategic victory over the
French invaders of Portugal at Buçaco. Military historians regard
the operation as a classic example of the correct use of superiority
at sea. His opponent, Masséna, six hundred hostile and difficult
miles from the Pyrenees, camped vainly before the Lines whose
defenders were supplied by the open sea lanes from London to
Lisbon. And when his enemy at last withdrew, it was from this
bridgehead that Wellington advanced in perhaps the greatest
campaign that Britain has ever fought in Europe, from Ciudad
Rodrigo and Badajoz on to the crowning mercies of Vitoria and
Toulouse.

Tôrres Vedras is probably better known abroad than any other
genuinely Portuguese place-name (for many languages have
given Lisbon and Oporto the compliment of distortion). It is
generally assumed, though, that the Lines defended merely

Lisbon and its outer suburbs. However, anyone driving the more than thirty miles out to Tôrres Vedras would agree that the bridgehead was the size of a small English county. Its defenders cannot therefore have suffered any of the usual claustrophobia of the besieged. Nor can there have been any lack of fresh foodstuffs, for the farms and market gardens which supplied—and still supply—Lisbon's markets were still in friendly Portuguese hands.

This rural hinterland could also supply fish. For Cascais, the first port beyond the mouth of the Tagus, though better known as a residence of exiled European royalty, is also the biggest fishing port between Peniche and Setúbal. To reach it we must follow from Belém the least rural, but also the most attractive, of all the roads leading away from Lisbon.

Both road and railway—Portugal's most important commuter line—run closely parallel to the Costa do Sol, a chain of residential suburbs and resorts facing south, first across the Tagus estuary and later into the open sea. In the centre of Oeiras, a mile behind the coast, the fine country house built for the Marquis of Pombal stands amidst a wholly appropriate eighteenth-century garden, with French-style statuary and water effects. Unhappily it is closed to the public since the Gulbenkian art collection was moved from here to its new museum in Lisbon.

Most of the other place-names, such as Carcavelos, Parede, or Monte Estoril, are unlikely to remain in the visitor's memory unless he has friends living in them. This is not as unlikely as it seems, for the Costa do Sol has shared with the Algarve the post-war immigration from Britain, so that it is now numerically well ahead of the traditional British colony at Oporto. A British preparatory school flourishes at Carcavelos. At Estoril itself there is an Anglican church, with an interesting modern interior behind a façade so plain as to conceal the building's purpose.

There are other things, too, to make the visitor feel at home in this best known of all Portuguese resorts. The small, *chic* beach beyond the somehow toy-like railway, overlooked by a terrace café on several levels and by a neo-Gothic tower, is probably already known to him from photographs. So are the ever-colourful and by night illuminated gardens before the recently-enlarged Casino. But just beyond each of the semicircular arcades of boutiques which lie on either side of these gardens lie two institutions offering amenities of which he may not at first be aware.

One is a branch of the largest Portuguese clearing bank, the Banco Espírito Santo e Comercial (the Holy Ghost and Commercial: surely the most glaring example ever of the juxtaposition of God and Mammon?). This not only provides a young lady linguist to deal with foreigners' problems, but also comfortable chairs where they can sit until she is free, and the *Financial Times* for them to read while they wait.

The other is the Tourist Office of the Costa do Sol, which provides not only information, but also a foyer where an artistic or photographic exhibition is generally on view, and a reading room where visitors can consult *The Times*, *Le Figaro*, *Allgemeine Zeitung*, or the Spanish *ABC*. It is worth drawing attention to this facility, for the geographic position of Portugal makes foreign newspapers almost a luxury for more modest budgets. (The *Sunday Times* costs 23p.)

There is little else to say about Estoril, pleasant, pretty and well planned as it is. It has only one characteristic in common with the country of which it is otherwise so unrepresentative. It is mild: in its climate, in the pleasures it offers, in the clientèle it attracts, and even in its modest architectural excesses. Accompanied by friends or family, or by a parcel of books, a month there can be a refreshing experience. Otherwise ennui can only be kept at bay by visits to Cascais.

Fortunately this is barely two miles away, by easy walk or still easier train journey to the line's terminus. Here there is a greater variety of shops and of eating-places, while after dark, besides night-clubs, there is all the fun of the fish market. The auction to the Lisbon merchants of the wooden trays, each shining with a different and still living hue of scales, can be watched from a 'strangers' gallery'.

On the left of the beach to which the fishing boats return stands a chapel. It was this setting which the stage designer must have had in mind for the best-known scene of that wartime musical, *The Lisbon Story*. After a long London run it toured every provincial theatre big enough to take it. The strains of 'Pedro the fisherman' still evoke, for anyone over thirty-five, a maritime Ruritania without blackout or rationing. There is, indeed, something of the operetta about Cascais, and the hospitality which it accorded in the later 1940s to so many crowned heads without thrones was wholly in keeping.

It has a park more satisfying to the spirit than Estoril's formal gardens. Where this touches the sea stands the former villa of the Count of Castro Guimarães, now a museum where the family's furniture remains in its place. Amongst the pictures, porcelain and nostalgic souvenirs of a friendship with the last Bragança queen, one notes, as so often in Portugal, some fine pieces of Luso-Indian furniture. The Estado da India, Albuquerque's inheritance, played as important a part in the life of Portugal as was played in the life of Britain by British India, its junior by two hundred and fifty years.

Beyond the park the coast road runs past a steep sea-hollowed gulf called the Boca do Inferno (Mouth of Hell), and wheeling north descends on the Praia do Guincho, the first of those storm-beaten beaches which follow one another all the way to the Spanish border. Careful driving is needed as it winds round the base of the Serra de Sintra. This drops to the sea in the Cabo da Roca, a 500-foot headland which is the westernmost point of Europe.

From the coastal highway we have followed several roads run up into the Serra de Sintra. As this is our first *serra*, something ought perhaps to be said about *serras* in general.

The word is, of course, of the same root as the Spanish *sierra*, and has much the same meaning: that of the French *massif*, a whole mountainous formation or even an entire range, rather than the single peak which is conjured up by 'mountain' in English. But Spain is so mountainous a land that '*sierra*', although so marvellously evocative a word, is at once too general and too variable in use to convey a satisfactory geographical concept. When we hear '*serra*', on the other hand, we know what to expect. Whether it be the mighty hog's back of the Serra da Estrêla rising to over 6,500 feet, or the Serra de Monfurado, barely distinguishable among the lesser undulations of the upper Alentejo, the term will designate a defined zone of hills or highland—of which one summit will naturally out-top any others.

This is in part because the great east-west *cordilleras* of Iberia break up as they descend towards the sea on entering Portugal, and partly because the higher rainfall of the Atlantic coast makes for valleys deep enough and wide enough to isolate these *serras* one from another. Thus the Serra de Sintra is one of a series of isolated highlands which rise to the 1,500–2,000 feet level in the long tongue between the Tagus valley and the Atlantic.

General rules, however, cannot explain special situations, and the situation of the Serra de Sintra is very special indeed. In the south one must go as far as the Algarve before finding anywhere higher than its 529 metres. Yet it is sufficiently near the Atlantic to collect an impressive amount of moisture in what is already a distinctly southern landscape. And the proximity to Lisbon of this ready-made summer retreat has led to the building there of several summer palaces.

Sintra has both private and royal palaces, not only in the town nestling on the Serra's north-east slopes, but scattered over the wooded range. Let our route take us past those which can be visited.

Continuing along the main road we followed from Cascais to Cabo da Roca, up through the wine-growing village of Colares, we reach Monserrate, now a state school of forestry. Here an English landscape gardener made use of the privileged climate, ample water, and a steep valley, to create one of the world's great gardens beneath an imitation Arab villa.

The native trees would have rendered this a luxuriant hollow even without the addition of magnolias, camellias and tree-ferns. But the ridge of the range, followed by another road which branches off before Colares, is barer, with large granite outcrops. Constructed on and in one of these is a tiny convent which from 1560 until 1834 held eight Capucin friars in tiny cells hewn from the rock, but mercifully insulated with cork—a product in which Portugal has always been rich. Though Philip II, fresh from building the magnificent palace-monastery of the Escorial, described it as the poorest convent of his kingdom, the minute hospital, kitchen and chapel have a certain cosiness, and its terrace enjoys a splendid view. It can be reached along an unmade track from the ridge road, or by walking up from opposite Monserrate. The path is confusing: entering a small gate where water flows into a tank, one should follow the iron pipe bringing this water, which occasionally juts above the surface, until the grove of trees around the steep outcrop marking the convent comes into view.

The road past Monserrate runs on past a number of other lovely, but unhappily inaccessible *quintas* (country houses). Just before dropping towards Sintra town it passes the luxury hotel which has been established in the private eighteenth-century palace of Seteais. Its fortress-like and rather isolated setting, with original Pillement murals and period furniture, is not to the taste of everyone even amongst those who can afford it. But those few to whose temperaments and purses alike it is congenial are amply rewarded.

It is indeed to rarefied eccentric beings that Sintra seems always to have appealed. At an equal distance on the other side of the town, where the direct road from Cascais meets the road from Lisbon, a girls' school now occupies the rambling yellow royal residence of Ramalhão, where Beckford of Fonthill Abbey fame lived for some months during one of his visits to Portugal at the end of the eighteenth century.

Travelling to Ramalhão by the ridge road we pass close to a residence where eccentricity has taken visible form. Pena palace was built in the 1840s by the King-Consort, Ferdinand of Saxe-Coburg-Gotha. Like his cousin our own Albert, his influence on his adopted country seems to have been for the good. Had his eldest son, the still-mourned Pedro V, not died at only twenty-four, the Republican Party which triumphed in 1910 might never have got off the ground. His wife, the early-Victorian looking Queen Maria II (often referred to, with a certain affection, by her full name of Maria da Gloria), whose portrait we see in so many royal palaces, died in 1853 in the very Victorian act of giving birth to her tenth child. The widower, remarrying a German singer, lived on in this his Balmoral.

Those *chefs-d'œuvre* of the neo-Manueline, the Rossio station and the Buçaco Palace Hotel, are later in date, more consciously nationalist in intention, and therefore more pure—if that word is not altogether out of place—in their style. The Pena palace, on the other hand, is at once Manueline, German Baronial, and Oriental. *'Parfois le baroque le plus truculent renchérit sur le manuélin'*, says the *Guide Bleu*, describing the 'window of the giant', beside which Tomar's famous window by Diogo de Aruda seems restrained.

Yet although no attempt has been made to harmonise these discordant styles, the general effect is not as shocking as it ought to be. Perhaps the marriage in styles reflects the marriage between Saxon Ferdinand and Latin Maria, itself symbolic of the successful marriage on Portuguese soil between Atlantic and Mediterranean?

The interior is just what might be expected from its period, and has the merit of being absolutely untouched. On one bed-head there still hangs a frond of palm sixty years old. It was left there on Palm Sunday, 1910, a few months before the Braganças left not only Pena but Portugal. The altar of the chapel has survived from the monastery which once stood here: it is one of the more exquisite productions of the French sculptor Nicolas Chantarène, who made his career here under Manuel and John III.

From every window, and even more from the walk round the fairy-tale battlements, are magnificent views. For Pena is perched like a fairy-tale castle on an abrupt peak. It is these views which help to lessen the shock caused by the clashing styles. For clearly something fantastic was called for in such a fairy-tale situation, with Lisbon and the Tagus in one direction, the line of the Serra and the Atlantic beaches in the other, the pile of Mafra in the distance, and another castle perched almost as precariously on a neighbouring peak.

This, the Castle of the Moors, was a Visigothic fortress even before it became an important Arab stronghold. Its capture was an essential preliminary of the siege of Lisbon in 1147. The battlements, more recent than the eighth-century foundations, have been restored by the Ministry of Public Works in their usual clean and discreet manner—which I personally find perfectly satisfactory. They offer, even better than Pena a hundred and fifty feet higher, a bird's eye view down into the main square of Sintra.

This is dominated by the Royal Palace, which again mingles Gothic, Manueline and Mauresque, but in an organic rather than an artificial unity. The four arches giving on to the square, and the kitchen whose curious chimneys recall the oast-houses of Kent or the *trulli* of Apului, belong to the reign of John I. His motto, *Por Bem*, is carried by the blackbirds which are painted all over the ceiling of another room. It has the sense of 'all to the good' —which was said to have been his riposte when caught by good Queen Philippa in the arms of one of her ladies-in-waiting.

If the Gothic parts of the palace remind us of the Master of Avis, the more extensive Manueline sections recall the last of his line, Sebastian, who here conceived and carried out part of the preparations for his ill-fated expedition against Morocco. Yet ironically the decorations of these rooms, the carved wooden ceilings, and some of the tiled floors and walls, are perhaps the greatest concentration of Moorish art in Portugal. These early tiles were made in Seville by *mudéjar* craftsmen (Moslems living under Christian rule). They can be distinguished from the later, exclusively Portuguese *azulejos* by their designs in relief, and by their unusual range of colours.

The quiet palace, and the quiet garden which borders it on one side, are in marked contrast to the everyday world of the busy little town. And the contrast is even more marked with the bustle each second and fourth Sunday of the month at S. Pedro de Sintra, barely a mile up the direct road towards Ramalhão. This is then the scene of a big fair, just as bucolic as those at Barcelos (see Chapter 9) or elsewhere in the provinces: proof if such were needed that there is still plenty of real country left within the Lines of Tôrres Vedras. I know of Englishmen who have chosen to farm in this very area, enjoying rural peace within easy reach of metropolitan amenities.

The direct route from Lisbon to Sintra runs along the first part of the unfinished Estoril *auto-estrada*. This crosses an impressive viaduct which crowns a complex system of flyovers connecting with the approach to the Salazar Bridge over the Tagus. It continues for some miles through the hilly wooded parkland of Monsanto, which at Montes Claros has a fine viewpoint with restaurant and garden. The turning off for Sintra leads also to one of the finest camping sites in Europe, with constant hot water and a swimming pool. It is so comfortable, so near the city yet so remote from city life, that scores of *lisboetas* park a caravan there permanently as a 'country cottage', leaving hardly enough room for the genuine tourists at the height of the summer.

Three miles later comes Queluz. Turning off where a gateway gives a tempting view into the park, we find ourselves in a few minutes in the cobbled square round which lie the subsidiary offices needed by even the smallest eighteenth-century palace.

Had this palace been any larger, had there been more than one storey to most of its galleries of salons, no doubt a heavier style would have been chosen. But it was built essentially as a country retreat by the brother of Pombal's King Joseph. It was only after his marriage to his niece—whose statue gives a melancholy dignity to the otherwise lighthearted square—and her succession to the throne as Maria I, that Queluz became for two decades the heart of the kingdom. It therefore succeeded in avoiding alike the austerities of Pombaline neo-Classical and the pomposities of Joanine Baroque to become the one important representative of Rococo in Lisbon and the south.

This is the artificial yet charmed world of the Petit Trianon. We are not surprised to learn that the French architect Robillon was here associated with the Portuguese Mateus Vicente. It is the nearest thing in Portugal to the Casa del Labrador at Aranjuez near Madrid. There are the same exquisite pieces of furniture and porcelain, with the addition, it being Portugal, of *azulejos*: there is also the bonus of a perfectly-proportioned ballroom, all mirrors and gilt and chandeliers.

The gardens are large in relation to the house, with box-hedges, topiary work, and fountains spouted by lead mermen. In one of the lower gardens a small stream has been canalised into a long basin, on the sides of which *azulejos* again appear depicting maritime life.

Yet there are neglected and little-visited corners of these gardens, and for all their size they do not seem out of proportion. In the late eighteenth century the courts of France, of Spain, and of Portugal were all reaching after a pastoral informality, however affected it may seem today. Gardens like those of Queluz are a witness of that unreal but delightful world, which was so rudely upset by the French Revolution and the wars which followed.

Queluz is on the scale which suits the Portuguese temperament: small sculptures, small cathedrals, small palaces. Mafra, eighteen winding miles to the north, offends against this canon, just as its massive, self-important style betrays the hand not merely of the foreign but of the Teutonic architect. He was Ludwig of Ratisbon, commissioned by John V on the birth of his son in 1714 to build a palace-monastery to surpass in splendour that other palace-monastery of the Escorial.

The design has been over-criticised. The immense dark granite façade, with a square pavilion topped by an unusual cupola at each end, may be cold but does not lack dignity. But this architectural criticism is really an extension of the moral indignation which Mafra inspires in many minds. They are incensed by the thought of the new-found riches of Brazil being squandered on a non-utilitarian construction with 4,500 doors and windows, which at one point absorbed nearly 50,000 workers.

With shocked delight they tell the story of how the casters of Antwerp, incredulous at the size of the order for a *carillon*, wrote to query it. Whereupon John V ordered two, so that the unexpected music of bells often sounds across the meadows of Estremadura, from the twin towers rising from either side of the basilica which occupies the centre of the façade. The critics say—quite rightly—that he was consciously modelling himself on Louis XIV. They add that he lacked the taste of the creator of Versailles.

But the exploration of the interior, conducted by a whole relay-race of guides carefully locking the door of one gallery before entering the next, will confirm the sureness of John V's taste to those who may have forgotten the church plate of S. Roque. The visit begins amongst the giant Baroque statues at the entrance to the basilica, and the kaleidoscope of marbles within. The nucleus of artists collected to carry out these and other decorations was not dispersed on Mafra's completion, but remained functional as an art school throughout the eighteenth century. The tour culminates in the library, whose leather bindings and priceless manuscripts are housed in a high light room with a colour scheme reminiscent of the best modern Scandinavian interiors. In between it passes through the long royal suites, with views over the vast *tapada*, or chase. These suites are of a cold magnificence very different from the humble quarters which Philip II allowed himself in the Escorial. Dr. Pais da Silva has aptly contrasted the two monuments in saying that whereas the Escorial was first a monastery, Mafra was first a palace.

If John V's extravagance was not devoid of taste, nor was it unpopular. From Afonso Henriques onwards the kings of Portugal were the embodiment of national independence, and the strength of the realm was identical with the royal power. When the barons of Portugal deposed Sancho II in 1248, his offence lay not in failing to give them a Magna Carta, but in failing to give them firm government. *'Um fraco Rei faz fraca a forte gente.* A weak king makes the strong folk weak', as Camoens put it. And when the common folk revolted, as in 1383 or in 1637, they wanted freedom not from royal oppression, but from Spain.

That readable but prejudiced historian of the last century, Oliveira Martins, enjoyed himself at John V's expense. He lingered with relish over the goings-on at Odivelas, eight miles out of Lisbon on the direct road to Mafra. Here, in what is now a select school for the daughters of army officers, was a convent founded by the great King Dennis, the Portuguese Edward I or St. Louis, of whom he was the younger contemporary. And while King Dennis, 'farmer king', castle builder, and husband of a saint, slept—as he still sleeps—in Odivelas church, his descendant John V enjoyed in the adjoining convent his illicit liaison with the nun Madre Paula. Voltaire, the enemy at once of absolutism and clericalism, sneered that his gaieties were religious processions, that when he took to building he built monasteries, and that when he wanted a mistress he chose a nun.

6. Sintra:
the Pena Palace

7. Sintra: looking down from the Castle of the Moors

But few of John V's subjects would have echoed Voltaire or Oliveira Martins. A more recent historian, and the acknowledged expert on the period, Dr. Borges de Macedo, told me that no king was more popular, or better understood the Portuguese character.

From 1580 the little country had endured sixty years of foreign domination, the loss of much of her overseas empire, twenty-eight years of an exhausting war of independence, and thirty years of financial bankruptcy. Better times had only begun with the arrival of the first gold from Brazil in 1697, and with the Portuguese army's early successes in the War of the Spanish Succession, culminating in its triumphant entry into Madrid in the very year of John V's accession, 1706. What nation would not go on a spending spree when a century and a quarter of decline and poverty were followed by a flow of sudden riches? In building Mafra, as in persuading the Pope to establish the Lisbon patriarchate, the king was doing what his people most wanted him to do: showing the world in general, and His Catholic Majesty of Spain in particular, that they were back on the map.

And when he embraced Madre Paula, did the shade of King Dennis really disapprove? For in spite of—or perhaps because of —his marriage to a saint, even the latter left at least one illegitimate son, the last great poet in medieval Portuguese.

The critics who deny the richest of the Braganças the taste of Louis XIV claim nevertheless that, like the Sun King, he prepared the way by his extravagance for the fall of his House. That fall was rather long in coming for such an argument to be sustained. But when, after the outbreak of the Republican revolt on 4th October 1910, the last Bragança monarch slipped away from Lisbon, it was perhaps appropriate that his last night on Portuguese soil should be spent at Mafra.

The next day he and the Queen-Mother sailed away in the yacht named after her, *Dona Amélia*, from the fishing village and resort of Ericeira. Six miles from Mafra, it is the only place of any size on the open, wave-lashed coast between Cascais and Peniche.

TAILPIECE: CASA DE BRAGANÇA

In claiming that Torres Vedras was the best-known Portuguese place-name I had not forgotten Bragança. To most minds, however, this conjures up not the most remote of the provincial capitals, in distant Trás-os-Montes, but the dynasty to which it gave a title.

I had intended to leave any discussion of the Braganças until a later point. But we have already been reminded of their glory at Mafra, of their fantasy at Pena, and of their departure at Ericeira. It is obvious that something must be said of the last royal House of Portugal before any more appearances by them confuse us still further.

To the English reader the House's most familiar representative is, of course, Catherine of Bragança, the Queen of Charles II. The still fledgling dynasty was desperate for help, and was prepared to buy it with the imperial dowry listed in the grudging verse of a contemporary London broadsheet:

> 'Three wonders to be seen:
> Bombay, Tangier, and a barren Queen.'

But though Portugal in Catherine's time was poor, her family itself was rich. Her father, its first member to become king under the restored monarchy of 1640, was by far the wealthiest man in the kingdom, with vast estates not only at home but overseas, and notably in Brazil.

The family was pre-eminent not only in wealth but in ancestry. In a sense it owed its very existence to the victory of Aljubarrota. For it sprang from the marriage of a bastard son of John I of Avis with the daughter and heiress of his ally and commander, the Holy Constable Nuno Alvares Pereira.

Throughout the rule of the house of Avis the Dukes of Bragança were almost an estate of the realm. We have seen how one of them probably figures on the Panels of Nuno Gonçalves. Another was executed by John II in 1484, for they ran the same risks as over-mighty subjects of the period in other parts of Europe. And they already held a claim to the throne when the last male of the house of Avis, the King-Cardinal Henry, died in 1580. For the Duchess of Bragança at that time was his niece—another Catherine.

Thus, although to non-Portuguese the Braganças in 1640 sprang apparently from nowhere, they were in fact the nation's only obvious choice. It was obvious even to the Spanish government, who attempted to get the Duke of Bragança away from Portugal by appointing him to the command of the Portuguese force they hoped to bring to their aid against France.

And the choice was the nation's, not their own. Only when others had conspired did the Duke, pressed by his ambitious Spanish wife, allow himself to be proclaimed as John IV.

For the Braganças had the cautiousness which so often accompanies great riches. We have seen how with the discovery of Brazilian gold in 1697 these riches became greater still, permitting the extravagances of the 'Munificent' John V. But for all its superficial glitter, his foreign policy was that of a cautious neutral. He himself declared that he must have the sea on his side. 'John V realised that the key to Portugal's security was, as it always has been, the English alliance,' said Dr. Borges de Macedo, looking straight at me across a lecture room crowded with French, Spaniards, Germans, Americans and Japanese.

To talk of the relationship between the Braganças and England recalls Manuel II's years of exile at Twickenham, and the British warship which carried his body back to the Tagus for a state funeral. It recalls, too, Pedro IV, who retired to London from Brazil, of which he had only nine years earlier been proclaimed the first Emperor, in order to work for the overthrow of the absolutist régime of his younger brother, Miguel. It recalls most of all Catherine of Bragança herself, although she is remembered in England for little more than her dowry, and for her reputation as a devout Catholic and a long-suffering wife.

In Portugal, however, where Nell Gwyn, the Duchess of Cleveland, and even the Popish Plot which almost deprived her of her private confessor, were alike ignored, she received a heroine's welcome on her return home after thirty years in 1692, and throughout the rest of her life the reverence accorded to one who had attained such distinction abroad. Just before her death in 1705 she acted as Regent of the Kingdom during her brother's illness. Her portrait when young, in the museum of Évora, is one of the better works of a dismal century for Portuguese art, and makes us wish her union had not been childless. How enlivened would have been British court life in the eighteenth century had our monarchs been Stuarts steadied by the blood of the Braganças.

It was between Évora and the Spanish frontier that the Dukes had their principal seat. For the Duke of Bragança was also Duke of Guimarães, Marquis of Vila Viçosa, Count of Barcelos, Count of Ourém, and Count of Arraiolos. In all these towns they had palaces or castles. And after 1640, of course, the royal palaces, too, were available for their use.

Vila Viçosa, however, was unquestionably their favourite residence. It has been said that British sovereigns when at Sandringham become ordinary country landowners, 'squires' just like any others. The same was true of the Braganças at Vila Viçosa, with the difference that their palance there, instead of being deliberately purchased as a retreat from affairs of state, had always belonged to them. As their carriages rattled between the orange trees which line the quiet streets of the white little town under the clear Alentejo sky, and drew up on the vast marble-paved square in front of the long, three-storeyed palace, they must have experienced all the emotions of homecoming.

The palace, like the paving and the lampstands and many of the houses, is of the marble cut from the quarries centred at Borba only three miles away. But over four centuries it has acquired a golden patina. And there is a profound yet princely peace everywhere, as peacocks strut unconcernedly out of the great garden and across the square.

Facing the palace is the Augustinian church where the Dukes all lie buried. On one side stands the Chagas convent where lie their Duchesses. And on the other is a smaller garden of box-hedges and water canals with blue and white tiles amusingly depicting all the kings up to the end of the eighteenth century.

In the centre of the square stands an equestrian statue of John IV, who set out from here to take up the responsibilities of kingship. To Vila Viçosa his pathetic elder son, Afonso VI, longed to return when in captivity. From here John V made the only recorded royal visit to Olivença, the Portuguese town beyond the Guadiana now occupied by Spain. As might be expected, his munificence left its Baroque mark here, notably in the chapel.

But the personalities who leave the profoundest impression on us as we visit the palace (allow over two hours!) are those of the last king but one, Carlos, and of his Queen Marie-Amélia, a French princess of the attractive Orléans family.

Opinions vary about Dom Carlos. We tend to agree with the more unfavourable ones as we see portrait after portrait of a corpulent little man, with close-cropped hair and bristling moustache, reviewing troops or shooting game with an almost Kaiser-like swagger.

But then we come upon the sensitive landscapes he painted, both in oils and water-colours. And we remember stories of his personal kindness, such as Raoul Brandão's account, in *Os Pescadores*, of how he once gave some fishermen of Olhão a tow behind the royal yacht to some grounds he had spotted teeming with shoals.

From here, by the railway which had only just been extended to Vila Viçosa, he left for Lisbon on 1st February 1908. After crossing the Tagus the royal family got into a carriage, which had only reached the far corner of the Terreiro do Paço when he and his eldest son were assassinated.

Here round his ancestral home he is mourned still. An elderly guide at the medieval castle, which was already nearly three centuries old when the palace was built, paused on the battlements and pointed out over the immense *tapada*, the chase where the Dukes and Kings used to hunt.

'It was in that clearing there that they gathered for the shoot, the very day before he left.'

Then he went on to extol the virtues of Queen Marie-Amélia. I had been interested by an extensive series of photographs of her last visit to Portugal in 1955—the only one she ever made after the proclamation of the Republic. I asked him if he had then met again the lady of whose kindness when he was a boy he had such happy memories.

'No. She went everywhere but here. She said that she had been so happy here that she could not bear to see it again.'

Both she and her son, Manuel II, left their large fortunes to the Portuguese State. With the good housekeeping which has characterised the national finances for the past forty years, these have not been absorbed into current account expenses, but have been used to set up a foundation which tends and nurtures this patrimony. Appropriately, this is centred at the palace of Vila Viçosa, where the visitor can purchase books recently published by the foundation about different aspects of the family's history, or personally consult Manuel II's priceless library.

The guides, therefore, who so courteously show you round, and the gardeners, who would fit so easily into the nineteenth century or even the sixteenth, are working not for the government, but with greater historical propriety for the foundation which is heir to the *Serenissima Casa de Bragança*.

3

THE HOLY PLACES

Wellington's method of defending Lisbon, by fortifying a line of hills between Tagus and Atlantic, was only practicable after the invention of artillery. In the fourteenth century it was necessary either to retire behind the city walls—as was done in 1384—or to give battle where the long peninsula between river and ocean began.

Here, then, took place the battle of Aljubarrota, a few miles north of the village of that name. A chapel dedicated to St. George, with at its entrance a pitcher even today regularly replenished with water, marks where Nuno Alvares Pereira raised his standard. His equestrian statue stands before the great monastery two miles further on which commemorates the Portuguese victory.

The erection of this statue set the seal on a 'tidying-up' of Batalha, both within and without, which has received many criticisms. Not having known it in its days of Baroque disorder, I can only express my wonder at its present purity: a reddish limestone fantasy rising at the heart of a hollow, and invisible therefore until the main Lisbon–Oporto highway drops suddenly upon it. The road now runs well to one side, and some distance above normal ground level, so that passengers in even the fastest cars can briefly feast their eyes on the maze of flying buttresses, the carved West doorway, and the aspiring columns of the Unfinished Chapels.

The statue of the Holy Constable provoked polemics on another plane: between those who wanted him shown on horseback, and those who would have preferred him on foot, as he would appear

on the plinth awaiting him in the Praça de Figueira in Lisbon.
This is not so pettifogging a distinction as it may sound. Nuno
Alvares Pereira was one of the few nobles to support the cause of
John of Avis and independence. And though a noble, he chose to
dismount his troops and, against all knightly tradition, to fight on
foot.

This was not in order to be a good democrat—though that is
almost what some of the advocates of a pedestrian statue tried to
argue. It was because he correctly calculated that it was the way to
win. For these were exactly the same tactics followed by Portugal's new ally, England, in her dramatic victories earlier in the
century at Crecy and Poitiers. Indeed, a detachment of English
archers was present at Aljubarrota to support these tactics: the
contribution of John of Gaunt, who was soon to become John I's
father-in-law.

There was English influence not only in the battle, but in the
building which rose to commemorate it. There is a very English
flavour about the lofty nave, and a strong possibility that Huguete,
the second architect in charge of the works, was an Englishman.

Even if he were not, the founder's chapel, for which he was
responsible, forms at least one corner 'which is for ever England'.
Here lies John I, looking well content after his successful reign
of nearly half a century. By his side, her hand in his, reposes
Philippa of Lancaster, who predeceased him by eighteen years.
With her dying breath she had blessed the great expedition riding
in the Tagus, ready to sail against Ceuta bearing her eager young
sons.

And round them lie four of those sons, hailed by Camoens in
one of his noblest lines as

'*Inclita geração, altos infantes.*'

'Superior generation, high princes.'

These are the 'holy prince' Fernando, who died in captivity in
Morocco; Pedro, later regent of the kingdom; John; and the
enigmatic but immortal Henry.

It is instructive to compare these men, who embarked on that first great Portuguese expedition overseas in 1415, with their cousins the sons of the English Henry IV. For they, too, were talented: the dynamic Henry V; the loyal John, Duke of Bedford; the cultured Humphrey, Duke of Gloucester. And this other 'band of brothers', to quote Shakespeare as well as Camoens, had their own victorious expedition in 1415. Thus, while one group of John of Gaunt's grandsons took Ceuta, another group triumphed at Agincourt.

But whereas the first had its eyes on the future, the second was looking towards the past. Within forty years Henry Plantaganet's dream of Continental empire was dead for ever. But the legacy of Henry the Navigator is with us still.

One of Philippa's sons, the eldest, is absent from the founder's chapel. For King Edward, whose *Loyal Counsellor* is the earliest major prose work of Portuguese, began a chapel, or rather chapels, of his own. There were to be seven, the eighth side of the octagonal building forming the entrance. It was again designed by Huguete, and might have risen as a chaste, almost Perpendicular construction had not the king died only five years after his accession. When his grandson Manuel I continued the work seventy years later, Portuguese architecture was under the influence of lands more exotic than England.

So the great doorway then erected seems at first to belong to Araby or the Indies, both in its intertwining ivy decoration, and in its Moslem-like repetition—365 times, say the guides—of the unfamiliar words, *tā yaserey* (even beyond my death), the last part of the motto of the melancholic King Edward.

Manuel had only half raised the great columns, incrustated with stone foliage, on which the roof of the chapels was to rest, when all his attention was drawn towards the Jerónimos at Belém. Hence the *Capelas Imperfeitas* remain unfinished still.

He again succeeded in transforming Gothic in the Royal cloister, part of the original monastery, filling the arches with delicate white marble tracery, suspended on slender columns. Off this leads the chapter house, where the visitor stepping across the quiet threshold is suddenly shocked by the clashing, rather than mere clicking, of boots, as two sentries spring to attention on either side of the Portuguese Unknown Soldiers (one killed in Flanders, and one in Africa). Its magnificent single-span roof proved so dangerous to build that it is said to have been completed by condemned prisoners.

Farther on lies the refectory, with a First World War museum, and then a plainer cloister of Afonso V which Manuel never got round to embellishing. Some of the surrounding rooms now serve as the Post Office and Parish Council offices of the little village which grew up around the monastery.

Both psychologically and geographically Batalha is as close as one can get to the heart of Portugal. Lisbon, though north of the Tagus, belongs in latitude and climate to the south. It is the sight of those red-gold pinnacles soaring from the basin below which marks the significant meridian.

'Batalha is beginning to make me feel guilty', said an English girl who for reasons best known to herself spent most of her weekends hitch-hiking between Lisbon and Coimbra. 'I sweep past it so often, and feel that I owe it a deeper obeisance.'

She was right. For it is indeed a holy place.

But it is not the only holy place in this Lusitanian heartland, where Estremadura and Ribatejo meet the Beiras. Many of them are visited in a long, crowded one-day excursion from Lisbon. Rather less are 'done' by that two-week coach tour optimistically entitled 'Northern Spain and Portugal', whose passengers I have often seen emerging exhausted from their charabancs to catch the train home at Hendaye. To do them justice, however, requires two nights away from Lisbon; or better still a whole holiday, or part of a holiday, on the adjoining coast.

Here there are four choices. The nearest to Lisbon is Peniche, on a rocky peninsula joined to the mainland by an isthmus only half a mile wide. It thus lives and breathes the encircling sea, and as befits the second fishing port of the country, has a well-deserved reputation for seafood. If those dubious Phoenicians ever did make a permanent settlement on this coast, it was surely here, less because of the doubtful etymology of its name than because the site so closely resembles Cádiz, Gibraltar and Calpe, where they are known to have founded cities.

Peniche's cliffs are strangely weathered, and some of the forma-
tions have been given unsuitable names like 'Palace of Queen
Leonor'. From the lighthouse at Cape Carvoeiro at the peninsula's
western end there is a good view of its continuation eight miles
out at sea: the Berlengas. Here, too, the rocks form caves,
grottoes and tunnels; and the peace and isolation make them a
'holy place' for the worship of nature herself. Those who wish to
enjoy this peace for more than a single day have at their disposal
either a camping site on the main islet (about two and a half
miles long), or an unusual *pousada* which has been installed in a
seventeenth-century fort, approachable only by a narrow
bridge.

The road north runs some way inland in order to avoid the
Lagoa de Óbidos, a melancholy but entirely unspoilt lagoon
whose shores are very hard to reach on four wheels. Óbidos,
from which the lagoon takes its name, stands out even in a
country with more than its fair share of castles and battlements. A
perfect medieval walled *cité*, it charms more than Carcassonne because it stands alone, and more than Ávila because it is smaller,
and set amidst low green hills instead of bare high *meseta*. Within
the grim grey defences—the whole length of which can be explored along the sentries' walk—all is white: white houses, white
churches, white craft shops where the folkweave and baskets on
sale can be seen in process of manufacture.

It is appropriate that such crafts should flourish here, for
Óbidos has a long artistic tradition. We have already noticed in
the Janelas Verdes some of the still lifes of Josefa de Ayala, the
woman painter whose serene work forms such a large fraction of
the somewhat barren artistic legacy of Portugal's seventeenth
century. Her uneventful, happy life was centred to such an extent
on this little town, where her father was also a painter (four of
his canvases can be seen in S. Pedro at Peniche), that she is often
known as Josefa de Óbidos. Her 'Mystic Marriage of St.
Catherine', with other pictures, can be seen in the church of S.
Maria, which also contains the fine tomb of D. João de Noronha
of 1525, attributed to Jean de Rouen, one of the group of French
sculptors who emigrated to Portugal under John III.

The square on which this church stands is the largest of several delightful paved spaces. On an adjoining one at a lower level is the Misericordia, with more of Josefa's work. And at the end of the quietest of main streets stands the castle. Part of this was rebuilt on more comfortable lines in the sixteenth century, with the addition of Manueline windows. It has more recently been made more comfortable still by conversion into a *pousada*.

Two brief halts should be made outside the town before proceeding on northwards. At the bottom of the hill stands the hexagonal church of the Senhor da Pedra of the 1740s: it captures both the monumental and the Baroque qualities of Joanine building.

Shortly afterwards we should pause to enjoy the crenellated silhouette of Óbidos against the skyline: a view hidden as we approached it from the south.

We are soon in busy Caldas da Rainha, where in my own experience it always seems to be market day. Certainly there is always plenty on sale there. Caldas is celebrated for its cakes, for its meringue-like *cavacas*, and for an atrocious green and yellow pottery twisted into every size and shape imaginable.

Even I did not imagine one particular shape, only obtainable 'under the counter', until two English girls assured me they had each received examples of it from their Portuguese boy-friends. The same custom exists at Amarante in the Douro Litoral (see Chapter 8), but only one day a year, and in the ephemeral form of a pastry. Whereas the phallic souvenirs of Caldas still lie in young ladies' secret drawers, realistic in their lurid colours, to remind them of an 'April in Portugal'.

Some regard the large collection of nineteenth- and twentieth-century painting and sculpture in the Malhôa Museum, down in the pleasant park, as almost as tasteless as the pottery. I myself find pre-industrial landscapes and society queens of yester-year at once restful and nostalgic. There is a poignant delight in recapturing a world so near in time, yet so infinitely remote. And has that world quite vanished from Portugal? Certainly not in this quiet provincial museum, where the occasional visitor is beamed in by unhurried guides in livery. The Francisco Franco after whom one of the galleries is named was a Portuguese painter, incidentally, and not a Spanish generalissimo.

Caldas da Rainha means 'hot baths of the Queen'. The hot baths are still there, and although the Queen Leonor who first came here to treat her rheumatism died nearly five hundred years ago, she left behind a hospital and the somehow cosy church of Nossa Senhora do Pópolo, on which sits an octagonal Manueline cupola.

Ten miles on we suddenly come upon what is almost the only stretch of calm sea-water in Portugal. There is plenty of calm water elsewhere, but it is fresh. There is plenty of sea-water, but it can be rough. S. Martinho do Porto, the second of our four resorts, offers on its perfect land-locked bay (*o porto*) a sheltered beach such as France's Atlantic coast offers at St. Jean de Luz, and Spain's at San Sebastian.

At our third resort it is not so much the beach that one looks at as the inhabitants. Yet despite all the photographs taken daily of the check woollen shirts and trousers of the men of Nazaré, and the several-layered striped skirts of their womenfolk, they go unconcernedly about their business of mending nets and gutting fish.

Indeed when I once settled down with a group of friends to fried sardines and wine in a small *taverna*, it was the proprietress and her daughters who gathered with their black kerchiefs over their gold ear-rings to stare at *us*. But that was the first day of our trip together up to the 'Holy Places'. By the time we had been stared at in inns at Peniche, Tomar, and Santarém we knew why we were of such interest. For we were a Czech, a German, and an Englishman accompanied by girls from South Korea, France and Brazil . . . and our only common language was Portuguese!

That particular *taverna* was up in the Sitio, the upper and older part of the town, accessible both by road and by a funicular up the cliff. From the Sitio one looks down on the lower town and the long open beach, along which are drawn up the characteristic tall fishing boats.

In the Sitio is Nazaré's oldest monument, the seventeenth-century church of Our Lady. It contains a Gothic statue to which no guides do justice. Legend claims that it appeared in order to halt a horseman pursuing a stag in the mist, who was about to fall off the cliff.

The working of economic laws is hard to follow. There are few fishermen left in the Channel Islands, or in many places along the French and Spanish Mediterranean, where tourism provides a living so much better and easier than the sea. But in Nazaré, which receives more foreign tourists for its size than anywhere else in Portugal, fishing remains the great and indeed the essential industry. I was surprised when I gave a woman a lift home from six miles out of town to hear that she walked that distance and back every day in order to sell the fish she carried in a basket on her head.

Alcobaça lies less than ten miles inland from Nazaré, but no greater contrast within a Portuguese context can be imagined. Whereas Nazaré is sea-orientated, architecturally simple, redolent of family life, and working class, Alcobaça is agricultural, monumental, monastic, and not merely aristocratic but royal.

It is impossible to separate these qualities, for they are interdependent. The first king of Portugal, Afonso Henriques, founded the monastery in 1152 in gratitude for his capture of Santarém from the Moslems. He handed it over to the fashionable new order of the Cistercians from his father's Burgundy, who were the most scientific farmers as well as the best builders of the age. Thus the fruit-growing potentialities of the surroundings were appreciated and encouraged; those who go through here at the right season can still enjoy the melons and pears—and perhaps even the peaches so appreciated by Sacheverell Sitwell.

Partly, then, from the riches which their own good husbandry had created, the monks were able to build a church which imitated but surpassed in size that of its mother-house at Clairvaux. Its thirteenth-century west door at the top of a wide staircase is now flanked by two eighteenth-century towers. This ought to be grotesque, but is oddly pleasing.

Within the church, as in even the most modern Cistercian churches, one's attitude turns to awe. The white fathers have left a vast white nave, supported by tall white columns with nine white chapels round the white apse which runs behind the high altar. And in the centre of each of the white transepts sits a white tomb whose intricate carving emphasises further the simplicity of everything else.

These tombs, the acknowledged masterpiece of Portuguese medieval sculpture, are of Portugal's most famous pair of lovers. He, Pedro, was the King's son and heir. She, Inés de Castro, was a Spanish lady-in-waiting who accompanied the Aragonese princess who had been chosen as the heir's bride. And though Pedro duly married the princess, it was with Inés that he fell in love.

On his wife's early death, he went to live with her; and their common-law marriage (though Pedro was later to claim that they had in fact been through a ceremony together at distant Bragança) lasted ten years and was blessed with four children.

Their domestic idyll was interrupted when certain royal counsellors, fearing—not without reason—the threats posed by Inés's foreign connexions, argued with their master that his son's lovely mistress should be done away with. Arriving at the country house near Coimbra where she lived, the King was persuaded by her tears to spare her: the scene has been a favourite alike with painters, poets, and playwrights. But as he rode away, his counsellors returned to the attack, until he bade them do what they thought for the best.

Thus in 1355 was Inés de Castro done to death. Two years later, however, her lover on his accession had her corpse exhumed and arrayed as Queen. The whole court was obliged to kneel before her and kiss her decaying hand. And brutally but understandably the unforgiving Pedro ordered her murderers' hearts to be torn from their living bodies beneath the window of the room where he was banqueting.

Critics are uncertain whether the carvings on their tombs represent events from their lives, or merely symbolic scenes: whether, for example, the Last Judgement actually shows Pedro and Inés gazing down from Heaven at her murderers in Hell! But the inscription 'Until the end of the world' certainly expresses his hope to achieve in a future life the reunion denied him in this. So does the position of the two tombs, with their effigies lying feet to feet, in order that on the Last Day they may rise to gaze at once on each other across the nave of Alcobaça.

Not in order to disturb this romantic story, but to emphasise the very special relationship of Pedro with Inés, it is worth remembering that he continued to have a sentimental life after her death. The year after his accession he had a son by a purely Portuguese mistress: the future victor of Aljubarrota, John I.

The monastic buildings include the beautiful Cloister of Silence, and the kitchen complete with huge chimney and stone fish-tank fed by a channelled stream. As an antidote to what that ultimate *milord*, Beckford, referred to as 'the most distinguished temple of gluttony in Europe', there is a narrow passage off the refectory which is said to have provided a practical test of obesity. Those members of the order who could not squeeze through it had to diet until they could!

Farthest to the north and smallest, but also perhaps the most attractive of our four resorts along this coast is S. Pedro de Moel. Its dangerous beach—fortunately supplemented now by an artificial pool—its modern construction, its tiny out-of-season population, and above all its hinterland of pines to which it owes its resin-scented air, all remind me strongly of the Atlantic resorts of the Landes and the Gironde.

But the pine forest stretching at the back of those little French *stations* is less than two hundred years old, whereas the plantation of the *pinhal* behind S. Pedro de Moel began almost seven centuries ago. The primary object of King Dennis (whose tomb we saw at Odivelas) in planting this oldest of artificial woodlands was the same as that of Brémontier in the Landes: to arrest the inland march of the sand-dunes. Tradition has it that his Queen, S. Isabel, whose homeland of Aragon then extended across the Pyrenees, began the work by scattering an apronful of pineseed from France. And Portugal has now returned the gift. For travelling across Gascony and Guienne I find that most of the workers in the pinewoods are now Portuguese immigrants.

The forest did more than halt the sand. Afonso Lopes Vieira, the poet of S. Pedro de Moel, could write:

8. Queluz: the Garden

9. Alcobaça: the tomb of Inés de Castro

10. Tomar: the famous window by Diogo de Arruda

'Pinewood of heroic trees so handsome,
It was out of thy soul and thy body
That were born our caravels
Eager for the Unknown.'

Its official name is that of Leiria, the pleasant little district
capital twelve miles inland, beyond the English-founded glass-
works of Marinha Grande. King Dennis often stayed there with
Queen Isabel in the castle built on the hill by Afonso Henriques,
and added the great keep which dominates the town. The castle
chapel, however, Nossa Senhora da Pena, probably dates from the
time of John I, and the Renaissance windows, which give the
whole construction such an airy appearance when seen from
below, from a century later still.

The cathedral, near the foot of the hill, was built after John III
had created four new dioceses in the mid-sixteenth century. Like
the others—Miranda do Douro, Portalegre, and Velha Goa in
India—it is an interesting combination of Renaissance columns
with a late Gothic vaulted roof.

The best view of Leiria as a whole is from the chapel of Nossa
Senhora da Encarnação, a short distance out of town on the
other side of the river. It is reached by the southernmost of those
elaborate monumental staircases which are such a feature of the
north of the country. And in the hills five miles to the north
stands the sanctuary of Milagres, southernmost of the isolated
Baroque pilgrimage churches, of which we shall later see so many.
This one is notable inside for its variety of marbles, and outside
for a hexagonal covered well.

Some miles farther north, on the very limits of Estremadura,
Pombal, to which the great Marquis retired on his fall from power,
lies on the main Coimbra highway. On the same latitude, just off
the road to Figueira da Foz, stands the leafy spa of Monte Real,
with the ruins of a medieval royal palace.

Alcobaça is the holy place of the Portuguese *reconquista*.
Batalha, only twelve miles to the north, is the holy place of
national independence. But the holy place which receives most
pilgrims today is twelve miles farther east again.

There is no space here to discuss or even to describe the series of monthly appearances made by the Virgin in 1917 to three Portuguese children. (One of them, Lucia, still lives as a Carmelite nun in Coimbra, and left her cloister to be present once again at the scene of the miracle on the occasion of Pope Pius VI's visit fifty years later in 1967.) But it is instructive to make a brief comparison between Fátima and that other modern place of pilgrimage: Lourdes.

It is simpler, at once in its plain sanctuary, at one end of a gently rising concrete hollow—which I find aesthetically very satisfying —and even more in its pilgrims. Our Lady of Lourdes, it is true, has become almost the patron saint for half a dozen departments round. Anywhere between Toulouse, Bordeaux and Hendaye you are likely to find a notice in the village church announcing details of the annual parish outing to visit her. But on arrival at Lourdes the charabancs of peasants from Béarn and Armagnac are lost amidst the coaches full of Belgians and Italians under the guidance of their urbane *monsignori*, and the trainloads of cosmopolitan devotees from the north.

At Fátima, on the other hand, because of its situation at the heart of Portugal, and of Portugal's remoteness from the rest of Europe, the pilgrims are overwhelmingly Portuguese. They are by definition, therefore, overwhelmingly rural.

And they come not for cures—though cures there have been— but for much the same reasons that they follow their local *romaria*. For the pilgrimage to Fátima, like that to some chapel only a mile or two from their home, is a day out. There is an aura of perpetual picnic on the outskirts of the sanctuary. The very first time I visited Portugal, on a motor-cycle in 1951, I met the statue of Our Lady of Fátima with a band of followers several miles from her home. In homely and bucolic fashion she was being carried round to bless a number of the surrounding parishes.

It is worth remembering, too, that Our Lady spoke to Bernadette in the patois of the tiny province of Bigorre. But she addressed Lucia, Jacinta and Francisco in the tongue of all Portugal and of Lusitania beyond the seas.

The twisting hilly road eastwards from Fátima provides good

views of the ruined medieval hill-town of Ourém, where in the
fifteenth century a palace was raised within an older castle by a
prince of the Bragança family (Count of Ourém was one of the
Duke's titles).

We have now entered the province of Ribatejo, the least helpful
and meaningful of the country's administrative divisions. Its
name means banks of the Tagus, and it does indeed straddle the
middle reaches of the river's course through Portugal. But
though its very existence creates in our minds a 'Ribatejo image'
of Cartaxo wines and lush flat pastures where bulls graze, it in
fact has no natural unity. The river separates two distinct regions.
The flat, sparsely-populated country to its south fades imper-
ceptibly into the Alentejo; while the well-watered hills and valleys
to its north differ in no essentials from Estremadura.

On one of these hills, and in one of those valleys, as we continue east from Fátima, we come upon Tomar. Many travellers
have remarked on the Italianate appearance of the steep mount,
shaded with pines and cypresses, which is crowned by the Convent of Christ. And Nossa Senhora da Conceição, a tiny basilica
three-quarters of the way up, would harmonise perfectly with an
Italian Renaissance setting, although her architect was probably
the Portuguese João de Castilho.

There is no need to fear driving up the hill, for there is a vast
parking space on top. It forms, indeed, one of the best of Portugal's many landscaped picnic places.

The site of the Convent of Christ was first given by Afonso
Henriques to the Order of the Templars, who played in the
Portuguese Reconquest much the same role as that played in
Spain by the Knights of Calatrava, of Santiago, and of Alcantara
(though these were also active in Portugal: from those of Cala-
trava originated the order of Avis of which John I was Master).

From the time of the Templars dates the original circular
church which formed the nucleus of the whole building. When,
early in the fourteenth century, the French king gave the example
to other sovereigns of dissolving this order (just as four hundred
and fifty years later Pombal was to give the example of expelling
the Jesuits), the statesmanlike King Dennis preferred to 'nationa-

lise' them, turning over their Portuguese property and estates to a new order he specially founded for this purpose.

This Order of Christ soon established its headquarters at Tomar. There, under its Grand Masters of the blood royal, including Henry the Navigator and King Manuel, it transferred its resources from the now-completed Reconquest to expansion overseas. The 'Maltese cross', which reappears so often in Manueline architecture, as well as on the sails of the discoverers' caravels, is that of the Order. Its bread, scattered thus literally upon the waters, returned multiplied after many days, permitting a rich accretion of buildings about the original round 'Temple'.

There are no less than seven cloisters. Two of the smallest are Gothic, built under Henry the Navigator. The others were added in Renaissance style under John III in the mid-sixteenth century. But it was King Manuel's architects who provided at once the synthesis and the features by which we shall remember Tomar.

Their work was in fact limited to the church, where statues and paintings were placed in the primitive circular building to which a rectangular nave was added. Its rich doorway, through which visitors enter the Convent, was by João de Castilho, whose later conversion to the Renaissance style is already latent in much of the detail. But the main body of the nave is in the 'pure' Manueline of Diogo de Arruda, brother of the Francisco de Arruda responsible for the Tower of Belém.

His famous window, with its rich and strange marine motifs, is best seen from the roof of one of the cloisters. It has often been described as 'overloaded'. But the weight of symbolic interpretation it has had to bear is heavier by far.

Given that the national style was still Gothic when Vasco da Gama returned from Calicut, how else could it be expected to react to the fantastic achievements and revelations of the discoveries? And even without the imposed order which was to come with the Renaissance influence, the most extravagant Manueline had a certain inbuilt discipline. Observe, for example, the vast spaces left uncovered round Diogo de Arruda's window. In spirit, if not in style, this is surely Camoens in stone.

The town of Tomar by the little river below has a parish church with Manueline tower and pulpit, and with some paintings attributed to Gregorio Lopes, one of several artists who made the early sixteenth century a worthy successor to the age of Nuno Gonçalves. And at Number 73 of the Rua Dr. Joachim Jacinto is a tiny square sixteenth-century Gothic synagogue, discovered and restored by a Polish Jewish refugee during the Second World War. He installed there the fascinating Jewish remains and inscriptions he collected from all over Portugal.

Tomar's stream after a few miles joins the Zêzere. Rising in the Serra da Estrêla this has more force than most other purely Portuguese rivers, and has therefore been harnessed to produce hydro-electricity. The traveller should be careful to take not the direct route to Constância, but the road which runs across the dam of Castelo de Bode, the base now of a long sinuous lake.

At Constância the Zêzere joins the Tagus. Nearby, an island in the river bears the picturesque castle of Almourol, placed there in the twelfth century by the same Grand Master of the Templars who built the original round church of Tomar.

Eight miles in the other direction from Constância lies Abrantes, the last place of any size on the Tagus before Talavera, a third of the way across Spain. Indeed, it was from Abrantes that Wellington began the advance which culminated in his victory at the Battle of Talavera.

The strategic importance of Abrantes is clear to anyone clambering up to the castle, built by King Dennis, who always recognised a good position. Within the wide ramparts, with the Beira highlands behind them, the Alentejo stretching away across the river, and the valley which the Castilians might be expected to follow at their feet, Nuno Alvares Pereira and John of Avis united their armies before Aljubarrota. The ruins of the castle chapel now constitute a small museum of sculpture.

Among the steep streets and tree-lined squares of the pleasant town below there are three churches whose present appearance owes most to the later sixteenth century.

Despite the high price of petrol in Portugal, people from Abrantes and all places north-east will go to any lengths to avoid taking the busy main road to Lisbon. They prefer instead what seems a long way round, biting into the Alentejo through Ponte de Sor and Mora, and running alongside the superb reservoir of Montargil.

Even when their destination is Santarém, which is situated on the main road, they will approach it through Golegã, famous for its November horse-fair, and through Chamusca and Alpiarça across the river. In Alpiarça stands a private museum, the Casa dos Patudos. Never having arrived there on a Thursday or a Sunday afternoon (when it is open), I have yet to visit its fine collections of Arraiolos carpets, Portuguese china, and pictures which include a Rubens, a Zurbarán, a Murillo, a Josefa de Ayala, and a Delacroix.

Santarém was important not only because, like Abrantes, it stands on a hill dominating the Tagus, but also because until the construction of the toll-bridge at Vila Franca de Xira it was the lowest point at which the river could be crossed by road. Even Ulysses is supposed to have got up here, according to a legend whereby he seduced the local ruler's daughter, from whom it derived its Roman name of Scalabis. It was still important when in Visigothic times it acquired its present name from S. Iria, when her floating coffin came to rest on a sandbank. The shrine which arose on the spot was later washed away. But enough medieval churches survive to make Santarém today the 'holy place' of Portuguese Gothic.

Around the two adjacent squares into which lead all the main roads are the fourteenth-century S. Francisco, the seventeenth-century seminary, and the curious octagonal chapel of Piedade of the same period. With the exception of S. Clara to the north, the other churches lie deeper amongst the maze of narrow streets which form the heart of the town.

Those of Marvila, of the Milagre, and of the Alcaçova are Renaissance reconstructions of earlier buildings. S. João de Alporão, now a museum, is of Transitional style. It shelters a glorious fifteenth-century tomb containing nothing more than a single tooth of Dom Duarte de Meneses: all that his widow retained when this nobleman was lost in one of the Moroccan campaigns of Afonso V.

But the glory of Santarém is the Graça, built in the same period and style as Batalha, but in a whiter stone. The famous tomb here is that of Pedro Alvares Cabral, discoverer of Brazil. The floor of the Graça is some way below the level of the street, and the view down into the nave is breathtaking. I was lucky enough to see it for the first time in an evening light, and in April. To round off my first memories of Santarém I walked down an avenue of flowering trees in full bloom, to the garden of the Portas do Sol to enjoy its famous view over the Tagus.

It is not a very easy river to approach by road. But in past ages, when water-borne traffic was more important, it was itself a highway. There used to be a royal palace at Salvaterra de Magos, now remote on the left bank. And at nearby Muge have been discovered traces of the first settled villages of Portugal. Skeletons uncovered there show short people with long heads, who lived in the Middle Stone Age perhaps ten thousand years ago. But they were of the same human material as the Portuguese of today.

Although the Ribatejo is the centre of the country's bull-fighting, and the only region where it can be considered as the predominant sport, the 'holy place' of this mystery is Vila Franca de Xira, back in Estremadura, and a mere twenty miles from Lisbon. Most of the villages on the road there from Santarém have their own bull-rings. A couple of miles across the Marshal Carmona toll-bridge there is an hotel, the *Gado Bravo*, with a private one of its own. Even Lisbon's red-brick ring at Campo Pequeno is on the way out towards Vila Franca (its etymology is not, as might be supposed, the same as Villefranche, 'free town', but comes from the *francos*, the Franks, i.e. the French knights of Afonso Henriques who were settled there).

In Portugal the bulls are never killed, and the whole ceremony is said to have an even greater ballet-like elegance than bull-fights in Spain. I can only repeat this at second hand, for I have never been present at one. Indeed the very fact that I am writing about a country where bull-fighting is of merely secondary importance emboldens me to say what I would never dare to confess in any book about Spain. This is that I find it rather a bore.

And having thus offended all those who love bull-fighting,

without winning the approval of those who hate it, I shall never-theless draw up, as I have drawn up so often, for a slow picnic beside the bull-ring at Vila Franca de Xira, in a rough park beside the river. But it is not of *corridas* and *quadrilhas* and *toureiros* that I shall be thinking, as I sip the wine of Cartaxo or of Vila Chã de Ourique. It will be of that significant crossing we are about to make over the toll-bridge, and of the whole new world which awaits us beyond the Tagus.

TAILPIECE: VELHA ALIANÇA

There had been friendly relations between England and Portugal ever since a force of English crusaders had helped Afonso Hen-riques to capture Lisbon from the Moslems in 1147. And after an English detachment had fought alongside the Portuguese at Alju-barrota—which was won by adopting the English tactics—the working alliance was converted into a formal Treaty at West-minster in the following year.

It declared that '. . . there shall be between the two . . . kings now reigning, their heirs and successors and between the subjects of both kingdoms, an inviolable, eternal, solid, perpetual and true league of friendship, alliance and union, not only between each other, their heirs and successors, but also between and in favour of their kingdoms, lands, dominions and subjects, vassals, allies and friends, wherever they may be, so that each of them shall have the obligation to assist and give aid to the other against all people now born or who shall come to be born and who shall seek to violate the peace of others or in any way make bold to offend their states'.

This Treaty has been renewed on various occasions, notably in 1642 after the restoration of independence, in 1654 under Crom-well, in 1661 at the time of Charles II's marriage to Catherine of Bragança, and in 1703. This last renewal took the name of the English negotiators, John Methuen and his son Paul, and in-cluded the famous commercial provisions whereby English woollens were to enter Portugal duty free, whilst Portuguese wine was to enter England paying only two-thirds the tariff on other wines.

The stimulus given by the Methuen Treaty to the development of British industry was considerable, but this is hardly the place to discuss it. And we must reach the Douro before considering its equally decisive stimulus for the Portuguese wine trade. But it was hardly a stimulus for the rest of Portuguese industry. French historians in particular are unanimous in their condemnation of what they see as one of the more dastardly machinations of perfidious Albion.

But this consequence could not be foreseen. Portugal in the late seventeenth century had suffered an acute economic crisis, beside which the worst nightmare of Sir Stafford Cripps or Harold Wilson would seem a pleasant reverie. There was a reverse trade gap of 400 per cent: imports, that is to say, were five times as great as exports. Financial salvation was on its way in 1703, with the gold which was beginning to arrive from Brazil. It was the sudden rise in purchasing power brought by this which destroyed the infant Portuguese industries, and not English competition.

In remote areas, almost untouched by a money economy, craft industries persisted, and persist still. You can buy hand-made blankets in Mourão or Reguengos de Monsaraz, while all over Trás-os-Montes cottagers spin and weave like characters from nursery tales. It was for this reason that Portuguese industrialisation, when it came, developed first in these remote areas, such as the unlikely Covilhã, on the farther slopes of the Serra da Estrêla.

One stimulus given by the Methuen Treaty was to the considerable British colony in Portugal, and in particular to the important fraction of it already centred on Oporto. The Oporto colony has given rise to an entire literature of its own. For although it depends on commerce, it is an exotic commerce, with an exciting history.

It was so self-contained as to invite literary treatment. For unlike other British colonies, it never integrated with its host society. All over France and Spanish America there are towns where a sprinkling of English names in the telephone directory is the only indication that as recently as the early years of this century there was an active British community there, drinking tea and sub-scribing to the *Illustrated London News*. A shift in trade or the exchange rate has removed its underpinning prosperity. A single generation of intermarriage has done the rest. The grandchildren, needing English for business, must expensively relearn it at Berlitz.

The inevitable comparison with Oporto is Jerez, the sherry town. There, although commercial relations with England are of less long standing, integration between English and Spaniards is total. The young men of the British sherry shipping families look and behave like any other prosperous Andalusian *señoritos*. The older men of the Spanish families, with their clipped English accents and their Savile Row suits, fit into the clubs of Pall Mall as well as any retired colonels or country landowners. They are probably in any case second cousins.

It is not so in Oporto, where for three hundred years two separate societies have coexisted without mingling. But ex-clusiveness has its perils. Takeovers by Portuguese capital, and the natural tendency of legislation to discourage employment of expatriates, has reduced the number of Britons making careers in port. The British colony, which numbered close on two thousand before the war, with a preponderance of men and women in the prime of life, is down to perhaps six hundred, with a much higher average age.

Such new recruits as do arrive are often only on short contracts to set up new plants, and lack both the attitudes which go with permanency, and the background which went with the colony's mercantile yet aristocratic tradition. Though the silver still gleams in the British Factory House, the continued existence of the essential British preparatory school at Foz poses constant problems. Though I would hate to exaggerate by using the word 'beleaguered', it comes to mind after a visit to Oporto.

Lisbon's long-standing British colony, on the other hand, has in recent years been strongly reinforced by the large numbers of retired people who have established themselves along the Costa do Sol between Carcavelos and Cascais. Their arrival can only benefit both themselves and the country they have adopted. It may even benefit the existing colony, which from the little I saw of it seemed exclusive in the wrong sort of way. I regularly attended the English church in Lisbon, but only exchanged words with two members of the congregation: a coloured South African, and a charming Portuguese convert to Anglicanism.

The greatest influx of British since the war, however, has been to the Algarve. Even here there was already a nucleus at Praia da Rocha, and in so far as a long thin band of coast can have a centre, there it remains. But such touchstones as the *Daily Telegraph* and branded marmalades are now available all the way from Lagos to Monte Gordo, with pockets of more intensive acclimatisation around such English developments as Praia da Luz and Vale do Lobo. I have no complaint against the price-dictated exclusiveness of these and others. As I suggest in Appendix 3, they offer a necessary alternative to the vulgarities of the Spanish Mediterranean.

For you are not obliged to buy into any of these exclusive developments, or to apply for membership of any of the exclusive British clubs. Like me, you can spend months on end in Portugal without seeing your compatriots or seeking their company.

But don't sniff at their failure to get to know the country or its culture. You owe them more than you think. For why are we made so welcome everywhere? It's not merely you or me the Portuguese are listening to, waving at, inviting out, forgiving. It's the *Velha Aliança*.

4

BEYOND THE TAGUS

'I expect you often go to Spain for your holidays?' I asked some friends who are members of the British Colony at Oporto.

To my surprise the answer was 'Never. When we don't go up the Douro to our *quinta*, or to the seaside cottage near Esposende, we drive down to my brother-in-law's home in the Algarve. It's such a different world down there that it's just as much of a change as going abroad.'

Portugal does in fact offer an extraordinary variety of scenery and atmosphere. But it is unnecessary to travel all the way from Oporto to Faro to experience the contrast. It is sufficient to drive across that bridge at Vila Franca de Xira near which we halted at the end of the last chapter.

The monotonous flat plain of popular imagination is crossed within the first few miles, and is characteristic only of the Ribatejo bull pastures. The Alentejo proper (*alem* = beyond, *Tejo* = Tagus) is a land of ancient mountains infinitely eroded. But the gentle undulations which remain from these all-but-vanished highlands enable us to see even farther than on the absolutely level *meseta* of Castile.

For the air is crystal-clear across the infinite wheatlands, and the white towns and villages, generally crowning a more pronounced hillock, can be seen from many miles. Several writers have commented on the distant view of Montemor-o-Novo on the main road from Lisbon to Madrid. Personally, I remember still more clearly my first sight of Beja from across a reservoir near Aljustrel. It was all of fifteen miles away. But with a small pair of binoculars I could make out every church and chimney on the skyline.

These centres are the more noticeable because they are few. The population of the Alentejo is sparse—less than a tenth of the country's total in almost a third of its area—but it is concentrated. Many of the villages number four or five thousand souls: they are towns in every sense except the one essential characteristic that distinguishes town life: diversification of work. The only activities in these rural centres—Alter do Chão or Moura or Ferreira do Alentejo—are agricultural.

In this the Alentejo closely resembles the adjoining Spanish province of Estremadura (which has nothing except its name in common with Portugal's Estremadura, the far western and most Atlantic of all her provinces). On both sides of the frontier, too, there is a scarcity of trees, except where the low groves of cork exhibit, when newly-stripped, their raw red wounds. (The manufacture of cork articles, from useless carvings to practical containers for keeping food warm, is one of the Alentejo's main industries, and cork itself, mainly from the Alentejo, is one of Portugal's main exports.) On both sides of the frontier large estates, lineal descendants of the Roman *latifundia*, are held by absentee landlords. And the frontier itself is artificial. For although since 1801 the Guadiana has divided the two states for a forty-mile stretch below Badajoz, a small fraction of the Portuguese nation still lives under Spanish rule beyond it.

In Roman times the heartland of their province of Lusitania stretched across today's frontier, from its capital of *Emerita* (Mérida, well inside Spain) to *Ebora* (Évora, which has the same etymology as York, the Roman Eboracum) and *Pax Julia* (Beja). Here, in a countryside relatively more densely populated than today, that noble rebel Sertorius had his first headquarters. And here the invading Moslems found a congenial environment, not unlike the plains of Fez or of Constantine.

What, then, made this frontier? For all its artificiality it is one of the oldest in Europe, having remained unchanged since 1253, except for that little incident in 1801 with which we shall deal anon. A French geographer has plausibly suggested that it was due simply to the balance between Castilian and Portuguese ambitions as both kingdoms advanced south.

Until they reached the line of the Tagus—the northern limit of the Alentejo—Portugal was still a country dependent on Leon, and rivalry between Christians was modified by the necessity of defending themselves against the Moors. But after Afonso Henriques's assumption of independence and the steady deterioration of Moslem power during the following century, a free-for-all developed. So the present boundary from the Tagus down to the mouth of the Guadiana does indeed seem to have been determined by the conflicting pressures of two rival spheres of influence.

But the same geographer adds that the regularity of the advance of the Portuguese was partly governed by the considerable use they made of sea-power, as in the capture of Lisbon, and later of Silves in the Algarve. And here he has touched on what constitutes the nuance separating the Spanish Estremadura from the Portuguese Alentejo. For all the large white villages, the big estates, and the cork trees they have in common, the *llanuras* and the *sierras* of Badajoz and Cáceres are essentially and utterly Continental; whereas the *planicies* and the *serras* of Beja, Évora and Portalegre have a taste, however attenuated, of the sea.

This sea, of course, is the Atlantic, along which the Alentejo even has a short coastline. But it is not of Somerset or Normandy or even of Galicia that we are reminded by the white pilgrimage chapels, the dry pinewoods, the infinite cornfields, yellow already in June. It is rather of Catalonia, of Sicily, or of Algeria. In crossing the Tagus we have crossed into that part of Portugal which Orlando Ribeiro described as essentially Mediterranean.

Even along the coast we seem to leave behind grey seas and heavy skies as we head south from Lisbon. Landing from the ferry amidst the fish restaurants and sardine stalls of Cacilhas, or driving over the slender-looking Salazar Bridge, with the tower of Belém like a toy fortress far below, we are conscious of entering a more meridional world, although for many miles beyond Setúbal we shall still be in Estremadura.

The Setúbal peninsula makes a striking contrast with the hinterland of Lisbon from which it was so effectively isolated until the opening of the bridge in 1966. The *auto-estrada* which runs on from the bridge crosses a stony sandy expanse redeemed by a large pinewood. If we turn right to follow the coast right round through the fishing village and resort of Costa da Caparica, a sandy track leads us past the lagoon of Albufeira. Its name recalls not only the Arab domination, but also that greater Albufera near Valencia, equally cut off by a thin tongue of land from the sea—but in its case from the Mediterranean.

The peninsula's south-western tip forms the high cape of Espichel, more impressive in the length of coastline it dominates from Cascais to Sines than the Cabo da Roca or even than Cape St. Vincent itself. Beside the lighthouse are a seventeenth-century chapel and the simple lodgings, usually deserted, which fill up with pilgrims for the *romaria* early in October.

Cape Espichel shelters the south coast of the peninsula. The additional protection this receives from the Serra da Arrábida, rising almost sheer to over sixteen hundred feet immediately behind, gives it an almost Riviera-like quality. We are driven to employ such a term, for the blue of the sea, the climate, and the vegetation (see Introduction) are alike Mediterranean. At Portinho da Arrábida only the clean, tide-cleansed sand reminds us that we are on the shores of the Atlantic. The average winter temperature of 14° Centigrade is only equalled in the Algarve.

Behind Sesimbra the Serra is not so high. This substantial fishing village beneath a twelfth-century castle is therefore more easily approached. And approached it certainly is, making it another Cascais for crowds though not for elegance. The recently-built *Hotel do Mar*, however, is an interesting example of contemporary Portuguese architecture, especially in its use of *azulejos* in the swimming-pool, and in its skilful adaptation to the different levels of the site.

There are a number of country palaces in and near Arrábida. That of the Duke of Aveiro is at Vila Nogueira de Azeitão. Not far away is that of Bacalhoa, rebuilt in the early sixteenth century by the son of the great Afonso de Albuquerque. Although its style is Renaissance rather than Manueline, there is a very natural Indian inspiration about some of the details, notably the cupolas of the towers. That of the Duke of Palmela lies in the other direction, at Calhariz: it dates from a century and a half later. But permission to visit them is not always easy to obtain. Even the Convento Novo, perched high above Portinho da Arrábida, requires an authorisation from the Palmela estate.

For the Palmela family, now as for centuries past, owns much of the property hereabouts—including the entire Serra da Arrábida. In the last century they threw up a great liberal states-man, a Lusitanian Lord Grey. Unhappily, while his English con-temporary was piloting the Reform Bill of 1832, Palmela could only effect his reforms by taking part in a civil war. But most of the Portuguese nobility, a small, tight, inter-related caste, took the side of Dom Miguel and absolutism, and were obliged to withdraw from public life after his defeat. With more Palmelas, the Crown might not have been quite so unprotected when Republicanism gathered strength.

Palmela itself is at the eastern end of the Serra. Its castle was built between the twelfth and the sixteenth centuries by the knights of Santiago, one of the military orders which operated against the Moslems throughout the Christian kingdoms of Iberia. It offers a panorama of all the peninsula, of the two wide estuaries of the Tagus and the Sado which create it, and of the two ports, Lisbon and Setúbal, which have grown up on those estuaries.

This panorama can be enjoyed even better from the *corniche* road which runs along the ridge of the Serra from above Portinho da Arrábida to Setúbal. This also gives a bird's eye view of the low, long, narrow tongue of land called Troia, which has one line of beaches on the quiet, lake-like estuary of the Sado, and another on the open sea. It has the ruins of a Roman community, destroyed by a tidal wave early in the fifth century. This was just the period when other half-mythical cities, in Cardigan Bay and Finisterre, disappeared beneath the waves as the barbarians streamed in from the east. These ruins are not easy to reach, and Troia itself is all but inaccessible by road. Things will alter, how-ever, when the first Portuguese holiday apartments company completes the development it plans there.

By sea Troia is a mere twenty miles from Setúbal, now the third city of metropolitan Portugal in population, and its biggest

11. The castle of Almourol on its island in the Tagus

12. Batalha: the Royal cloister, whose original Gothic has been transformed by Manueline

13. Batalha: the *Capelas Imperfeitas* or Unfinished Chapels

fish-canning centre. Amongst a number of religious buildings the most important is the Church of Jesus, the earliest work of Boytac, himself the earliest of Manueline architects. Dating from 1491, seven years before the King's accession, it is indeed Manueline before Manuel. Its spirally twisting pillars are often regarded as a trade mark of the style as a whole, as they certainly are of Boytac in particular. Its cloister is more 'mature' Manueline.

A series of pictures of the same period taken from this church now hang in the municipal museum, in the adjoining former convent. Their unknown author, the 'Master of Setúbal', was one of the most gifted artists of the golden century of Portuguese art stretching from Nuno Gonçalves to the loss of independence.

Setúbal has produced distinguished practitioners of other arts: the pre-Romantic poet Bocage whom Portuguese quote almost as much as Camoens himself; and—better known outside Portugal —Luisa Todi the singer.

It is a busy, noisy town, and the route through it involves about half a dozen sharp right-angled bends. But once outside the quietness descends, and the kilometres peel away peacefully from these wonderful Portuguese roads. Without the many-laned panache of the motorways of other lands, they carry us with greater safety and as swiftly as we need, integrating us into the landscape instead of merely channelling us through it.

On such less-frequented and less-pretentious highways a cross-roads is a more romantic feature than in regions nearer to the heart of the consumer society. Inevitably, in view of its situation there are several such on the way east from Setúbal. Thus I have often stopped, for a cup of tea or a night's sleep, where white signposts in the middle of nowhere read 'MONTIJO E PONTE', 'LAGOS', 'FARO', 'BEJA', 'ÉVORA', 'ELVAS', and even 'ESPANHA'; and I have felt as the legionaries marching up Watling Street from London to Wroxeter must have felt when at High Cross they met the Fosse from Bath to Lincoln.

Tempting though the roads to Évora and Elvas may be, let us drive south before going inland. We are forced away from the sea by the wide, marshy estuary of the Sado, which we can only cross at Alcácer do Sal, and even then by a bridge which rises to allow the passage of small ships. For the Sado, with the Mira and the Guadiana, is one of the few navigable rivers south of the Tagus.

The 'Sal' of Alcácer do Sal is the salt still extracted from the Sado marshes. It is the best and most savoury in Portugal, and formed the foundation of Setúbal's fish preserving industry. In these marshes malaria was once endemic, and something of its lassitude seems to have entered the spirit of the white little town, sleeping below its ruined castle.

Thirty miles on, after the Serra de Grândola—first of the low lines of hills which run parallel to this coast—comes Santiago do Cacém. Again it lies at the foot of a castle (one of the Templars'). Just before entering the town a signpost indicates the entry to the important excavations of a Roman city. Friends who have worked there tell me they may prove more extensive even than those of Conimbriga.

From here a detour through Sines adds less than ten miles to the route south. It enables us to see the house built on the site of the one where Vasco da Gama was born, and the chapel he himself erected above the little port. It is the only place of any size on the westward-facing coast south of Setúbal.

Despite the exposed aspect which has prevented other ports from developing, there has always been a mildness in the air and a Mediterranean blue about the sea whenever I have gazed from the Cape of Sines on the vast expanses of beach in either direction. Perhaps I have been lucky. But the visitor to this most unspoilt of all Portugal's carefully-developed coasts can be assured of miles of sand to himself. The side roads to little *praias* like Melides or Vila Nova de Milfontes lead on nowhere else. The latter, incidentally, has a unique country-house hotel.

Vila Nova de Milfontes lies at the mouth of the Mira, which has given its name to Odemira, the last town on the main road before the Algarve. As in Spain, Portuguese railway stations tend to be a long way from the towns they are supposed to serve, and nowhere more so than in the Alentejo. '*Estação de Odemira*' lies no less than thirteen miles east on the road to a huge reservoir named after Dr. Marcello Caetano, the biggest of several which are transforming the agriculture of the lower Alentejo.

I have already referred to another of these reservoirs, between Aljustrel and Beja. A crow's flight there would take us across the Campo de Ourique, which may have been the site of Afonso Henrique's famous victory over the Moslems which gave him the excuse for assuming the title of King. But in 1139, eight years before the fall of Lisbon, this was deep in enemy territory. Modern historians regard Chã de Ourique near Santarém as a more probable site, itself still a Moslem city until 1147.

Aljustrel is the Alentejo's only important centre of industry. Even this industry is of the primitive extractive kind which can so easily be adversely affected by outside factors. For copper is mined here, at the western end of the same belt which over in Spain gives rise to the great mines of Rio Tinto and of Tharsis. The latter takes its name from the kingdom of Tarshish which 2,500 years ago supplied copper to the Phoenicians. It is still British-owned, as was Rio Tinto until 1954. And nearer to them than to Aljustrel on the same copperbelt lay a British-owned mine in Portugal: S. Domingos.

The son of a former manager recalled to me his childhood at S. Domingos before 1914: the home-made entertainments, the 'living off the land' in grand style, the shooting parties on horseback. For the guns and for their plentiful game alike, the frontier was then simply an imaginary line!

It was not a rich mine. But it had the advantage of cheap water transport for its ores after they had been taken a few miles on its private railway to the banks of the Guadiana.

Like Tharsis and Rio Tinto, however, the company which owned S. Domingos was quoted on the London Stock Exchange. A takeover bid placed it in the hands of a management with little mining experience, who diversified unsuccessfully into land in the Algarve. The company failed. The mine closed. Now the neat, clean little town is dead. Its population is down from 7,000 to 1,500. Such is always the danger for communities with only one string to their bow.

In less dramatic fashion a similar danger menaces every village in the Alentejo. Twenty years ago their future, albeit a poverty-stricken future, seemed assured. Though the only work they could offer was on the land, at least the land would always be there. There was a sadness greater than that of Wordsworth's solitary reaper in the chants of the long lines of harvesters, sickle in hand, bent beneath the burning sun. But at least there was a permanent background to their lives; and during the previous century there had in fact been considerable interior colonisation by landless peasants who had become smallholders in the process.

Wages were low, and for many years frozen. Critics of the government have made up songs of their own about a particular incident near Serpa, when police were sent in to break an agricultural strike, and a pregnant young woman was accidentally killed. But Serpa was no Sharpeville; and given the special problems of the Portuguese economy in general and of Portuguese agriculture in particular, it is very hard for the outsider to make any useful judgement.

'Industrialise,' cry the critics. 'Raise the wages.' And indeed that is just what has happened, less by intention than by the operation of external market pressures.

Farming became mechanised. Less labour was required. The *alentejanos*, in the past the only Portuguese never to leave their homes, began to emigrate to France, whose attractions had just become apparent. Soon there developed a shortage of seasonal workers. By the laws of supply and demand wages rose. This pushed up costs, and in turn the prices of fruit and crops. On some occasions they were even priced out of the market, and therefore not worth harvesting.

As a result land, that 'one safe hedge against inflation', stands in some places at a quarter of its value in the 1950s. The small land-owner, who half a generation ago enjoyed a comfortable standard of living—somewhere between that of a squireen and that of a yeoman farmer—is reduced to little more than penury.

When I arrived in Portugal early in 1969 Dr. Marcello Caetano, who had only been Prime Minister for a few months, was making a tour of the Alentejo. Like every other tour he has made, whether at home or in the overseas provinces, it turned into a personal triumph. On his return to Lisbon he gave one of his televised Roosevelt-style 'fireside chats', in which he expressed his determination to encourage an efficient agriculture capable of absorbing the younger generation and of giving them a sufficient standard of living.

British farmers in Portugal will tell you that there is indeed as much protection and aid for farming there as in the U.K., though with a different emphasis. Many of them have been tempted out there by the activities of an enterprising estate agent in the Home Counties, but find that land is not always easy to purchase in economic units at a price which will ensure an economic return on their capital (for the good reason that the larger landowners are unwilling sellers). Curiously enough, it is in the Alentejo where a majority of these expatriates wish to establish themselves—and certainly the most famous British farm in all Portugal is in the province.

An earlier generation of British in Portugal also liked it here, though they had no intention of settling. These were Wellington's troops during the Peninsular War. They were always glad to be posted to the Alentejo, because they could be sure of clean billets.

Such in fact is the cleanliness of the *alentejano* cottages, their walls whitewashed early each spring, that it often disguises the poverty which may lurk within. The occasional cottage without windows, however, is evidence neither of poverty nor of a hatred of fresh air. Its builder rightly believed that the absence of openings strengthened its structure against earthquakes.

Occasionally a sparkling white cottage—with windows or without—will have the unlikely name of '*a casa do preto*', the house of the black man. The Alentejo had a considerable population of Negro labourers from the sixteenth right up to the nineteenth century. But the great tradition of *assimilação* has done its work. Today only a very rare nose or lip recall the black men whose dwelling-places are still remembered.

Probably the greatest attraction of the province for the British farmers is its soil. This is still the good earth which made prosperous the Lusitania of the Romans, and of their Visigothic and Arab successors. Three towns had a continuous life throughout these periods, being sufficiently far south of the devastated no-man's-land between Sueves and Visigoths, and later between Christians and Moslems, to avoid the fate of Conimbriga. But what they have retained from these periods is uneven.

The farthest south is Mértola, the Roman *Myrtilis*, on a hill above the Guadiana only a few miles west of the mines of S. Domingos. It has always enjoyed a minor importance as a river-port and crossing. Some authorities regard the present bridge as partly of Roman work; and the Moslems contributed both to the quays, and to the castle above the town.

But the really interesting building is the white crenellated parish church, halfway up the hill. Step inside. It is low and square, with no less than four rows of pillars. The door of the sacristy has an unusual, irregular shape, reminding us of Córdoba and Gránada. And there beside it, but blocked up, is another similar door. Yes: it is a converted mosque, the only one in Portugal, given a Renaissance doorway and its present internal appearance in the time of Manuel I.

I had often read of the humane Portuguese custom of allowing prisoners to talk from their windows with the general public in the street outside. But it was coming down from Mértola's church that I had my first experience of it.

Suddenly I was hailed from a low, barred window in what was otherwise a perfectly ordinary white house. Behind it were eight men, held there for various offences which they were only too glad to tell me about in the friendliest manner. Their self-assured spokesman owed his confidence to having worked for a year in France, from which he had returned in a car. After his holiday he had unsuccessfully attempted to carry some of his friends out of Portugal without passports, and was now fatalistically awaiting trial.

Beja, thirty miles to the north, disappoints many visitors. Although four times the size of Mértola, it still numbers only 20,000 inhabitants. Its undistinguished streets lack the personality which should go with its position as capital of the lower Alentejo.

However, it has a Roman gateway, the Porta de Évora, and the small basilica of S. Amaro from the Visigothic period, with rare geometric motifs on its columns. From later periods, the thirteenth century has given it a fine castle keep; the fifteenth the church of

S. Maria and the hermitage of S. André, a curious fortress-church with triangular crenellations.

But the big draw at Beja is the museum near its centre—and not for its contents, interesting though some of these are. For it occupies the fifteenth-century former convent of Conceição, the home in the seventeenth century of Sister Mariana Alcoforado. Her putative love-affair with the Chevalier de Chamilly may have given a French writer the idea of constructing the passionate *Letters of a Portuguese Nun.* The originals have never been found. Literary critics today claim that they never existed. Yet I find it hard to go along with those who claim that love-affair and letters alike were a total fabrication.

There is a certain intangible flavour of erotic piety, or pious eroticism, about the century following the Portuguese Restoration. John V at Odivelas was no innovator. Indeed he, who so well understood the Portuguese character, was perhaps translating into reality a national fantasy, a fantasy to which testify such survivals of convent cuisine as 'nuns' bellies' and 'nuns' breasts'.

The liaison became possible because Chamilly was stationed at Beja when French forces were sent to help fight the Spaniards during the long wars of the Restoration. Today a joint German-Portuguese air-base has been established about five miles north of the town. But the Conceição, like all the other convents in Portugal, was dissolved in 1834. So that any sentimental adventures enjoyed by the bronzed, blond young aviators from the *Bundesrepublik* will lack the delicate, forbidden flavour of their predecessor three centuries ago.

Third place in the region with a continuous history of 2,000 years is Évora. It lies on a hill and almost entirely within walls which rest on Roman and Visigothic foundations. And on the very crown of this hill stands the most notable Roman monument of Portugal. This second-century 'Temple of Diana' repeats on a better site but on a smaller scale the plan of the *Maison carrée* at Nîmes, distant about a quarter of the way across that gigantic empire.

The granite of its columns and the marble of their plinths were to be the materials of many other monuments in the city during the succeeding centuries. For since the Reconquest Évora has been the acknowledged capital of the Alentejo.

It has at times even come near to becoming the capital of the kingdom. Here in 1340 Afonso IV gathered the last Portuguese army to march with the Castilians against the common Moslem enemy. Here John II carried out his plans to humble the too-powerful House of Bragança.

The palace which this monarch began in gardens just within the walls was continued by his successor Manuel I. Its remains are of mingled Renaissance and Arab styles. For although the Moslems ruled longer in the Algarve, they left a stronger imprint on the native architectural tradition of the Alentejo.

John II also founded the church of S. Francisco a little way above the palace. In this case it is Gothic which mingles with *mudéjar*. Attached to it is the macabre Capela dos Ossos, its walls entirely covered with bones. A pertinent sonnet framed for the visitor's edification begins:

> 'Where are you off to so fast, passer-by?
> Stop . . . proceed no further;
> You have no business more important
> Than this, presented to your sight . . .

Under John II, though not actually by him, was also founded the Convent of the Loios (an Order following the rules of St. Eloi), just opposite the Roman Temple. It now shelters one of the most attractive of all the government *pousadas*, with carpets round the cloister and armchairs in the chapter house! But its church (of St. John the Evangelist) still serves its original purpose, and contains some fine tombs, notably that of the humanist Francisco de Melo by the French sculptor Nicolas Chantarène.

The palace of the Melos, now owned by their descendants the Dukes of Cadaval, stands on the other side of the church. It has Arab-influenced windows, and a private art-gallery which can be visited.

Manuel's son, John III, gave the city an aqueduct, and the extraordinary church of the Graça. Here Roman Renaissance becomes

Lusitanian. Atlas giants above the pediment support globes—
King Manuel's emblem.

The globe reappears in the form of a fountain in the best-
known square of Évora: the Largo das Portas de Moura. On one
side stands an early sixteenth-century house with a delicate
Mauresque *loggia*, surmounted by one of those curious pyramids
which appear quite frequently on *alentejano* buildings of the
period.

It is difficult, however, to separate what Évora owes to John III
from what it owes to his brother, the Cardinal-King Henry. For
he was its Archbishop for many years before his brief reign from
1578 to 1580. He built, for example, the collegiate church of S.
Antão, on the square where stands a Renaissance fountain of 1571.

Although under his archiepiscopate the flames of the *auto-da-fé*
rose seven times in the city, there rose at the same time a university which made it for two centuries a centre of learning. Being
under Jesuit control, however, it was suppressed by Pombal at
the same time that he dissolved the rest of the Order. Its monumental Renaissance courts now shelter a school and a seminary.
But the attached church of the Conceição has a richer, more
Baroque interior decoration, and below the high altar is a
monument to its founder, the last king and the only cardinal
of the House of Avis.

The cathedral where he presided is one of the wonderful group
of buildings up by the Roman temple. Being entirely of granite,
it is the most sombre amongst them. Its transitional style has been
well summed up by Dr. Pais da Silva, who described it as at once
the last Romanesque and the first Gothic cathedral in the country.
There is a marble doorway by Nicolas Chantarène in the left
transept, and a rich treasury. But the greatest collection of art in
Évora is in the museum installed in the former archiepiscopal
palace.

A large proportion of the exhibits were produced in Évora,
which with Coimbra and Lisbon was one of the three centres of
the Portuguese Renaissance. This was characterised by a return to
European norms after the fascinating digression of Manueline.
The patronage of the crown, then at its wealthiest, was used to

establish artistic links with abroad. Thus we can study here a further series of works by Nicolas Chantarène, the earliest and most gifted of the school of French sculptors who emigrated to Portugal in the first half of the sixteenth century. John III actually went so far as to send Portuguese artists to study in Italy. And a friar from Flanders, Frei Carlos, combined both the profession and something of the style of Fra Angelico in the work which he carried out over twenty years at Évora.

But it is the less important paintings of the silver age of the seventeenth century which will interest the British visitor. There is a room of rather homely canvases of the earliest members of the Bragança dynasty, including one of Catherine of Bragança at her prettiest.

We sympathise with her, thrown unwillingly into competition with all those brash beauties of Charles II's court whose likenesses Sir Peter Lely has preserved at Hampton Court. It is pleasant to think that she came back here to spend part of her retirement at the Manueline palace of the Counts of Basto, overlooking the former university. In the street leading to this palace stands the Library, whose collection ranks with those of Braga and Coimbra, and often draws scholars from Lisbon for a long weekend of study.

The Library, however, is simply an excuse. For many a cultivated Portuguese, especially since the rebuilding of Coimbra's 'Alto', Évora is the white 'museum-city' of his dreams. Walking on the cobbles and under the arches of its quiet streets, and outside its still complete walls to the curious fortress-church of S. Bras, or a mile or two farther to the Charterhouse, or to the convents of S. Bento de Castris or of Espinheiro, he can imagine himself back in the world before the Dutch had rounded the Cape of Good Hope, and before King Sebastian had sailed away and forever to Morocco.

I have now described the Alentejo's coast, and its essential historical background, on the ascending scale of Mértola, Beja, and Évora. To describe the rest in detail would require a book in itself. It would also be needlessly repeating work which has been better done by other hands. But the traveller who at his con-

venience follows three general routes, will have seen a great deal
of the rest of the province.

His recollections of all three routes will be at least as much of
the cornfields and cork woods and unexpected reservoirs as of the
occasional towns and villages. And in those towns and villages
he will probably remember less the Manueline windows or
Renaissance houses than the spring water gushing cool in the
sunshine from the *bicas* of a score of white marble fountains, and
the dark silhouettes of as many grim castles, guarding this easily-
invaded region against Moslem or Castilian.

The first of these routes is the main road from Lisbon to
Madrid. It has something of interest every twenty miles or so.
Thus Vendas Novas has a palace rushed up in nine months for
John V. Montemor-o-Novo has a good castle: Arraiolos an even
better one, with only half a mile away the unforgettable Quinta
dos Loios. Its chapel has a Manueline doorway and is buttressed
by inward-sloping supports topped by spheres.

Arraiolos has a long-established tradition of carpet making by
hand. It is essentially a cottage industry, with only two factories.
But though there is little to indicate this activity in the quiet little
town, Arraiolos carpets are found in better-class homes all over
Portugal. Their excellent yarn and their tight knit enable them to
be handed down from generation to generation. The industry
was just as active in the seventeenth and eighteenth centuries,
when with the introduction of motifs borrowed from Persian
carpets, Arraiolos returned the compliment paid by Persian
carpet makers to Portugal.

Next comes the much busier town of Estremoz, where the
marble we met at Vila Viçosa eleven miles away is used for quite
ordinary buildings. There are more important buildings, too. On
the vast double square are the Misericordia with two cloisters, the
seventeenth-century Tocha palace, and the thirteenth-century
convent of S. Francisco. Next to the Misericordia is a museum of
alentejano crafts; even without entering it the visitor will see in
many of the shops artefacts of cork and the sheepskin coats and
split aprons worn by countrymen hereabouts. (The *alentejana*
women have an equally unusual working dress, tying their skirts

up in the middle in such a way that they look almost like bloomers, and muffling their mouths with the black headscarves they wear under felt hats reminiscent of the Peruvian *altiplano*.)

On the hill behind the squares rises the old quarter, dominated by a thirteenth-century castle within which King Dennis built a palace, now converted to a *pousada*. His widowed queen, Saint Isabel, died here, though her place of retirement had been Coimbra. The chapel marking the site of her resting-place, however, is the work of a later and slightly less saintly queen, the ambitious Spanish wife of John IV, Luisa de Guzmán.

Borba, at the heart of the marble quarries, has one of the best of the *alentejano* fountains. And then comes Elvas, which unlike Estremoz is concentrated almost entirely on its hillside by its constraining fortifications of Vaubanesque complexity.

These enclose several churches of interest besides the Manueline former cathedral and the octagonal Renaissance Nossa Senhora da Consolação. The fountain of the Misericordia dates from 1622, the year when the massive aqueduct which had been a century and a quarter in building was at last completed.

Eight miles after Elvas the road reaches the busiest complex of *alfândega*, *policia*, and *cambio* offices in the country. For here an insignificant tributary of the Guadiana called the Caia marks for a mile or two the frontier with Spain.

The importance of this particular frontier crossing is due, like the size of the fortifications of Elvas, to the fact that this is the main road between the two capitals. But Elvas is only one of a whole series of fortified positions. Our second route will follow them along this frontier of few natural defences.

The southernmost, Mértola, we have already visited; the road from there past the mines of S. Domingos takes us north to Serpa (with a quiet *pousada* on a hill outside the town) and to Moura. Both owe their castles to King Dennis of whom it was said:

    'Dizia Dom Denis:
    "Serpa e Moura fiz;
    E mais fizera se quisera,
    Que quem dineiro tiver
    Faré o que quiser".'

'Quoth King Dennis:
"I built Serpa and Moura;
And could have built more had I wished,
For he who has money
Will accomplish all he wants".'

The lines might appropriately have been adopted as the device of another great ruler of Portugal, who came to power just over six hundred years after the death of King Dennis.

Moura's name, of course, refers directly to the Moors. And like Lisbon itself and many smaller towns it has a street called the Mouraria. The next town north, Mourão, shares the same etymology. But its castle is less impressive than that of Monsaraz, facing it a few miles away across the Guadiana.

I spent a night in my motor caravan parked outside the gate of Monsaraz, high above the Guadiana valley looking into Spain. The village within its walls now numbers only some three hundred inhabitants, and there are many houses in ruins. But I have since met two people who have acquired such houses as 'country cottages'.

Keeping close to the frontier, which since 1801 is here the Guadiana, we come to Terena, with a castle above the village, and the crenellated fortress-church of Boa Nova a mile down a side-road. Everyone was white-washing their houses the April day that I was there.

Alendroal has more than the guide books allow it: not only a castle of King Dennis and the chapel of Consolação with its tomb of Diogo Lopes de Sequeira, but also an Indian Virgin brought back by this governor of the Indies; and what I regard as the loveliest of all the *alentejano* village fountains.

Juromenha, right on the present frontier, has a very ruined castle, but a fascinating view into Spain.

Twelve miles north of Elvas, Campo Maior is large for its position in the middle of nowhere. Its castle has a Manueline window; and near—not actually inside—the vast parish church is a chapel of bones of the same type as in S. Francisco at Évora.

Nearby the Caia has been dammed to make a reservoir more

extensive and liberating to the spirit than the long narrow *barragens* in the valleys farther north. But the rolling plains which make this possible are almost over. We soon find gradients getting steeper as we approach the Serra de Portalegre.

It is towards Portalegre that our third route will lead. North from Arraiolos or Estremoz quiet country roads will take us to Avis, where the castle and attached convent were the headquarters of the Order of which John I was Master. The road running on north follows for ten miles a long, narrow reservoir fed by a stream over which a Roman bridge survives from the highway which once linked Santarém to Mérida.

Alter do Chão is a large, quiet rural township at whose centre a fine fourteenth-century granite castle faces an equally fine sixteenth-century marble fountain. The *chão* is the surrounding plain, which lends itself well to horse-breeding. The national stud is situated two miles outside the town.

Seven miles on lies Crato, which at once rings a bell for the student of Portuguese history. It strikes a softer and a sadder tone than that of Avis, a mere twenty miles away, but its note is the same. For in 1580 it was António, Prior of Crato, who stood for national independence in very similar circumstances to those under which John, Master of Avis, had stood for national independence two centuries earlier at Aljubarrota.

On the death of the Cardinal-King Henry, last legitimate male of the House of Avis, the common people rallied round the bastard son of one of his brothers, just as in 1383 they had rallied round the bastard brother of the last king of the first dynasty. But Portugal, reeling under the shock of the defeat and death of King Sebastian in Morocco, was now faced not merely by Castile, but by the whole Spanish Empire, then the greatest power on earth. Philip II's general was the same Duke of Alva who had struck terror into the Low Countries, while poor António had no Nuno Alvares Pereira to command his ragged troops.

It was the Holy Constable's father who in fact founded Crato's convent of the Order of Malta. Although its prior had a house—still standing at the top of the village of Crato—the convent proper is at Flor de Rosa a mile to the north. It stands on one side of a vast space where horse-fairs are held. When the work of restoration is completed it will constitute a monument ranking immediately behind Batalha and Alcobaça.

Continuing north from Flor da Rosa, and crossing the main road to the frontier we reach Nisa, the northernmost place of any size in the Alentejo. It has a characteristic brown pottery incrustated with patterns of small white stones. Two gateways and large stretches of its fourteenth-century walls still stand: unusually they enjoy no advantage of height or terrain. But then this leisurely, spacious little town has natural defences of another kind: to the north the Tagus which divides it from Beira Baixa, and to the east and south-east a whole series of *serras* along the frontier.

Arriving by this route, after traversing the undramatic distances to the south and west, we can appreciate the name given by the late Huldine Beamish to a restricted region with a character all its own. In *The Hills of Alentejo* she described life and agricultural practices in what will forever remain the most famous English-owned farm in the province, if not in all Portugal. I have spent a night there myself, and have met several people who have recaptured there the English country-house life of their youth at the beginning of the century.

Huldine Beamish described, too, the 3,400-feet high Serra de S. Mamede on whose slopes the farm lies, and the little city of Portalegre near its foot, with its cork factories and former convents. Its cathedral, like that of Leiria, is one of John III's foundations, though its façade and sacristy date from the end of the eighteenth century. In a house in the street alongside is an excellent small museum, with some good sculpture.

She takes us, too, to Castelo de Vide on the other side of the Serra, one of the most attractive small towns of Portugal. Besides several churches, palaces and a castle, it has a lovely fountain in 'country' Renaissance, and a Judiaria with several Manueline doorways and windows. Many may prefer it as a place to stay to the *pousada* of Marvão, ten miles nearer the frontier, and chilly at nearly 3,000 feet.

But the remote little walled town of Marvão within which it stands should not be missed. Its windy cobbled streets have probably never known very much activity, but it was not built as a commercial centre. To perceive its purpose we must climb its keep to enjoy an immense view in all directions—and especially to the east. As José Amaro wrote:

> '*Marvão, por lindo que és,*
> *Sentinela da Aramenha,*
> *Tens Portugal a teus pés,*
> *E a abrirte os braços a Espanha.*'

> 'Marvão, how lovely you are,
> Sentinel of Herminium*
> You have Portugal at your feet,
> And in opening your arms . . . Spain.'

TAILPIECE: PAIS VIZINHO

It was below the eastern wall of another castle keep—that of Pinhel near the frontier in Beira Alta—that the retired Portuguese major who had appointed himself as my guide commanded me to look up. Raising my eyes I beheld high above me two gargoyles of an unusual shape. To emphasise the already obvious he went on:

'You see what they are. One is the nether parts of a man. The other is the nether parts of a woman. They are both relieving themselves in the same direction. Towards Spain. You will find similar gargoyles on many of the frontier castles, always pointing in the same direction. That is what they thought of the neighbour land, *o pais vizinho.*'

And indeed the sense of the gargoyles' gesture, even when expressed less forcefully or more politely, is inevitable. For ever since Afonso Henriques established the right of the little country of Portugal to independence, she has had a neighbour with several times her size and several times her population.

Moreover, since the reconquest from the Moslems ended over seven hundred years ago, she has had no other neighbour. Like

---

* The Romans' name for the Serra.

.. Nazaré: fishermen
mending nets

15. Berlenga Islets:
fortress converted
into *pousada*

16. Obidos: scene within the walls

17. Obidos: general view

Scotland she is a country with only one frontier. But whereas Scotland's frontier is a mere seventy miles, Portugal's is almost seven hundred and seventy. Her very existence was an act of defiance.

Spain looms as large in the Portuguese consciousness as it looms on the map. It is significant that the only irregular adjective of nationality is *espanhol*. Semantically speaking, indeed, Portugal's achievement could be described as the assertion of the separateness of Lusitania from the Hispania of which it once formed part.

The effort of such an assertion has unexpected results at all levels of history and culture. Towards the end of Chapter 2 we referred to the support which the crown always received as the embodiment of national independence. There was no room here for such luxuries as barons' revolts, when at any moment the chill wind might blow from the east.

> *'De Espanha nem bom vento*
> *nem bom casamento.'*

> 'From Spain neither good wind
> nor good marriage.'

For it was his marriage to a Portuguese princess that brought Juan I of Castile to Aljubarrota. And it was his father's marriage to a Portuguese princess that carried Philip II of Spain all the way to Lisbon.

Being a small country under pressure, with a king whose authority received ready recognition, had a further result. This was that the king was readily approachable by his subjects as he travelled around his small and then sparsely-inhabited realm. It was therefore unnecessary to set down in writing many aspects of law which were early codified in the legal systems of larger and more populous lands.

As a result there subsist even today big gaps in Portuguese law which are filled—and are expected to be filled—by the direct action of government. The Portuguese man-in-the-street understands this, and regards it as normal. Where an Englishman or an

American instinctively calls on the law, he tends instinctively and with just as much historical reason to call on authority.

The geographical situation and historical development which led to this attitude shaped also his attitude to the rest of Europe. With only one European country did Portugal invariably trade and communicate directly by sea, and with that country she established a special relationship enshrined in the *Velha Aliança*. Europe except for England was what lay beyond Spain; and it was a long way off. The very distance evoked *saudade*,* as in Cesário Verde:

> *'Batem os carros d'aluguer, ao fundo,*
> *Levando à via férrea os que se vão. Felizes!*
> *Ocorrem-me em revista exposições, países:*
> *Madrid, Paris, Berlim, S. Peterburgo, o mundo!'*

> 'The carriages throb, down below,
> Bearing by railway those who are departing. Happy ones!
> In my mind's eye appear exhibitions, countries:
> Madrid, Paris, Berlin, St. Petersburg, the world!'

Thus, too, could the novelist Camilo Castelo Branco speak of *'Essa Europa'* ('that Europe'), as if he were referring to a distinct entity of which his country formed no part. European wars, and even European diplomatic activity, have indeed been of interest to Portugal only when her vital interests have been concerned through her overseas possessions—or through Spain.

This is not only because of her distance from those wars or diplomatic activity. It is also because the presence of a single powerful neighbour has denied Portugal any possibility of European territorial expansion.

This may at first seem a statement of the obvious. But its implications for the national consciousness are profound. It has made the Portuguese soldier fight with reluctance on foreign fields, whether in Flanders, Roussillon or Valencia. But conversely it has made him the most redoubtable of opponents on his own soil,

---

* See note on spelling and pronunciation on page 18.

as at Aljubarrota, Buçaco, or in those great Restoration battles in the Alentejo at Elvas, Ameixial, and Montes Claros.

It is this love of his own land, and his realisation of how finely-balanced have been the retention or the loss of its independence, that gives to the Portuguese a special sense of *saudade* as he gazes across the Guadiana from Monsaraz or Juromenha. For he is looking on soil which until 1801 was Portuguese, and which he regards as Portuguese still.

As an outpost beyond the river Olivença was as important as Moura or Serpa. It was also a good deal more exposed, with less natural advantages, and with the great Spanish fortress of Badajoz only fifteen miles to the north. Like Campo Maior, it guarded one of the flanks of Badajoz's opposite number, the Portuguese fortress of Elvas, whose most characteristic gateway still bears the name of Porta d'Olivença.

Its position invited attack whenever the two countries were at war. It fell to Spanish arms a number of times—though it also resisted a number of sieges. But it was regularly handed back when hostilities ended.

After it had again been occupied by Spain, then in alliance with France, in the short 'War of the Oranges' in 1801, it was specifically laid down that it should be returned to Portugal in the Treaty of Paris of 1814. On this occasion, however, the Spaniards chose to ignore this provision, although ironically they owed their own liberation from the French to the Anglo-Portuguese armies which had operated from Portugal.

To find out how Portuguese Olivença remained after 168 years of Spanish occupation, I spent three days there at the beginning of April 1969. Superficially it looked like any other Estremeño rural township of about 12,000 souls, with more animation, but also with a more untidy appearance, than if it had been in the Alentejo. It had more, and bigger, and more modern bars, and there were more people in them. On the other hand the streets were not as well made-up, and the public garden was a dustbowl. It is the contrast one notes wherever one crosses the frontier: Spain active, but fly-blown; Portugal perhaps dormant, but tidy.

Wandering from one bar to another in the evening I heard only

Spanish spoken. But next morning, as the older men and women went about their shopping, there were plenty of greetings and gossip being exchanged in Portuguese. And as I penetrated deeper beneath the surface of life I found many more survivals of the older Olivença.

Almost everyone, including even the children, could understand Portuguese, though not necessarily speak it. The extent to which it was used in daily life varied with age, and from family to family, depending very much on the extent to which intermarriage had taken place with 'Spaniards'.

Thus a man of twenty-six born in Olivença always spoke Portuguese with his wife, aged twenty-five, who was also a local girl. His sister of twenty-four could speak it just as fluently, and sometimes used it with her husband. On the other hand his younger sister and brother, aged fourteen and twelve, understood Portuguese but never spoke it.

Obviously education conducted in Spanish was having its effect. But this obvious pressure has not always been applied. Until fifty years ago, older people told me, there was only one public school, and everything was taught there in Portuguese. Those who wished to learn Castilian had to go to one of several fee-paying schools, where instruction was in Spanish!

There was a feeling amongst some of the inhabitants that they were better off economically as part of Spain. But their Portuguese comparisons were always made with poor hamlets immediately across the border, forgetting that Olivença's municipal territory used to be one of the most fertile stretches of farmland in the Alentejo. It included a number of outlying villages, such as Vilareal opposite Juromenha, where Portuguese must be in even more regular daily use.

Vilareal is almost halfway to Vila Viçosa, as the crow flies. From there in 1718 Olivença received its only recorded royal visit: from the much-maligned John V.

There are two churches: S. Maria and La Madalena. Anyone with lingering doubts as to Olivença's essential character should step inside the latter. It has just the same twisted columns as the Convent of Jesus at Setúbal, the hall-mark of Boytac, architect

of the Jerónimos. Can Manueline ever be anything but Portuguese?

And a small incident confirmed in my mind that whatever
language they speak, Olivença's inhabitants will always remain
Portuguese at heart.

All over Spain one meets people who at the drop of a hat will
recite poetry—anything from Cervantes to Rubén Dario. I was
not therefore surprised when a man, hearing of my interest in the
place, came up and started to intone a long poem in Spanish
about Olivença. When he had at last finished I inquired who it
was by. It was all his own work! Only in Portugal does one find
people who not merely recite poetry, but compose it themselves!

It is not in the Portuguese character to hate. The gesture by the
gargoyles of Pinhel was directed against the generalised concept
of 'the enemy', and not against individual Spaniards. The average
Portuguese knows and understands Spain far better than the
average Spaniard knows and understands Portugal. He can follow
Spanish without difficulty, whereas the reverse is anything but
true. The Spanish ambassador speaking on Portuguese television,
or a visiting Spanish lecturer addressing a Portuguese audience,
can speak his own language at his own speed, and know that all
he says will be understood.

Understanding does not always make for friendship. Olivença,
and eight centuries of diverging interests and policies, form a
deep gulf.

Yet the gulf has been bridged. One of the greatest of the many
achievements of Dr. Salazar's government was to sign a Treaty
of Friendship with Spain in 1939. By one of its articles neither
party was to enter into an alliance or treaty directed against the
other. This contributed largely to Spain's neutrality during the
Second World War.

Today, therefore, there is a warm note, almost of complicity,
in the voice of the radio announcer, referring to some item of
news from across the frontier, when he speaks of 'o pais vizinho'.

5

DEEP SOUTH

❦

Of the eleven official checkpoints where one can legally cross from Spain into Portugal, ten are undramatic in the extreme. The eleventh, however, offers almost as much of an experience as crossing the Channel. For the Guadiana, though it only acts as the Alentejo's frontier opposite the stolen Olivença, divides the Algarve from Spain during thirty bridgeless miles.

Arrival at Ayamonte, therefore, after the long drive from Seville, has something in common with arrival at Dover. The traveller can see the other side, hardly a mile away, but its detail is sufficiently blurred to multiply the mystery. There is a wait until the next ferry is ready to sail, and a period of suspended animation, or statelessness, between the final clearing by *aduana*, and the quieter but more punctilious reception by *alfândega*.

Those ten minutes crossing the Guadiana, like the eighty minutes crossing the Straits of Dover, sharpen the traveller's anticipatory antennae. Because he expects everything to be different, it is different. As Vila Real de Santo António comes into sharper focus there is the same sense, as at Calais, of a new world beginning. There are different uniforms and subtly different expressions on the quayside. There is even a train, waiting at its terminus to convey passengers to the capital.

Vila Real is indeed very different from Ayamonte. Pombal, who built it, meant it to be. Profiting from his experience with the Lisbon Baixas, he imported much of the building material in 'prefabricated' form. In the 1870s or perhaps the 1970s the result might have been less than happy. But in 1774 it led to the construction of a model 'Georgian' village, with all the charm of a

London square but with an added southern warmth from the red tiles beneath the blue sky.

The central Praça do Marquês de Pombal is paved with a particularly attractive mosaic pattern resembling the schematic rays from a sun; and there are more mosaics, of marine life, beside the flower-lined avenue which runs along the river.

I therefore had the impression of arriving at a place not only pleasing, but also typically Portuguese, when my first two visits to the country began at Vila Real in 1951 and in 1969.

But on both occasions my initial enthusiasm waned as I continued my journey west along the coast. The mild pinks and blues of the unpretentious one-storey cottages, the lack of monuments, the undramatic quality of the scenery, contrasted disappointingly with the glaring white cities of Andalusia, with their Moorish palaces and Renaissance churches, set against a background of lush *vegas* and snowy *sierras*.

My mistake, though inevitable, lay in ever making the comparison. The Algarve is not Andalusia. It should be judged independently and on its own merits. After two or three days of both visits I had begun to develop a taste for certain of its aspects; and this would soon have spread to embrace the province as a whole. But in neither case, in my anxiety to get up to Lisbon, did I give myself time.

For the Algarve must be seen in its proper context. It is not Andalusia's Far West, but Portugal's Deep South. It should be visited first by the foreigner who has already been in Portugal for several months—ideally winter months.

Then indeed it seems, in the words of my friends in Oporto, 'such a different world down there that it's just as much of a change as going abroad'. Then, as the traveller breasts the Serra de Espinhaço de Cão, and coasts down towards the blue bay of Lagos, he will realise delightedly that he has reached a true riviera, a land of figs and flowers and almonds between villages of pastel-shaded cubist cottages: a balmy southland as essential to Portugal as the green Minho or the frugal Beiras.

The Algarve is a little more than this climatically-privileged coastal strip. It owes its privilege, like other rivieras elsewhere, to the protection from cold winds given by mountains running parallel to the coast. One or two townships lie north of these mountains. In the east, for example, there is Alcoutim on the Guadiana. In the west there is Aljezur, whose municipal territory embraces the little-visited westward-facing strip of *algarvio* coast, with good beaches such as Odeceixe.

The eastward and westward routes to the Algarve take us near Alcoutim and through Aljezur, to a certain extent outflanking the protective mountains, of which there are two distinct ranges. But there are two more exciting routes which take us right through them.

The route through the eastern range is the main road from Lisbon to the provincial capital of Faro. This Serra do Caldeirão is said to have been largely brought under cultivation over the last century by 'internal immigrants'. But I found it deserted enough, with some good *miradouros* where one could draw up to enjoy the view and the scent of wild herbs.

Views are even better, however, on the route through the western range, from Odemira to Portimão. Even in kilometres this is no short cut. Nor is it to be recommended for easy driving. What it offers are deep valleys and woods, wild scenery more appropriate to a northern land, transfigured by a southern sun. It is the miraculous marriage, yet again, of Atlantic with Mediterranean.

This western range is called the Serra de Monchique, after the town which nestles between its two summits. The higher of these, Foia, at just over three thousand feet, can be reached by road. It offers vast and windy views in all directions, especially of the peninsula of Sagres narrowing towards Cape St. Vincent.

Monchique itself is unlike anywhere else in Portugal. It reminded me of certain high-set hamlets in the Canary Islands. There, as here, unlikely plants grow side by side, and the cottager in the timeless street proves to have returned last week from a job thousands of miles away. They make a rather expensive honey here, and an excellent almond-flavoured *eau-de-vie*. This is not on sale; but the lucky and talkative, like myself, may be invited to taste it!

High above the white streets and the parish church with its Manueline doorway, beyond a ruined convent is an utterly peaceful *miradouro*. Its benches, lined with *azulejos*, surround the clear 'spring of the little birds'.

The lower slopes of the Serra de Monchique are the favoured retreat of certain newcomers to the Algarve who want country life as well as the beach. One enterprising Englishman has started one of the better of the new restaurants, *Les Rossignols*, near the little spa of Caldas de Monchique.

He is only one of the latest in a series of invaders who have come to the Algarve since the earliest times. The rulers of the Bronze Age kingdom of Tarshish beyond the Guadiana were overlords here when the Phoenicians came trading. The Greeks, who also traded here before the Carthaginians closed the Straits of Gibraltar to them, were to return in an unexpected way more than a thousand years later. The defeat of Hannibal and of Carthage was followed by six centuries of Roman peace, during which a city like Ossonoba could rise with all modern conveniences at Milreu, six miles north of Faro.

Roman rule in Portugal is often regarded as having ended fore-ever when the Sueves, Alans and Vandals succeeded in passing the Pyrenees in A.D. 409. But in fact there was a re-occupation at least of parts of the Algarve during the second half of the sixth century and the first quarter of the seventh.

This occurred when the Emperor Justinian, who had already reconquered Italy and Tunisia from the Ostrogoths and Vandals, turned his arms against the Visigothic kingdom too. But although Justinian himself was a Latin speaker, the Byzantine empire he ruled was Greek. Thus it was Greek sailors who between about 560 and about 630 patrolled from Lagos to Ceuta, along the same route where Prince Henry the Navigator's sailors were to learn so much seacraft eight centuries later.

Barely three generations after the Visigoths had expelled the Byzantines came the Arabs, and stayed here until 1249, longer than anywhere else in the peninsula except Gránada. I have been careful elsewhere to use the word 'Moslem' to describe the opponents of the Christian north, for though of one religion they were of several races. But in the case of their principal city in the Algarve, Shalb, 'Arab' is a perfectly appropriate description. For it was settled by Yemenis who spoke a pure Arabic.

Silves, as Shalb is known today, lies beneath the Serra de Monchique on a river which was then navigable. It was up this waterway that a fleet bound for the Third Crusade (the one which helped in the capture of Lisbon belonged to the Second) sailed alongside the Portuguese to reduce the city in 1189.

Although it was recaptured by the fierce Almohads from Marrakesh less than two years later, its glory had gone. All that remains today of the Arabs are two great underground cisterns within the walls of the massive thirteenth-century castle, over which triumphs a statue of the conquering Sancho I. Yet there was surely an Oriental hospitality about the way I was invited to pick oranges just outside the town, in a grove opposite the 'Cross of Portugal'. This remarkable Gothic monument shows the crucified Christ on one side, and his descent from the Cross on the other.

But if the Arabs have left little to mark the five and a half centuries they ruled here, the Christians for their part seem to have erected remarkably little in the Algarve during the seven which have followed. There are a few isolated Manueline details, as in the churches of Alvor, Acantarilla, or Luz; a few Renaissance details, as at Tavira, or Loulé; a few fortifications, as at Castro Marim a couple of miles up river from Vila Real de S. António; and a Rococo palace at Estoi near the ruins of Milreu. But the overall picture is of an obviously ancient land without the human trade marks of antiquity.

Faro the capital, for example, has a rebuilt Gothic cathedral and a rebuilt Renaissance Misericordia. It was not its sack by the English under the Earl of Essex in 1596 which made the rebuilding necessary, destructive though this was. It was the earthquake of 1755, which was as violent here as in Lisbon.

Indeed this province has always suffered from seismic activity more than any other. It is this which has effaced much of the legacy of former centuries. For obvious reasons news of earthquakes elsewhere, in Persia or Peru, is given especial prominence in Portuguese newspapers. But nowhere does it receive more concerned interest than in the Algarve.

I have first-hand experience of what a minor tremor can do. After my arrival at Vila Real de S. António in 1969 I spent three days at Portimão before driving on up to Lisbon. On my very first night in the capital I was woken at about 3.45 a.m. on February 28th by the violent shaking of my motor-caravan. Thinking that some intruder was trying to force his way in, I shouted antagonistically, seizing the weapon I have to hand for such emergencies.

The shaking ended. But there was no tell-tale shuffle of re-treating feet. I had a wild surmise. Reaching for my transistor, the first station I could locate was Radio Madrid. Sure enough, the announcer was busy calming listeners who were ringing the studio in alarm at the earthquake which had disturbed them. She was able to comfort them with the assurance that 'It has been much worse in Portugal'.

And in Portugal, as so often before, it had been worst in the Algarve. The epicentre had been some distance out in the Atlantic, to the south-west of Cape St. Vincent. The resulting concentric bands of force gave Lisbon a tremor of the order of 6·7, most of the Algarve one between 7 and 8, and the peninsula of Sagres itself one of over 8—the point at which buildings start to tumble.

Damage in Lisbon was minimal. The greatest fright was suffered by people on the upper floors of blocks of flats, for whom the shaking of the ground floor was multiplied. A French girl on an eighth floor told me she was so scared that she rushed out and drove through the night all the way to Oporto!

What a slightly stronger tremor could do I saw when I drove down to Portimão again three months later. There were wooden supports across many of the narrow streets, to reinforce the houses on either side. The friends who had accompanied me found their flat damp and draughty. Cracks had appeared in walls. Window-frames had been loosened.

When we drove to Cape St. Vincent, and entered the small area which had suffered a tremor of the order of 8, we found scaffolding all round the tower of the church of Vila do Bispo. This was the place where the earthquake claimed its only victim, an old lady who died as much from shock as from injury.

Portimão stands on the estuary of the river which comes down from Silves. It has taken Silves's place as the natural centre of all the western Algarve, or Barlavento. Although it lives on catching and canning fish, it is in fact a pleasant place to stay, with good shops and restaurants. Here, as elsewhere in the Algarve, wait the curious one-horse *carinhas*, last surviving relatives of the pre-1914 Russian droshky, ready to convey the traveller the couple of miles to Praia de Rocha at the mouth of the estuary.

As the best-known and longest-established resort on this coast, Praia da Rocha's physical and social characteristics may already be familiar to many readers. Physically it is distinguished by the immense red rocks which make its beach a ready-made setting for hide-and-seek—especially when illuminated as they often are by night.

Socially it is a between-the-wars celebration of the *Velha Aliança*. The line of hotels and pensions along the top of the cliff, leading to the restaurant in the cleverly-converted Fort of S. Catarina, recall both in architecture and in tone the 1930s. Then the upper-middle classes of Portugal and of England were perhaps nearer in outlook than they have ever been before or since. It is England which has suffered most change in the interval. Any Englishman over forty is bound to feel profoundly at home in Portugal, as he recognises sensations and attitudes he has forgotten since his infancy.

Though I can briefly luxuriate in this *recherche du temps perdu*, I feel a little ill-at-ease when my compatriots try to revive a vanished world. This they have attempted at other places along the coast: in luxury hotels at Albufeira and Vale do Lobo, and in developments where property prices begin at five figures sterling. 'Domestic help available', these gloatingly advertise. And unthinkingly another generation of the middle-aged moves into houses and gardens which will prove all too big for them in a few years' time, when the domestic help is no longer quite so available, and when inflation has overtaken the fixed income of the typical 'retirer to the sun'.

Each to his own taste, however. I admit that the style of some of the new houses and hotels is not for me. But I must admit also that they are in every way preferable to the alternative: the chips-with-everything of the Costa Brava. And it is with Spain's mistakes as an example that the government has cautiously evolved its development plans which encourage a more selective approach.

And if some of my compatriots have moved into the Algarve as into a colony, others have caught its essential spirit as very few Portuguese even have succeeded in doing. I have already indicated that it lacks the vivid contrasts of some other holiday regions. But the absence of sharp edges makes for more subtle nuances, and these have been beautifully interpreted in word and drawing by David Wright and Patrick Swift in *Algarve: a portrait and a guide*. They describe the sardine-fishing, the eating out—you will never regret following their recommendations—the wine, the fairs, the fascinating variety of *algarvio* chimneys, and above all the people.

To catch these nuances required a whole book. With only a chapter at my disposal I shall refer briefly to merely two aspects of life in the province.

One is its agriculture, which makes a sharp break with that of the Alentejo immediately to the north. It is in many ways nearer to horticulture, with small irrigated farms concentrating on intensive crops such as fruits and almonds. It is therefore less susceptible to mechanisation. Even the irrigation is still often carried out by an ancient device operated by a horse walking round and round a well—much as threshing and cider-pressing are still carried out in some parts of the world.

Another is culture. The Algarve is no cultural desert. Folklore is cherished at Loulé, and at Alte up in the foothills of the Serra do Caldeirão. Poetry is still composed in Silves, though no longer in pure Arabic. I know someone who is writing a thesis on the poetry of a Silves doctor! For its population, the province is probably more culturally aware than anywhere else except the big cities and Coimbra.

Apart from Portimão, the coastal villages of the cliff-girt

Barlavento to the west of Faro are for the most part small. Carvoeiro, where Patrick Swift himself has settled, will stand for them all. When foreign residents adopt them, they can quickly acquire a cosmopolitan atmosphere. Here I am not necessarily using 'cosmopolitan' in a pejorative sense. Nothing can be more agreeable than to come across sophisticated company far from where it might be expected.

The flat, island-bordered Sotavento to the east of Faro, on the other hand, is not only less likely to attract newcomers, but is better able to resist their influence. It would take a good many foreigners to alter the character of the 'cubist', flat-roofed Olhão, or of the charming Tavira.

Right at its eastern end, however, the vast beach of Monte Gordo offers a special situation. Here, backed by pinewoods, foreign visitors are able, all the year round, both to enjoy the Algarve climate, and to profit from the strength of the escudo by making certain of their purchases across the river in Ayamonte.

It is usual to treat the entire coast under these two divisions. However, the peninsula of Sagres is so different from the rest of the Barlavento that I propose to deal with it on its own. It is windier and barer: with more of the Atlantic in its make-up than of the Mediterranean. As we have seen, it is subject to worse earthquakes than anywhere else in the country.

Yet Lagos, at its base, preserves two of the most interesting monuments in the Algarve. One is an arcaded building where were auctioned off the slaves who inevitably were acquired when the Portuguese discoverers began to trade with African lands where slavery was an established institution, and slaves an article of commerce.

The other is the church of S. Maria, from the Manueline window of which King Sebastian is said to have addressed his troops before they sailed to meet disaster at Alcázar-Quibir. And here, where his own less pretentious but more successful expeditions used to gather, sits a statue of Prince Henry the Navigator.

Historians dispute the claims of Lagos and of Sagres as his main port. It seems likely that Lagos's far more sheltered bay should have been at least his rear-base. The cliffs which guard it to the west are carved into shapes and caves hardly less fantastic than some of the marvels his mariners were to discover. They can be visited by parties of up to about six in small fishing-boats.

They are the first of a whole series of high cliffs, ringing the windswept plateau which juts from here into the Atlantic. Every-where broods the memory of the Prince who spent so many of his later years here that he became known as *o Infante de Sagres*. In the chapel of Nossa Senhora de Guadeloupe he used often to pray, while staying at his *quinta* at Raposeira near Vila do Bispo. And at the cape to the west of the fishing village of Sagres he estab-lished a school of navigation where he gathered seamen, carto-graphers, astrologers and anyone else who could further his purposes. The outer walls still stand, and within there are some buildings of doubtful identification, with on the ground a great design in stone of the points of the compass. His exact motivation remains a mystery, as do certain aspects of his character. He still fascinates the Portuguese more than any other of their country-men. A debate even continues as to whether or not he was a virgin! That he was something of a recluse no one who has visited this bare peninsula can doubt.

But then we are on mysterious ground. At Cape St. Vincent, four miles farther west, the ancients believed that at sunset the sun, appearing a hundred times its natural size, could be heard sizzling as it disappeared beneath the waves.

TAILPIECE: A LÍNGUA E A HISTORIA

There is one more, invisible survival which still preserves Prince Henry's memory in the peninsula of Sagres. It is the accent of its inhabitants, which is distinct from that of the rest of the Algarve. Most noticeable is the way they pronounce certain vowels, especially 'u', to which they give a French rather than a Portu-guese value.

This particularity is found in two other places. One is part of S. Miguel, largest island of the Azores, where it has been ascribed to the settlement of Bretons. But it seems far more probable that it was carried there by Prince Henry's colonists.

The other place is a more extensive area in the upper Alentejo and Beira Baixa, around the middle Tagus to the east of Tomar. Here again there seems to be a link with the Prince. For this was just the district where the Order of Christ, of which he was Master, had its greatest concentration of estates.

But from where did the French 'u' get there in the first place, to be later carried by the Prince's activities to Sagres and to the Azores? Strangely enough, the answer seems to be 'from France'.

Afonso Henriques's father was from Burgundy. Frenchmen played a prominent part in his counsels and his campaigns. As the reconquest from the Moslems proceeded, the devastated marches of the middle Tagus had to be not only defended but repeopled. The Templars whom he established in Tomar, and from whom the Order of Christ inherited their lands, were themselves predominantly a French order.

The nationality of some of the colonists they brought in is still shown by the names they gave their settlements. Nisa, of course, comes from Nice, nearby Tolosa from Toulouse, while Ródão above a narrow cutting of the Tagus recalls the swirling Rhone. Proença-a-Nova a few miles off in the direction of Tomar is a deformation of Provence.

Place-names also tell us that farther down the Tagus more Frenchmen settled at Vila Franca de Xira, Leonese at Benavente (named after a town in Leon), and Galicians at Montijo, which used to be known as Vila Galega. There are many more such clues up and down the country to the history of the resettlement. But in most cases settlers were too few in numbers to leave any mark on the local speech like the French 'u' they left in the upper Alentejo.

There are a variety of other ways, however, in which the Portuguese language reflects the history of Portugal.

The historical atlas which was my favourite textbook at school had on its very last page a map of Europe after the 1919 Peace Treaties. The new national boundaries were superimposed on an unfamiliar and quite different pattern of colours which repre-

18. Evora: the *chafariz* or fountain in the Largo das Portas de Moura

19. Evora: the Roman 'Temple of Diana'

20. Monsanto in Beira Baixa

sented the languages spoken. A note made the point that Portugal was the only country on the Continent with no linguistic minority; and indeed the dark green representing Portuguese flowed right up to the frontier.

The lighter green of Spanish, on the other hand, was broken by yet another shade of green for Catalan, by stippled white for Basque, and up in Galicia by bands of the dark green to represent the use there of that close relative of Portuguese, *gallego*. Even Great Britain had its overall red disturbed in Wales and in north-west Scotland by bands of mauve signifying the survival of Celtic-speaking minorities.

The pedant could claim that this statement about Portugal was a simplification. There are one or two frontier villages, such as Barrancos, a tongue of Portuguese territory surrounded by Spain, and Montalvão, in the 'hills of Alentejo', where a limited number of Castilian locutions and vocabulary have permeated local speech. And up in Trás-os-Montes, as we shall see, there are two exiguous pockets of Leonese. These last, however, are hardly 'minorities'. For Leonese is no longer spoken over the border in Leon, and survives in its purest form—and that far from pure—only in Portugal.

It is not in these peripheral exceptions, fascinating though they are, that Portuguese history is reflected, but in the broad development of the written and spoken language.

It is often said that Portuguese has no dialects, and that speech is identical throughout the country. Certainly it shows a remarkable homogeneity by comparison with other tongues. But it is not altogether without variations.

A linguistic map on a much larger scale than the one which so intrigued me at school would show everywhere north of the Douro marked in one colour, everywhere south of the Tagus marked in another, and an irregular mixture of the two colours in the central region between these rivers.

The first of these, north of the Douro, would represent a more conservative, archaic speech. Even the newcomer with only a slight command of the language notes that it assumes a more homespun texture as he travels north. He is in fact listening to the nearest living relative of the Portuguese of Afonso Henriques, and of the earliest documents.

The colour to the south of the Tagus, on the other hand, would represent a speech which has undergone more development and innovation. This was the result of the long Moslem domination there, which brought about an evolution and simplification in just the same way that the Norman domination of England brought about an evolution and simplification of English. There were inevitably borrowings from Arabic, but this was not the essential feature of the process: sometimes, when north and south have different words to describe the same thing, the southern word is not an Arabism, but a more modern word derived likewise from Latin at a later date.

The speech between Tagus and Douro is that of the debatable land between Christian and Moslem rule.

The kings of the first dynasty were for ever travelling around their realm. The nearest they had to a fixed capital was Coimbra. It was the events leading up to Aljubarrota: Lisbon's support of John of Avis, and its defiance of the Castilian army which laid siege to it, which made him definitely establish the capital there, linguistically very much to the south.

The same events led to the eclipse of the old aristocracy of the north who had supported Castile, and to their replacement at court by the smaller nobility of the centre and south, and by the Lisbon merchants. The language of all these was the more developed language of the south.

The political revolution of 1383–5 was therefore followed by a linguistic transformation. Portuguese has changed less since its beginnings than any other modern language except Italian; and it would therefore be an exaggeration to say that within a generation it made the jump from Chaucer to Shakespeare. But it was a jump in that direction.

Nearly four centuries later there occurred another abrupt transformation, though this time in the written rather than the spoken language.

We have already noticed how the Marquis of Pombal, rebuilding Lisbon in neo-Classical style, gave Baroque in the capital a

blow from which it never recovered. This change of style in architecture was paralleled by the change in style of government from
John V's politics of prestige to Pombal's enlightened despotism.
And it was paralleled also by a change of literary style from a
florid, involved Baroque to a simpler, more functional writing.

Further, but less important changes of this sort were brought
about by the Romantics. This was partly due to the personal role
played by some of their number—and especially by the greatest
of them, Almeida Garrett—in the victory of liberalism.

More recently there have been changes of the opposite kind:
changes, that is, in the spoken language which have not yet been
reflected in the written. The newcomer, indeed, listening to the
bewildering variety of forms of address expressing the simple
'you', and being told that each is in fashion in a particular social
class or age-group, feels that in certain fields at least evolution is
overdue. It will be interesting to see if future historians of the
Portuguese language will be able to recount how the technocrats
of the Corporative State, busy building their dams and roads and
strong *escudo*, built also, if less consciously, a new and appropriate form of the language to reflect their achievements.

6

THE HIGH PLACES

The 'hills of Alentejo' are a foretaste of the highlands which await us after we cross the Tagus at Ródão into Beira Baixa. Though this is not all mountainous country, mountains are generally within view, and the level of land is rising all the time. When we reach the next province to the north this average level is between two and three thousand feet, which is why it bears the name of Beira Alta.

The giant amongst these hills, and the backbone of Portugal in a more valid sense than the Pennines are the backbone of England, is the Serra da Estrêla. Its long mass, continued by the Serra de Louzã to the south, interposes itself between Beira Baixa and the rest of the country.

Despite its geographic position, however, the Serra da Estrêla is far from being central in the Portuguese consciousness. Many people have travelled widely between the Minho and the Algarve without ever going near it. And we must go a long way back in history before we find a period when it did play a central role.

There was such a period, however. Then the Mons Herminius, as the Romans called the Serra da Estrêla (the Serra de Marvão they called the lesser Herminius), was the fastness of their great Lusitanian enemy, Viriatus. Though he died as long ago as 139 B.C., it is interesting to note that he excelled in operating far from his base, and in arranging widespread alliances with other tribes opposed to Rome—both of them qualities retained by the modern Lusitanians.

Even remoter from the centre of history has been Beira Baixa, the region between the Serra da Estrêla and the frontier. Yet it, too, had its moment of glory in 672, when a Cincinnatus-like character called Wamba was summoned from his lands near Egitania to be king for a few years of the unstable Visigothic realm. Egitania is today Idanha-a-Velha, a village occupying a mere corner of the area enclosed within the still standing walls.

The road there runs through the provincial capital of Castelo Branco, a quiet white town beneath a castle with a pergola-approached *miradouro*. The bishop's palace, which is in process of being transformed into a museum, has a famous formal garden. Its low hedges and pools are twisted into fantastic shapes, for it was finished in 1725, at the height of the Baroque age of John V. The often-photographed line of kings' statues along the balustrade has been continued to include his son Dom José. Every one of them is given a titular virtue: 'the strong', 'the good', and so on. Even 'Dom Felipe I' (Philip II of Spain) is characterised as '*o prudente*'.

The garden stands near the edge of the town, and its formality contrasts uncannily with the stony, *maquis*-covered countryside which makes up much of Beira Baixa. It is great shooting country. I arrived one night at the hill town of Idanha-a-Nova, to find a bustle untypical of rural Portugal. I learned that it was full of *caçadores*, just arrived for the opening of the season. And next morning, as I enjoyed a picnic breakfast in superb country overlooking Idanha-a-Velha, I was hailed by a lanky figure in camouflage-patterned combat jacket, dangling a hare. He proved to be the *guarda* of the ruins of Egitania.

From where the Tagus ceases to act as the frontier, and disappears into Spain—soon to be crossed by the great Roman bridge of Alcántara—there is even less than usual in the way of physical obstacles to separate the two countries. However, this semi-wilderness, good for little but rough shooting, acts as an insulating no-man's-land, and is continued by one of the remotest areas of one of Spain's remotest provinces. In this unlikely setting there stands on the very border the spa of Monfortinho. A good road brings Lisbon sophisticates to take the waters.

Monsanto, on the other hand, a few miles north of Idanha-a-Velha, seems well suited to its setting. Its crowded granite houses clamber up and between and even within the boulders of the steep outcrop to which it clings. They are not all poor cottages. There are one or two more substantial dwellings with carved coats of arms down by the church and the tiny Misericordia. But the most interesting religious building is the ruined hermitage above the village and below the castle. Though a roofless shell it preserves a carved Romanesque doorway and frieze.

The silver cock which once crowned the early fifteenth-century tower of Lacarro has been placed in safe-keeping by the municipality, which has replaced it with an equally effective substitute in aluminium. For there have been plenty of outside visitors to Monsanto since in 1940 it was declared 'the most Portuguese village in Portugal', a title which neither its remote location nor its dark, forbidding appearance would seem to justify.

From Monsanto can be seen the even bigger outcrop of Penha Garcia standing over near the Spanish border, and ten miles to the north Penamacor. Nestling beneath its castle keep, this is far nearer to the archetype of the clean, white little Portuguese town. Everything is there, including the sixteenth-century pillory, and the Misericordia with Manueline doorway. (The Misericordia has not been pulled down, as claimed by one excellent guide.)

A few yards up a turning off the Castelo Branco road is the Convent of S. António, unmentioned in any book, with a fine gilded roof and high altar, and a delightful two-tiered cloister. I would never have discovered this empty, echoing building had I not been accompanied round the town by three senior schoolboys from Penamacor's *colegio*. They had appointed themselves as my guides not only in order to practise their French, but out of interest in foreigners, and above all out of that spontaneous friendliness the stranger meets everywhere in Portugal.

I had a similar experience at Alpedrinha, a village fifteen miles to the west, on the direct road from Castelo Branco to Guarda. Here it was the local 'Teddy boy' who insisted on accompanying me. The smallest village has one of his type, in appearance halfway between Almeida Garrett and a Rolling Stone. But until Alpedrinha I had managed to avoid them.

To my surprise he proved a guide not only intelligent, but

innocent. Without him I would never have found the elaborate fountain of the reign of John V at the top of the village, between a ruined palace of the same period and a cobbled causeway supposedly untouched since it was built by the Romans.

But it was after we had returned to the main road that he proudly showed me what he regarded as Alpedrinha's greatest claim to fame. Leading me through the hall and bar of the *Estalagem S. Jorge* he opened a door to release billowing clouds of heavy smoke. By a low red light I could dimly perceive a couple of his own age slowly gyrating. He turned to me with a smile of pride:

'They come from as far away as Coimbra, for they haven't got one even there. This is the only night club in the interior of Portugal!'

Alpedrinha is already high on the southern slopes of the Serra da Gardunha, a steep range of hills which, at over four thousand feet, would anywhere else in Portugal seem mountains. But they are dwarfed by the Estrêla, running parallel a mere fifteen miles away. Its shelter gives a Mediterranean rather than an Atlantic appearance to the *maquis*-covered Gardunha, and indeed the province as a whole. But in no part of Beira Baixa is this more manifest than in the fertile strip which lies between the two Serras. The farmers nearer Penamacor or Castelo Branco speak of this 'Cova da Beira' with the tone of envy used by those of the Lincolnshire Wolds when referring to the rich Fenlands.

It owes this garden-like fertility to the fact that it is not only sheltered but watered. It is the valley of the Zêzere, one of the most important of Portugal's secondary rivers—we saw it dammed at Castelo de Bode near Tomar, just before it enters the Tagus. Its 'capital' is Fundão, which despite two or three old churches struck me as an expanding, modern little town. New shops and banks line the wide avenue from which the lorries set off with the fruit for which the Cova is famous, and to which modern transport has given a wider market.

This new-found agricultural prosperity contrasts with the depression of an old-established industry near at hand. Covilhã, only twelve miles away on the other side of the valley, became the centre of the Portuguese textile industry for two reasons. Its situation on the farther slopes of the Serra da Estrêla protected it from British competition in the days of poor communications. And the flocks on those slopes were at hand to provide the wool.

But now EFTA, which elsewhere in Portugal has brought about a boom in the labour-intensive manufacture of shirts and knitwear from artificial fibres, has dealt Covilhã the blow which Methuen failed to deliver. The knock-out came from sterling devaluation, which in bringing English suitings within the range of the average escudo-lined pocket, put several hundred operatives out of work in this steep little town.

With some twenty-five thousand souls, it is the biggest in all the area covered by this chapter. Yet it has little of the appearance of a manufacturing town, and still less of the setting. For like a smaller Grenoble it is at once an industrial and a winter sports centre, offering the easiest access to the highest point of the Serra da Estrêla, and thus of Portugal.

This is known as the Tôrre, because a tower twenty-nine feet high has been erected to bring its altitude up to the magic figure of two thousand metres. A road has been built up to it from the road joining Covilhã to Seia across the mountains. Penhas da Saúde, the only properly equipped ski-resort in Portugal, stands at four thousand nine hundred feet, five miles before the Tôrre.

There is an abrupt climb from Covilhã of two thousand five hundred feet in only seven miles. But after Penhas da Saúde the road levels out, and on one side there opens below us one of the transversal valleys which distinguish this range. For in many places it is 'split down the middle', giving rise to two separate crests, and to some very wild, unspoilt country between them.

'Since last week's snowfall you'll never get beyond Penhas da Saúde,' I was assured with a tolerant smile at the Covilhã *Turismo* on the morning of May 18th. And indeed I felt like an Arctic explorer as I drove on beyond the ski-station between ever-rising banks of snow. I was finally brought to a halt just where a track branched off down the transversal valley mentioned above. But the sun was up, and my time was my own. So I decided to spend the day working up there, in the bright mountain air.

There followed many hours of profitable silence. They were broken only at six in the evening, when just as I was preparing to return on my tracks I heard a distant car. The sound came not from the direction of Covilhã, but from the transversal valley. As a Mini emerged from the track on to the main road I stepped out to inquire how it had got through.

'The snow's been melting all day,' its driver told me. 'Except for one small patch the track is clear now all the way to Manteigas. If we've managed to come up it, you'll have no trouble. Because for you it will be downhill all the way!'

Jolting down the unmade road I soon felt at home. It was a Pyrenean landscape, the only one I have yet encountered in Portugal: bright green with a damp feel to the air as soon as the sun went in. Waterfalls cascaded, and a stream tumbled down a stony bed, with all the eagerness born of melting snow.

The stream was the infant Zêzere. This flows north-east along this transversal valley, before bending round through a hundred and eighty degrees after passing the leafy spa of Caldas de Manteigas and the small town of Manteigas itself. Here is manufactured much of that excellent sheep's cheese, *queijo da serra*, which Lisbon grocers sell for up to 5op a pound. As with Brie or Camembert, the more it 'oozes', the better its taste and quality.

The Zêzere is not the only river to start its life in the wrong direction by taking advantage of the 'splits' in the Serra da Estrêla. High above Manteigas on the magnificent road to Gouveia, beyond the *pousada* of S. Lourenço, an artificial basin has been built to receive the spring which marks the beginning of the Mondego. But before we follow the precipitous early descent of the longest river whose entire course lies within Portugal, let us take a last backward look at the mountains which give it birth.

They are not only the highest in the country, but the most extensive. They provide its only natural lakes, in small depressions formed long ago by glaciers, with names like 'The Round Lake', 'The Long Lake', 'The Dark Lake'.

They provide, too, important mineral deposits, including unexpectedly arsenic, and that mysterious wolfram which the Germans did everything possible to acquire in the closing stages of the Second World War. (It yields tungsten.) As at S. Domingos, English capital has been active here. Beralt Tin and Wolfram has an honoured place amongst the four thousand-odd companies quoted on the London Stock Exchange. Its name was known to me for long before I knew any Portuguese; and I had several times scanned the map for the unlikely place-name of 'Beralt' before it occurred to me that it was a convenient contraction of 'Beira Alta'.

And it is into Beira Alta that the Mondego now leads us. Just before it starts its own one hundred and eighty-degree turn, in the opposite direction to the Zêzere, it passes beneath what is perhaps the greatest road in Portugal. This is not to disparage the Great North Road from Lisbon to Oporto. For this is really its international extension, providing both cities with their main route to northern Europe. The roads to Vigo, Orense, and even Seville offer only provincial changes of scene. That to Madrid is primarily to the *pais vizinho*. But this leads to '*Paris, Berlim, S. Petersburgo, o mundo!*', as Cesário Verde expressed the *saudade* of the far west for the wider world.

Frequently it also offers to visitors from that wider world their first view of Portugal. It is an approach far wilder than the quiet crossing of the Guadiana, or the plain of Badajoz. Rodney Gallop described how, many miles before the frontier, the passenger by train momentarily glimpses 'three small white triangles, like the topsails of a schooner, hull down upon the horizon', a tantalising signal from the Serra da Estrêla. But although the traveller by road will notice a change at the border, from the monotonous Spanish *meseta* to a more varied and wooded countryside, he will only be plunged into a new culture when he pulls up in Guarda.

At three thousand five hundred feet it is the highest city in Portugal, and after Avila in the entire peninsula. The austerity associated with this altitude is disguised by the prevailing white of its buildings. But the underlying reality surfaces in the grim, almost black granite of the cathedral. Its exterior is of the period and inspiration of Batalha, but the nave owes much to the great Boytac, working in the Manueline style a century later.

This granite reappears in three gates along the line of the

former city wall, outside which in a great half-moon dominating the hills of Beira Alta, a fascinating fair is held each Wednesday. And it appears again in Guarda's oldest monument, the Romanesque chapel of Milreu, which the traveller arriving from Spain passes on the long steep climb to the city.

There is just as long a descent towards the valley of the young Mondego, which the road then follows for some miles to Celorico da Beira, with a ruined castle. From there the Lisbon highway winds through numerous pinewoods along the northern flanks of the Serra da Estrêla. The interesting little towns of Gouveia and Seia, from which lead the mountain roads over to Manteigas and Covilhã, lie higher still.

The most interesting building along this road involves a detour of only a mile. It is the tiny basilica of Lourosa, with 'ERA dccccx' inscribed above the entrance in archaic characters. This date of 910 makes it with S. Amaro at Beja, S. Pedro at Balsemão, and S. Frutuoso near Braga one of the four pre-Romanesque churches in Portugal.

Lourosa is already technically within the next province, Beira Litoral. The tangled heartland of Beira Alta lies north of the road through Guarda to the frontier. Until the end of the thirteenth century this frontier lay several miles farther back, along the River Côa.

The strip of Portuguese territory then added was protected by the fortress of Almeida, now an elaborate Vaubanesque design sheltering a tiny town. Arriving there on Corpus Christi day, I fell into conversation with a farmer, who invited me to taste his home-made garlic sausage and wine. He drank quite as much as I did, and at the sound of a distant band dragged me into the street and the middle of a procession. Together we marched through Almeida between a Youth Group and that most popular of all Portuguese community organisations, the Voluntary Fire Brigade!

Being on the point of leaving Portugal, I bought a large loaf of the excellent rye-bread, *pão de centeio*, which is found all over Beira Alta, but never in Spain. To my surprise the baker told me that he did very little business, as most people purchased their bread a few pence cheaper, across the frontier in Fuentes de Oñoro, only ten miles away.

The strip of territory acquired at the end of the thirteenth century was also defended by a castle at Castelo Rodrigo, twelve miles north of Almeida. It is completely ruined now, just as the village around it has decayed. Only a perfect Manueline pillory, a huge water cistern, and a delightful little church survive from its days of importance. For most of its population has long since transferred itself to Figueira de Castelo Rodrigo down in the plain. Two miles up another road is the remote Convent of S. Maria de Aguiar, with a well-restored square Gothic church, and a Renaissance *loggia* on the farmhouse into which the convent buildings have been converted.

The fortress in the rear, defending the line of the Côa, was Pinhel. As described in the Tailpiece of Chapter 4, I was lucky enough to be shown round by a retired Portuguese major. We wandered from the little museum for which he had made himself responsible, past the Manueline doorway of the Misericordia, and along a narrow street on the edge of the town which he told me was the old Judaria. Each house, he pointed out, had both the usual narrow door, and a wider one 'for the shop'.

I asked him if there still survived any 'New Christians', the forcibly-converted Jews who sought refuge from the Inquisition in these distant provinces. Conspiratorially he assured me that there were several, one of whom, at least, still practised Jewish rites in secret!

The major himself was named Falcão, and traced his ancestry to a Sir John Falconer who had accompanied Philippa of Lancaster when she arrived for that happy marriage alliance which followed Aljubarrota.

The castle with those so suggestive gargoyles was built by Dennis, the king who acquired the territory beyond the Côa. His own marriage to the princess from Aragon who became Saint Isabel was celebrated twenty miles to the west at Trancoso, a small walled town amidst magnificent countryside. It, too, has a good castle, as has Penedono eighteen miles farther north.

Travelling west, there is something to suit every taste. Aguiar da Beira offers a tiny but perfect ensemble of pillory, keep, and what *The Selective Traveller in Portugal*, which rather goes to town on Aguiar, judges to be an unroofed medieval council chamber. Moimenta da Beira, like several centres in the Beiras, has a wine co-operative where I was able to purchase five litres straight from the press for only twenty escudos—less than 5p a bottle. And if you wish to even accounts with those friends who sent you a postcard from Hell in Norway, why not return the compliment from Sátão (Satan)?

Penance for this sin can be performed on a pilgrimage to S. João de Tarouca, a Cistercian church richly decorated in a very un-Cistercian way. It contains a picture by Grão Vasco of St. Peter wearing the Papal tiara, which may be the original of a similar one in the Grão Vasco museum at Viseu. All around the monastery buildings decay: the roofless dormitory shelters a kitchen garden.

Within five miles of S. João de Tarouca are a fourteenth-century fortified bridge at Ucanha; another former monastery at Salzedas; and the church of Ferreirim, which will be better able to show off its pictures of the Portuguese Renaissance when its untidy restoration is completed.

Beira Alta is everywhere high. But to the west it becomes noticeably wilder, in a series of *serras* running from the Douro south to the Mondego and cutting it off from the coast. A servant woman in Lisbon had told me grim stories from her country childhood near Viseu of wolves driven down to her village by the snow—very much Atlantic rather than Mediterranean Portugal! But I had tended to discount them until I saw a newspaper photograph of a shepherd beside a wolf five feet eleven inches long, which he had killed in defence of his flock, only a few miles from the same city. And after I had travelled the lonely road from Lamêgo to Castro Daire, over the desolate flank of Montemuro, I was ready to accept any reports of the region, however horrific.

Castro Daire, a small town in the middle of nowhere, had several houses sufficiently imposing to have been the home of the very innocent villain of Castelo Branco's best-known novel, *Amor de Perdição*. (His only fault was that he loved the heroine, and that unlike the hero he was in a position to keep her!) But none of them looked the choice of 'an English lawyer, retired from Nigeria, who has established himself in some place at the back of beyond called Castro Daire, to get away from it all'. In these vague terms I had been given an introduction to him, with no more precise address.

'Does an Englishman live in Castro Daire?' I asked the first person I saw.

'Not actually in the town, but eight kilometres away at Reriz,' the reply came pat.

And sure enough, at the end of a long unmade road, a lovely house stood in beautiful grounds beside a stream full of trout: a sizeable enough 'corner of some foreign field'. Its owner proved to be the friend of another Englishman retired from Nigeria, whose home I had come across in an even less likely setting in the lunar landscape of Lanzarote in the Canary Islands. To both men their years in West Africa had given the self-sufficiency to live the civilised life anywhere.

Perhaps it was the imperial assumptions with which they grew up which enabled both to do something more. The retired tin-miner on Lanzarote has created his own genre of painting from its extraordinary volcanic landscape. And a few days after my visit to Reriz I got into conversation at Coimbra University Restaurant with a student from another valley near Castro Daire. He told of '*o inglês de Reriz*', who had introduced a giant race of pig which had brought about an economic revolution in the sties of Montemuro. Evidently the Large White has taken over from the thin red line in support of the *Velha Aliança*.

The Mondego, though it starts its life in Beira Alta, belongs to all Portugal. More essentially of the province is the Vouga, which flows from a steep ridge behind Aguiar da Beira past Sátão into a deep and lovely valley dividing the Serra da Gralheira, the southward extension of Montemuro, from that of Caramulo. In this valley lie two interesting little towns. S. Pedro do Sul has a good Misericordia. Vouzela has a Romanesque parish church, in the chancel of which hang some 'Grandma Moses' type primitives of quite recent local saints. On my visit there it was carpeted with herbs.

The Serra do Caramulo, though lower and less desolate than Montemuro, can be even bleaker. But its smaller area enables it to dominate more extensive views, embracing the Serra da Estrêla in the east and the coastal plain of the Bairrada in the west. It is well worth enduring a buffeting from the winds to climb one of its belvederes, the highest of which, Caramulinho, can be reached by road.

Some of these views can be enjoyed at Caramulo itself, the only inland Portuguese resort which is not a spa. And it offers views of another kind in two museums such as one hardly expects to find two thousand seven hundred feet up a mountainside. One of these holds Portugal's only Vintage Car collection, including three Rolls-Royces of 1911, 1920, and 1930.

The other museum contains a haphazard assemblage of individual bequests of porcelain, tapestry, sculpture, and above all painting, of every country, every school . . . and every quality. It taught me the importance of the curator's role as a selector, providing exhibition space only for the typical model of a style, the unique, or the best, and consigning the dead wood to reserve. But donors must be humoured, and at Caramulo the dead wood lives on, while the great names—of which there are plenty, including Picasso, Chagall, Dali, Sutherland—are not always represented by their masterpieces.

If an art museum had to be placed on a mountainside, then this was the most appropriate mountain to choose. For Viseu, the district capital almost at the foot of Caramulo, is despite its remote location what the French call a *ville d'art*. Almost twice the size of Guarda, and at less than half the height, it has more movement in its tree-lined streets. It smiles less austerely, too, in no less than five Baroque churches, many of them with memorable *azulejos*.

Its thirteenth-century cathedral, however, is of the same dark granite as Guarda's, with plain square towers on either side of a seventeenth-century doorway, and with an even plainer town palace in the same stone alongside. It is inside these two buildings that Viseu reserves its greatest surprises. The cathedral has a

Manueline roof, criss-crossed by the ropes of the caravels, a double cloister of which the lower is a beautifully proportioned work of the Renaissance, and a rich treasury of sacred art.

The plain palace alongside is the Grão Vasco museum, named after Vasco Fernandes, the early sixteenth-century painter who founded a school in Viseu. It is not devoted exclusively to him. In particular the Baroque sculpture, removed from various churches and convents, is worth a second and indeed a third look. But it is he who presides, just as his St. Peter (of whom we saw what may be an even older version at S. João de Tarouca) reigns over the entire museum.

Neither Grão Vasco nor his younger Viseu contemporary, Gaspar Vaz, were isolated provincials: both had probably studied under King Manuel's Court painter, Jorge Afonso. But their hearts remained here where they worked. And in that work these high places of the Beiras made again an essential contribution to Lusitania, as seventeen hundred years before in the time of Viriatus.

An octagonal Roman camp on the outskirts of Viseu is indeed appropriately though mistakenly named the Cava de Viriato. And from the windows of the museum can be seen, above the narrow streets of the older part of the city, far away on the other side of the Mondego valley, the long mass of the Estrêla from which he came.

TAILPIECE: PAIS IRMÃO

Belmonte stands on a hill above where the main road from Covilhã to Guarda crosses the Zêzere. It is not therefore as remote as scores of more isolated localities in Beira Baixa. Yet it seems so, especially at its dusty summit, where a squat little castle, unadorned save for a Manueline window and a coat of arms, stares across at the Estrêla and the unending ranges of Beira Alta. Here, surely, is interior, inward-looking Portugal, as far as it is possible to reach from the influence of either Atlantic or Mediterranean.

Yet in the modern church at the other end of the little town is

21. In the Serra da
Estrêla

22. Aveiro on its canalised lagoon

an ancient statue of the Virgin which long ago travelled across the South Atlantic. And before the castle stands a cross donated in 1969 by an airline with the unfamiliar name of VARIG. For here, five hundred years earlier, was born to the family who bore that coat of arms, a scion who was to make possible that airline, and infinitely more: Pedro Alvares Cabral.

In a sense, of course, he was merely an instrument in the great process of discovery. Others could equally well have been appointed to command the second expedition to India which left the Tagus on 9 March 1500. Vasco da Gama himself was available. So were Francisco de Almeida and Afonso de Albuquerque who were soon to carve out the Portuguese empire in the East. But with our hindsight, the young noble born in a province so close and so alike to the Estremadura of Cortes and Pizarro certainly seems the most appropriate commander for such a sweeping voyage.

For sweeping it was. The main destination of the armada of thirteen ships was India, so much the nation's object of yearning since Vasco da Gama's return that Oliveira Martins could write: 'The whole of Portugal embarks for India in Cabral's fleet.' It was almost incidental that on the way it touched at the land Cabral named after the True Cross, thereby claiming for the Portuguese Crown the vastness of Brazil.

Was he a discoverer in the same sense as Columbus? There exists a flourishing and fascinating literature arguing that the Portuguese already knew that lands existed to the west when King John II deliberately refused to sponsor the great Genoese. This argument finds support in the famous Treaty of Tordesillas, which in 1494 drew the line of demarcation between Spanish and Portuguese spheres of interest three hundred and seventy leagues to the west of the Cape Verde Islands. For this conveniently handed Cabral's 'discovery' to Portugal six years before he set out to make it.

Certainly the 'Machiavellian' John II, a highly intelligent realist, would have been quite capable of remaining silent about any of his captains' discoveries which he could not immediately exploit. The resources of a small Atlantic nation of a million souls

were limited. They must be channelled towards the main chance—
the route to the East.

It was the East which continued to demand the overwhelming
share of those resources long after Brazil was discovered. The
illusory road to riches for Camoens and so many of his contemporaries lay by Moçambique and Melinde, Malabar, Malacca
and Macau.

But while they sought, all too often in vain, to build their fortunes by trade, warfare, and sometimes even piracy, the first
colonists in Brazil were achieving wealth through the more prosaic
but certain medium of sugar plantations. And their numbers and
prosperity continued to grow while the empire in the East with-
ered during the grim years of subordination to the Spanish Crown.

A main reason for the decline of that empire was the attacks
launched against it by the Dutch. These had always bought their
spices and other Oriental products from Lisbon, until Philip II,
against whom they were in rebellion, became King of Portugal
and closed its ports to their ships. They were driven to fetch their
own goods from the East; and there followed the foundation of
the Dutch East India Company, the occupation of Ceylon and the
Moluccas, the settlement of the Cape of Good Hope, and even
the capture of the Portuguese trading posts in Angola.

Nor was this attempt by the Dutch to supplant the Portuguese
limited to the Old World. Born colonists, they yearned for a more
substantial footing in the Americas than the New Amsterdam
they had just established on and around Manhattan Island. Their
expeditions against Brazil were perhaps the biggest the United
Provinces ever launched overseas. Soon all the northern part of
the country, then the richest and most important, was under the
rule of their viceroy Prince Maurice of Orange.

The spirit which brought about the restoration of independence
under the Braganças was not, however, confined to European
Portugal. The colonists themselves expelled the Dutch from
Brazil. And it was they, too, who sent a fleet across the South
Atlantic to liberate Angola. Thus, three centuries ago, Brazil had
already shown at once her ability to stand on her own feet, and
her sense of partnership in the 'Lusitanian community'.

The loss of much of the East had given her a major position in that community. With the discovery of gold in 1693 in Minas Gerais she became its treasury.

The munificence of John V and the rebuilding of Lisbon were alike made possible by that gold, and by the cotton plantations encouraged by the Marquis of Pombal when the mines showed signs of exhaustion. When in 1807 the royal family and their ministers sailed to Rio de Janeiro, only a few hours before Lisbon was occupied by the invading French, it could be said that the seat of Portuguese government was transferred to the seat of Portuguese resources.

This became manifest when the Brazilians, who had sheltered King and Court for fifteen years, were alienated by the arbitrary measures forced on that King by the liberals who had obliged him to return to Lisbon. For the secession which followed in 1822 brought Portugal to a state of near-bankruptcy, from which she only emerged more than a century later.

Thus, even before independence, Brazil's relationship with Portugal was nearer to one of parity than that of the other American colonies with their European mother-countries. And her secession, unlike theirs, involved no bitter fratricidal war. The famous cry of Ypiranga, 'Independence or death', was uttered not by a cotton-planting squire or a Creole general, but by the King's son and Regent. Thus the Regent became Emperor, and Brazil passed its first sixty-seven years as a sovereign nation under the rule of Braganças.

The continuity of this non-violent transition, and the equality of status between the two countries, has prevented the development of many of the unpleasanter complexes which still bedevil Anglo-American relations, and make impossible all but the loosest cultural ties between Spain and the fragments of her erstwhile viceroyalties. Brazil is not an ex-colony which has successfully revolted, nor a penal settlement which has grown rich, nor even a daughter who has set up her own home. She is—excuse the change of gender—the *pais irmão*, the brother-land.

It is a measure of Portugal's achievement that she has not only established this healthy and normal relationship, but that she has bequeathed so much of her way of life to a land so different from her own. Spain in Mexico and Peru found the reflection of her own fertile coastlands and bare *mesetas*. The Puritans in austere New England, like the Cavaliers in mellow Virginia, found country appropriate to their style of living. But Portugal is small and poor and temperate, whereas Brazil is vast and rich and tropical. Yet the churches of Belém and Bahia and Minas Gerais, the mosaic pavements of Rio, and even some of the daring developments of Brasilia, alike speak of a common and still continuing cultural heritage.

So do the very names. For perhaps the greatest gift from the older brother-nation to the younger has been their shared language. Inevitably this has suffered a sea-change as profound as English or Spanish in crossing the Atlantic. Portuguese, which in its homeland has evolved less since its medieval beginnings than any other European language except Italian, has developed rapidly in the luxuriant soil to which it has been transplanted.

The foreign tourist who, having taken the trouble to learn a little Portuguese, is politely asked if he is *brasileiro*, may conclude that it has changed beyond recognition. This was indeed the avowed aim of Brazilian nationalists of a generation ago, such as Vargas: a new language for a new nation.

But the 'United States of Brazil', the federal republic which succeeded the second Bragança emperor in 1889, welcomed immigrants from every corner of Europe just as warmly as that other United States, of North America. Germans and Italians, in particular, flocked to the southern states, from S. Paulo to Rio Grande do Sul, in sufficient numbers to form indigestible minorities. America had found unity by insisting on a knowledge of English before granting citizenship. Thus Brazil decided to continue its work of assimilation through the medium which for five centuries had enjoyed such striking success in every continent of the Old World: Portuguese. Formal institutions were given by treaty to the concept of the Luso-Brazilian Community.

This has been established to encourage co-operation in other fields besides linguistic. In the linguistic, indeed, co-operation has been evident as much in the breach as in the observance. A joint agreement on syntax and orthography which made many concessions to Brazilian usage was ratified in Lisbon but not in Rio. So the Portuguese must write '*perguntar*' for 'to ask', although he still pronounces '*preguntar*'. For this and other reasons '*a Comunidade Luso-Brasileira*' is sometimes referred to in deprecating terms reminiscent of those applied all too often in England to the British Commonwealth.

But in both cases the creaking institutions, conferences of academies or of prime ministers, mask living realities. Were they to disappear tomorrow, others would have to be invented to take their place. President Quadros of Brazil may have sympathised with certain of Dr. Salazar's opponents—though he was not allowed to stay in power for long enough to do much about it. Some of the hundreds of *brasileiro* students who matriculate each year in the Portuguese universities may be regarded by their hosts as a little brash, excitable, and noisy. But they are regarded no more as foreigners than are Australians in London—and a good deal less than are Americans. For how can they be *estrangeiros*, these transatlantic Lusitanians from the *pais irmão*?

7

THE BELOVED CITY

The Mondego, whose source in the Serra da Estrêla and early
course beneath its northern flank we traced in the last chapter,
receives only one sizeable tributary from the hills of Beira Alta.
This is the Dão, from whose mild arcadian valley comes what I
am not alone in regarding as the best table wine in Portugal.

Shortly before its junction with the Mondego, the Dão meanders
between the little town of Santa Comba Dão and its dependent
hamlet of Vimieiro. The quiet road between them crosses the
stream by a stone bridge watched over at one end by a tiny
chapel. And half-way up the gentle hill down which straggles
Vimieiro stands a single-storeyed cottage, as simple and as solid
as the man who was born there in 1889.

Not even a commemorative plaque marks his birthplace,
though a statue of Salazar does now sit before the courthouse of
Santa Comba. 'You notice how he turns his back on Justice,' say
the wits who in Portugal, as elsewhere, are ready with their cheap
jibes against the establishment.

I was more impressed by the attitude of an old woman to
whom I gave a lift from the bridge up to the town. She had
known his family all her life, and spoke of him with pride mingled
with affection. It was early in April 1970, and his recovery from
his sudden stroke eighteen months before was proceeding apace.
Buttercups and daisies covered the meadows round the cottage
where two of his sisters still lived. And this old family friend
hoped that he would soon be coming to stay for many weeks in
his own home and amongst his own people.

Within three months he was dead, and even his bitterest

opponents had to admit that Portugal had lost a giant. To whom can he be compared? His self-effacement and frugality recall the austerity of Prince Henry the Navigator. But far from retiring to Sagres he dwelt at the very centre of power.

That power was as much in his hands as two centuries earlier it had been in the hands of Pombal. But his tenure of it lasted for thirteen years longer than Pombal's, and was terminated only by his own illness. And whereas Pombal, despite the riches of Brazil, left an Army and a Navy in decay, and a depleted Treasury, Salazar inherited an escudo which in five years had sunk from five to the pound sterling to more than a hundred to the pound, and left it as one of the strongest currencies in the world.

Yet it is his activity in the financial and economic fields which is today the most disputed aspect of his policies. I have deliberately separated 'financial' and 'economic' because, as one young critic put it to me, 'Salazar was perhaps a good financier, but he was certainly a bad economist. A developing country cannot afford the luxury of a hard currency. He should have let inflation rip, as Franco has done across the frontier.* Then today our industry, like Spain's, would have reached the take-off point, and there would be no need for all the young people of our villages to emigrate to France.'

But this young neo-Keynesian, like the majority of his kind, had never earned a penny, let alone saved one. Only those who have suffered personally from inflation can justly value a statesman who aimed, with considerable success, at ensuring that an escudo in the pocket was still worth an escudo in the shops.

Even that industrial 'take-off point' was on the horizon when the war in Africa arrived to cream off the annual increase in Portugal's gross national product, which has been achieved in every year since 1961. And here the same critics who attack his economic policies also attack his policy overseas. For them Portugal should have abdicated, like Belgium or Britain, washing her hands of any Angolan Katangas or Guinean Biafras which might have followed her departure.

* In 1950 the £ sterling bought 70 pesetas, but 80 escudos. In 1970 it bought 167 pesetas, but only 68 escudos.

But they cannot have it both ways. Industries of today's scale and techniques demand home markets with sufficient purchasing power to absorb those industries' production. The nine million people of metropolitan Portugal, four-fifths of whom are in the agricultural sector, and mainly in the poorer levels of the agricultural sector at that, are simply not enough to form such a home market. But the thirty million people of *'o espaço português'* are; and the Portuguese troops of every colour in Africa are guarding not only its mineral but also its human resources. Prosperity requires consumers as well as producers. The ex-Professor of Economics of Coimbra University may have understood his subject better than his critics imagine.

Coimbra was central in his life. From this beloved city he was called to power; and to it he gladly returned when to begin with his terms for budgetary reform were not accepted. For anyone born at Santa Comba Dão, Coimbra must indeed occupy a place at least as central as Oxford for anyone born at Witney, or Cambridge for anyone born at Grantchester. Towards Coimbra from the high places of Beira Alta rush both road and river, following a valley which narrows almost to a gorge between the steep hills.

Five miles up a side-road amongst those hills stands the former Convent of Lorvão. It is no less impressive for being hidden by them until one is directly in front of its long plain façade, the result of an eighteenth-century reconstruction. To the same period belong the vast interior of the church, many of the vestments and quaint Baroque furnishings of its sacristy, the wrought-iron grille which separates off the choir, and the elaborate silver coffins which lie on either side of that choir.

But although these coffins date from as recently as 1713, they hold the bones of two princesses born in the twelfth century, who retired to Lorvão and died here. They were daughters of King Sancho I, whose capital was Coimbra, which until the conquest of southern Portugal lay at the centre of the kingdom. Even when the Court moved south to Lisbon, Coimbra remained a favourite royal residence. In this chapter, therefore, we shall be visiting other convents patronised by royalty, and remembering other queens and princesses.

This was a favoured residential region earlier still. For Conimbriga, the Roman city ten miles to the south, was a Pompeii or a Bath rather than an Olisipo or a Londinium. Its destruction by the Suevi in 468 was almost as complete and as sudden as that of Pompeii, and left, as at Pompeii, a good deal more for posterity to gaze at than would have been spared by the slower but surer attrition of continued human occupation. Its site, deep in the country, with a generally empty car park beside the little museum where many of the choicest fragments are gathered, is strangely like that of Volubilis, the deserted Roman city in Morocco.

The survivors of Conimbriga moved with the name of their city to a site better adapted to their less peaceful age, on a steep hill protected on one side by the Mondego. Like Toledo on the Tagus, it was a spot which appealed in turn to Visigoths, Arabs, and the lords of the *reconquista*. There grew up one of those densely-packed mazes of narrow streets which constituted a city for medieval man, whether Christian or Moslem.

An Islamic specialist has written that what distinguished those cities from the cities of the modern West, and what still distinguishes the cities of the modern West from older-style Moslem cities such as Fez, is less the crowded humanity with its smells than the all-pervasive sense of religion. And just as at the heart of modern Fez lie the great mosques, so at the heart of medieval Coimbra lay its cathedral.

A cathedral no longer, the Sé Velha lies there still, half-way up the hill in a little square, surrounded by steep streets whose plan can have changed little since it was built eight centuries ago. In many respects it is the most unspoilt of Portugal's Romanesque cathedrals. The view of the main façade, with its doorway repeated to form a window immediately above, or of the dark nave, would be recognisable by King Afonso Henriques.

Elsewhere it owes features to the Renaissance, when John III, reacting against the late Gothic which was Manueline, welcomed artists from abroad. Those who settled at Coimbra were mainly sculptors, and mainly from Normandy: one of them is even known as Jean de Rouen. It was he who carved the altar in the chapel on the left of the *altar-mor*, itself a Flemish masterpiece of a generation earlier. And colleagues of his carved the porch added to the north façade in the local stone of Ançã. It is amenable to the chisel, but to the elements too, so that this sixteenth-century portico looks as if it has suffered far more exposure than the twelfth-century granite on which it has been grafted.

There is the same unusual combination of Romanesque with Renaissance, in this case with Manueline overtones, in the other major religious monument of Coimbra: the monastery of Santa Cruz. This now lies at the heart of the newer town which has grown up beneath the hill. It stands between the town hall and a restaurant of the *belle époque* installed incongruously in the vaulted chamber of a former convent.

Santa Cruz was founded by Afonso Henriques himself, and his Manueline tomb, with that of his son Sancho I (father of the princesses of Lorvão), lies up in the choir. Of the same period is the Cloister of Silence: cloisters, as we have seen, generally received special treatment from Manueline architects. But there is a Renaissance fountain at its centre, and paintings by masters of the Portuguese Renaissance in the sacristy. And the beautiful pulpit is by one of the group of French sculptors we have met at the Sé Velha: either Jean de Rouen or his still more brilliant contemporary, Nicolas Chantarène.

In the Middle Ages kings' wives as well as kings' daughters often retired to convents in widowhood. Queen Isabel retired thus to the Convent of S. Clara across the river when the great King Dennis died in 1325, forty-three years after they had married at Trancoso. Her rich tomb, and a famous modern statue of her by Teixeira Lopes, almost pre-Raphaelite in its willowy languidness, stand in the church of the seventeenth-century S. Clara-a-Nova on the crest of the hill.

It was rebuilt there after her original foundation lower down had been half filled with sand by the shifting Mondego. Its ruins, on the left soon after crossing the bridge, are one monument which children will enjoy visiting. They can scamper amongst the upper capitals of its thirteenth-century nave and choir, with thirty feet of sand between them and the true floor. But accompanying grown-ups should make sure they keep away from the occasional crevices and drops which all such old buildings contain.

For a more carefree visit, they can move on a few yards to Portugal dos Pequenitos, a children's playground on the grand scale, where churches, castles, and town and country houses from every province both at home and overseas are reconstructed on the scale of the 'little people'. To squeeze in so much, there has had to be condensation, and one building often contains features from several. So while the children scramble in and out of the cottage from Nazaré or the pagoda from Macau, their adult companions can enjoy recognising the tower of the castle of Guimarães, or Diogo de Arruda's window at Tomar.

The road to S. Clara-a-Velha and Portugal dos Pequenitos leads half a mile on to the Quinta das Lágrimas. Here in the years before 1355 lived in blissful though unwedded domesticity another figure from Coimbra's royal past, Inés de Castro— though she was only to be crowned Queen after her death. Her story was told in the account of Alcobaça in Chapter 3. Though the present Quinta is a private residence, the Fonte dos Amores in the quiet shady garden behind can be visited for a fee. There is generally more than one young couple from Coimbra University sitting or walking beside the quiet pool, evoked in memorable lines by Camoens, which is the traditional site of her murder.

But if Inés de Castro receives as pilgrims the young and poetic, the Queen of Coimbra for the town rather than the gown remains S. Isabel. Her *Festas* early in July every other year fall outside term-time. Though she was Aragonese by birth, and died at Estremoz in the Alentejo, the *conimbrigenses* feel for her an affectionate possessiveness. Even at local *festas* in the surrounding villages there is always a procession of little '*Rainhas Santas*', of whom one or two may be accompanied by their little brother dressed up as '*Dom Diniz*'.

Yet it was he who founded the University which was to make Coimbra more celebrated than royal or even saintly residents had ever done. The best and most complete view of the city as its loving *alumni* remember it is from the terrace in front of S. Clara-a-Nova. Gazing thus across the Mondego, even those who studied there before the great reconstruction of the early 1940s can imagine that the Coimbra spread before them is still the beloved city of their youth. The poplar grove a mile downstream is still the broad *Choupal* where they strolled in philosophic or romantic converse, for the recent depredations of the Mondego sandbanks are from here invisible. And the *Alto*, that clock tower crowned acropolis, is still the medieval labyrinth whose every twist and turning is visible to their mind's eye.

But on returning across the river, and passing under the thirteenth-century gateway called the Arco de Almedina, and up beyond the Sé Velha, we soon find that the ancient narrow streets around it are a mere remnant of those which once covered the whole hill. Before 1940 Coimbra indeed resembled Fez, the great Moslem centre of learning, in that the university, like an organic growth with which it was in symbiotic relationship, spread along its arteries and around its very heart.

As usual, there are critics in plenty of the clean sweep which was made, and of the monotonous 'office block' style of some of the buildings which have risen on the sites thus released. But university expansion demanded fresh accommodation. The other options were a complete new 'university city' two miles up river, or messy agglomerations of new faculties on the outskirts, as at Oxford and Cambridge. The plan adopted at least contained the academic world within its traditional precincts. If the Army can be persuaded to relinquish certain adjoining properties, it may even be possible to extend these precincts to cope with the undreamt-of subsequent increase in student population.

At a recent exhibition of photographs of the vanished Coimbra, handkerchiefs were raised to moist eyes in the mingled pleasure and suffering of a particularly poignant moment of *saudade*. But the present generation will no doubt feel an equal attachment to today's wider spaces and longer vistas, which surely blend better with the older university buildings amongst which they stand than did the undisciplined streets they replaced.

For just as the foundation of the university was an act of the royal will, so the major stages in its expansion have all been initiated by the government of the day. They therefore bear the marks of order and design, which have features in common alike in the sixteenth, the eighteenth and the twentieth centuries. For it is to these three periods that the buildings of the university belong almost in their entirety. King Dennis established it in the first place at Lisbon in 1290, and it was only at Coimbra between 1307 and 1338, and between 1354 and 1377, before John III finally transferred it there in 1537. He gave it the old royal palace there, which had been restored by Marcos Pires as recently as the end of the previous reign. But of this Manueline restoration only the chapel remains.

The rest of the *patio*, with the exception of the seventeenth-century entrance gateway and the room where doctorates are granted, were John V's contribution to learning from the gold of Brazil. Under him were built both the clock tower we have seen from afar, and the magnificent library, with its painted ceilings and the best-known portrait of the munificent prince himself, smiling enigmatically through the double frame provided by two carved and crowned archways.

The *patio* around which all these monuments stand remains the heart of academic life, and retains the proportions of its palace origins. So do the quadrangles of the Oxford and Cambridge colleges, whose models were the great houses of the aristocracy. But none of those has a site like *o Alto*; and the fourth side of Coimbra's quadrangle has been left open to give a view over the Mondego valley towards the Serra de Louzã.

Another square on the *Alto* shows how well the old can blend with the new. Two sides are formed by the modern Faculty of Medicine. A third is dominated by the seventeenth-century Jesuits' church; a provincial version of the Order's mother church in Rome, which has superseded the Sé Velha as cathedral. The fourth is formed by the former episcopal palace, now a museum named after Portugal's greatest eighteenth-century sculptor, Machado de Castro (best known for his statue of King Joseph in the Terreiro do Paço).

Although its paintings are by no means negligible, it is this museum's sculpture one remembers. The main part of this is not by Machado de Castro himself, or even of his period, but by that group of Frenchmen who were invited here by Portugal's Renaissance Prince, John III, just as da Vinci was invited to France by his contemporary, the French Renaissance Prince, Francis I. There are works by both Jean de Rouen and Nicolas Chantarène; but the most arresting exhibit is of nine almost life-size statues by Philippe Houdart. These originally stood in the refectory of Santa Cruz, and most of the other sculpture has likewise been transferred from former convents and monasteries. So have many of the priceless religious ornaments on view, which include one or two Romanesque pieces from the earliest years of the kingdom's existence.

John III's activity in Coimbra went as far as personal designing. Such, at least, is the traditional origin of the unusual Jardim da Manga, a curious arabesque of four tiny chapels round a domed gazebo set over water. The king is said to have sketched his ideas on his stiff sleeve or *manga*; but the actual execution of this centre for a cloister was entrusted to Jean de Rouen.

It now forms the smallest of Coimbra's various public gardens, which range in size up to the Botanic Gardens on the other side of the *Alto*, founded by Pombal as part of his far-reaching scheme of university reform. Its vast greenhouses and long paths beneath the aqueduct built by Filippo Terzi in 1570 are even more soothing than those of the Botanic Gardens at Oxford, for here no roar of traffic penetrates from Magdalen Bridge.

This is indeed the quietest side of the city. Despite Coimbra's importance in the life of the country, it numbers less than forty thousand souls, and we have soon passed through a peaceful residential suburb to the edge of the country. Another garden has been developed where the ground drops steeply to provide a view. This is the Penedo da Saudade, a name commemorating the national emotion experienced here by the generations of Portuguese poets who have reached literary maturity in this most Portuguese of cities. None felt it more keenly, nor expressed it better, than António Nobre.

> '*Foi Coimbra. Foi esta paisagem triste, triste,*
> *A cuja influência a minha alma nao resiste.*'

'It was Coimbra. It was this sad, sad countryside,
To whose influence my soul offers no resistance.'

A minor poet of the last century who died young, he succeeded
as minor poets sometimes do in leaving his own clear message.
This was of the allegiance felt by her sons towards Coimbra. And
Coimbra has repaid him, not only in renaming the square squat
tower near the Misericordia where he lodged the *Torre de 'Anto'*,
but in engraving various extracts from his *Só* on stone tablets
scattered about the Penedo da Saudade. A tribute by another poet
on one of these tablets likens him to 'a Byron of the south'.

There are two monuments on the same side of the town to tempt
the curious as well as the simply soulful. The monastery of Celas
was founded early in the thirteenth century by one of the princesses whose tombs we admired at Lorvão. It contains work of
every century from then to the sixteenth: from the Transitional
cloister to the Manueline ceiling of the church.

A mile farther up the hill is the tiny chapel of S. António dos
Olivais, on the site of the convent where St. Anthony of Padua—
the site of whose birthplace we visited in Lisbon—became a
Franciscan in 1220.

In this century Coimbra's long monopoly of higher education
has been broken by the foundation of universities at Lisbon,*
and Oporto, and at Luanda and Lourenço Marques overseas.
Although with eight thousand undergraduates Coimbra has a
student population several times as great as thirty years ago,
Lisbon alone now has nearly twice as many. It seems unlikely,
therefore, that the self-conscious *élite* of the country's youth will
ever again gather in the intimacy of their beloved city to plan the
regeneration of Portuguese literature, as did the group round
Teófilo Braga and Eça de Queiróz in 1865. The shift in power is
shown by the succession in 1968 to Dr. Salazar, former Professor
of Economics at Coimbra, of Dr. Caetano, former Rector of
Lisbon.

* There are now two universities at Lisbon. The 'Classical' has the usual 'academic'
faculties of Letters, Law, Medicine and so on. The 'Technical' has been formed by
upgrading a number of vocational training institutes—in the same way that the
Colleges of Advanced Technology have been upgraded into universities in Britain.

It may be due in part to this relative decline in importance that Coimbra's traditions are so jealously guarded. The black *capa* or cape is seen more frequently than the *batina* or frock-coat which it protects, which is still worn, however, at all significant moments of academic life. This is regulated at an informal level by the *Praxe*, a code of customs and initiation ceremonies. And although the *Queima das Fitas*, the round of festivities accompanying the symbolic burning of the coloured ribbons which mark a student's faculty, has been adopted by the other Portuguese universities, it nowhere else reaches such intensity as at Coimbra.

Pride of place in all Coimbra's academic lore, however, is taken by the self-governing residential clubs called *Repúblicas*. They are so famous that it is often mistakenly assumed that they play a preponderant part in the university's life, as do the colleges at Oxford and Cambridge—the earliest of which, indeed, had a similar origin. I was surprised to learn that only about two hundred and fifty students live in them, although there also exist less formally-organised lodging-houses called *solares*, one of which will sometimes apply to the *Concelho das Repúblicas* for membership.

The number and make-up of this council is never steady for long. For of today's twenty-odd *Repúblicas* the oldest only dates from 1936, although the institution as such has existed for centuries. Though each has its own particular ethos, they live in mutual tolerance, with the exception of one ultra-right wing and monarchist republic which keeps itself very much to itself.

With their short, fluctuating lives they are unable to build up much in the way of material endowments. Improvisation and imagination are the keynotes of their furnishing and decoration. But their members have the self-discipline required for community life, and for this reason are always pleased to see visitors, and able to show them round.

On my own visit to what I later learned is one of the best known, I was pleasantly surprised by the efficiency of its organisation. '*La plus haute fantaisie*', as the *Guide Bleu* puts it, certainly described the embellishment of the bedrooms, covered with do-it-yourself murals usually featuring sex or politics. But there was a

23. Coimbra: the
patio of the
University

24. Lamêgo: the six hundred steps leading up to Nossa Senhora dos Remedios

dimly-lit and psychedelically-painted room upstairs for parties
and dances, and downstairs a dining-room with a good solid
table covered with a cleanly-wiped oilcloth. I was told that they
employed a maid to clean the rooms, and to cook the food they
purchased after deciding on their menus.

'But surely it would be cheaper for you to eat the subsidised
meals at the University Restaurant?' I asked.

'No: it comes to just about the same. And here we can eat what
we want, cooked as we like it.'

On the dining-room walls were the lists of former members,
dating back to the Republic's foundation in 1956. There were also
some of their famous sayings; deliberate or involuntary shafts of
wit preserved for as long as the community might last. A
member remains a member after he has gone down from the
university, and when revisiting Coimbra invariably stays in his
old republic.

As I ended my visit, the member who had welcomed me in and
showed me round gave me a sheet of their printed notepaper as a
souvenir. It bore their device, adapted from two famous lines
from the *Lusiadas*:

> '*Aqueles que por copos volumosos*
> *se vão da lei da sêde libertando . . .*'

> 'Those that through generous glassfuls,
> Free themselves from the law of thirst . . .'

in which 'brave works' and 'death' had been replaced by 'generous
glassfuls' and 'thirst'.

Although such a hilly city, Coimbra is the capital of Beira
Litoral, the only relatively flat province in the country. The
Mondego, which we followed through a narrow valley only a few
miles above the city, wanders slowly over a plain to the sea
twenty-five miles away. To the south the land is soon broken up
by the hills of Estremadura, and just over the border the village
of Louriçal has a convent where the nuns are once again in
residence. It was market day when I was there; and it was a
strange experience to move from the worldly but alien, pre-

industrial hubbub to the unworldly but equally alien, pre-industrial atmosphere of the blue-tiled eighteenth-century church, where the Poor Clares were singing out of sight behind the grille.

The school of sculptors of French origin who worked at Coimbra in the sixteenth century made great use of the white stone of Ança, quarried a few miles to the north-west; and some of their work has survived in the countryside around. Thus the church of the former Convent of S. Marcos near Ança has a reredos by Nicolas Chantarène, and a whole series of both Gothic and Renaissance tombs. It is reached from the main road west, which passes through Tentúgal (famous for its pastries) and Montemor-o-Velho (famous for its castle), which both have more examples of this sculpture in their churches. This road reaches the sea at the Mondego's mouth, or *foz*, at which the little port of Figueira da Foz has grown into an uninteresting resort, very popular for Portuguese family holidays.

North from Figueira the road crosses an isolated hill and runs some miles inland. The only village it goes through is Tocha: the plain white church on the vast open space at its centre has an impressive baldachin over the altar. Then comes Mira, on the southernmost of the interconnected lagoons which distinguish the district of Aveiro, the northern half of Beira Litoral. They run for thirty miles north to Ovar, separated from the ocean by a thin tongue of land, and creating, with their creeks and inlets, a labyrinth of peninsulas and islands.

Until the advent of motor transport, and to a certain extent even today, communications throughout this area were easiest by boat. Because conditions in the lagoons were so different from those in the open sea sometimes only a few hundred yards away, a whole race of craft and navigational lore were developed to deal with them. Much of this escapes the casual visitor, as the only roads which approach the lagoon are the one from Aveiro to the depressing little resort of Costa Nova, past the only break in the protecting sandbank, and that from Ovar right down the sandbank itself to the other side of this break. The latter passes the *Pousada da Ria*, built as its name indicates on the lagoon itself.

For those who do not intend to stay in this *pousada*, or who are not 'collectors' of lagoons, a prolonged visit to this area is not to be recommended. Fortunately they can learn more in half an hour at the little Museum of the Sea at Ílhavo than during a week's diligent investigation amongst the salt pans and the gradually disappearing *moliçeiros* (designed for the harvesting of the *moliço* or seaweed). Examples of these boats are preserved here, some with quaint sleeping arrangements, and all with brightly-painted prows. Some have primitive paintings with figures dressed in the fashions of the 1920s, with inscriptions in which *b* is substituted for *v*, an archaic confusion in the spoken language which is only found from here northwards.

Ílhavo lies directly on the road we have followed from Figueira da Foz. A little to the left a mile earlier another museum is attached to the porcelain factory of Vista Alegre. This far from Satanic mill, founded in 1824, is a most civilised adaptation and extension of a seventeenth-century *quinta*.

Perhaps I have been a little hard on the *rías*. But though they do have undoubted attractions, and though they are quite different from anywhere else in Portugal, and from any other lagoon complex anywhere, their general atmosphere of unruffled vaporous monotony can be better gauged on the Norfolk Broads which are easier to reach, or at Venice where there are monuments to turn to when Nature palls.

Nevertheless Aveiro—sometimes called the Portuguese Venice because of the canalised lagoon which charmingly bisects its heart—has its monuments too. The greatest of these spreads its plain, massive walls from the corner of a quiet square some distance from the canal. The Convent of Jesus reveals itself as a more elaborate structure after the visitor has penetrated within the Manueline doorway. For its chapel has one of those Baroque interiors of carved and gilded wood in which the nuns of seventeenth- and eighteenth-century Portugal delighted. Refectory and chapter house likewise have their Gothic origins concealed by *azulejos*.

All this was in honour of yet another princess, who died here in 1490. But this princess, whose warrior father Afonso V himself longed for the cloister at the end of his reign, actually took the veil. Even in her own day the combination of royalty with sanctity had a strong appeal, and a famous portrait attributed to Nuno Gonçalves (who painted her father, brother and uncle in the great Panels of the Janelas Verdes) hangs in the regional museum which now occupies many of the conventional buildings.

But two centuries later, in that atmosphere of mingled mysticism and eroticism of Restoration Portugal which we remarked at Beja, this appeal was irresistible. To this period belong the gilt decoration of the chapel, many of the *azulejos*, and a series of paintings in the chancel which illustrate scenes from the life of S. Joana, as she was called, with costumes and furnishings of the reign of Pedro II. It was this monarch who ordered the Renaissance tomb of inlaid marble where she now lies. Completed in 1709, after his death, it is an extreme example of the persistence in Portugal of styles which had elsewhere been superseded.

It is characteristic of Portuguese religiosity that the convent should be so much larger than the pleasing sixteenth-century cathedral on the opposite side of the square, with façade and some interior furnishings of two centuries later. There are several smaller churches nearer the canal, where a busier square is surrounded by a number of public buildings, including the Misericordia, built under Philip II (Philip III of Spain), with a well-proportioned doorway.

Aveiro's royal and religious past is so far forgotten that the city has on several occasions—the last as recently as 1969—acted as congress centre for the Republican Party, which toppled the monarchy in 1910, and which still pervades one corner of Portuguese political life with its nineteenth-century ideals. The nuns are daily celebrated, however, in the continuing confection of delicious sweetmeats from eggs and sugar called *ovos moles*. One or two form a delicious dessert to a picnic lunch.

Ovar, near the northern end of the lagoon, has no such royal past to inhibit the expression of its essentially proletarian personality. Here traditionally originated the *varinhas* (*ovarinhas*), the Lisbon fishwives.

However, a young man from Ovar whom I came to know very well had never met a fishwife from his native place during his five years at Lisbon University. Of impeccable manners, he dressed in the traditional, well-groomed clothes still favoured by most Portuguese students, and spoke French and Spanish, as well as his own language, in accents of almost exaggerated correctness. Though I soon learned that he was from Ovar, it was many months before he indirectly revealed that his parents were humble fisher-folk. Though his eager and successful *embourgeoisement* might well be a means to advancement, I reflected that he had encountered no difficulties in embracing it. So many English rebels are frustrated *bourgeois*, denied by accent, ignorance of etiquette, or even the habit of taking high tea, entry to the middle class whose ideals are really theirs. Portugal is a more homogeneous society than is allowed by those shallow progressives who speak dogmatically of 'only two classes' and 'downtrodden peasantry'.

The main N1 from Lisbon through Coimbra up to Oporto runs far from the coast, through a prosperous region called the Bairrada. From the grapes grown there an excellent sparkling wine is produced at the small town of Anadia, as I have good reason to remember.

For after riding through Anadia in 1951, when English motor-cycles were seldom seen on Portuguese roads, I suddenly found myself chased and halted by three men on motor-cycles at whose intentions I could only guess. They turned out to be the local agents for BSA, the firm which had made my own machine. To celebrate my safe arrival in Beira Litoral on a diminutive 'Bantam' they invited me back into Anadia to sample its speciality. It was a wonder that my journey continued safely after the long hour I passed in those cool *adegas*. My first impressions of the lagoons of Aveiro were even more misty and featureless than those left by subsequent visits.

Five miles before Anadia an important road—the N2—branches off towards Viseu and ultimately Chaves. It soon goes through the spa of Luso, where a table water, sold elsewhere in bottles, can be acquired at no expense from a many-mouthed fountain.

From Luso several routes lead up into the Forest of Buçaco, a last projection of the *serras* of Beira Alta. Its highest point, the Cruz Alta at 1,800 feet, can be reached either by road or by a path which winds past chapels, hermitages and fountains of a devotional *via sacra*. The features for which one visits Buçaco lie lower down, and are even more accessible.

The first is the forest itself: nine hundred walled and protected acres of primeval woodland, to which various species have been added from overseas. Some of them have only been introduced by the State forestry office since they took over from the Carmelite friars in 1834. But these, from soon after their arrival here in 1628, had introduced other trees, notably the 'cypress of Buçaco' as it is now called, from Mexico, which has become the king of this sylvan Sintra.

Buçaco is indeed nearer to my own idea of a 'glorious Eden'. Like Sintra, too, it has the convent of a contemplative order—the Carmelites—with a more ample chapel, but with almost equally comfortless cork-lined cells, in one of which Wellington spent the night of 26th September 1810. Adjoining this convent stands Buçaco's Pena, the neo-Manueline *Palace Hotel*, built as a hunting lodge during the years of nationalist feeling following Lord Salisbury's Ultimatum of 1890. The same theme inspired the *azulejos* which decorate its verandah and hall with some of the more glorious incidents from the *Lusiadas*.

The gardens round the hotel merge into the forest: I spent there my two most peaceful nights in this utterly peaceful country. Yet here on 27th September 1810 a battle took place where several thousand lives were lost. Wellington was proved right in his deliberate choice of this excellent defensive site. Though the immediate outcome was a studied retreat behind the Lines of Tôrres Vedras, there passed to him at the battle of Buçaco the initiative in all the Peninsular campaigns which were to follow. It is commemorated by a monument just outside the wall of the forest.

By the roadside stands a fascinating little museum, with contemporary engravings and other souvenirs. Though the command of the Portuguese army had been handed over to the English General Beresford, Buçaco, like every other victory of the war, was as much a Portuguese as a British achievement. No victorious nation has given more and lost so much as did Portugal between 1807 and 1814. The only comparable sacrifice was that of the equally victorious Portugal between 1916 and 1918.

The main N2 beyond Anadia goes through a district of small towns which, despite their insignificance, constantly figure on the Portuguese radio. I never seemed able to switch on my transistor without hearing a request for a record from a lady at S. João da Madeira, or a reply to a query over insecticides from a farmer at Vale de Cambra. Vale de Cambra lies some miles up the side road into the *serras* which must be followed by those wishing to visit the remote convent of Arouca.

Founded in the twelfth century, Arouca still preserves relics of its early years in a small museum. But the buildings as they stand belong to the seventeenth and eighteenth centuries, as do a series of giant-sized statues of nuns in the choir of the church: statues which earned encomiums from that expert on the period, Sacheverell Sitwell. To 1734 there also belongs the silver tomb of another royal nun: Queen Mafalda of Castile, who retired here after being divorced. We have come full circle. For she was the sister of those two princesses whose silver coffins of 1713 we admired at Lorvão.

TAILPIECE: FUNDAÇÃO GULBENKIAN

Founded by Dennis, re-established by John III, embellished by John V, and reformed by Pombal, Coimbra University is the living evidence of Portugal's long history of cultural patronage. Through Coimbra, too, this *'fim do mundo'* has maintained relations other than political and commercial with the rest of Europe. Dennis, grandson of Alfonso the Wise of Castile, was himself the greatest poet of his generation in the Galaico-Portuguese which was then the vehicle for poetry throughout the peninsula. John III invited to Coimbra not only sculptors from France but also savants like the Scot, George Buchanan. Pombal's Botanic Garden was designed by an Englishman. Today, besides the public lectures given from time to time by visiting professors, Coimbra enjoys the more continuous influence of a French Institute, a German Institute, and a delightful little branch of the British Council.

Kenneth Witcomb went out as Assistant to this *Casa da Inglaterra* in September 1940, to undertake a task at once more vital and more congenial than many other forms of national service. In teaching English and moving about amongst the academic *élite* of the younger generation he was to do more than mere diplomats can ever do to preserve the *Velha Aliança*.

I have his letters of the war years to an old friend of his and mine. They would enable him to occupy an honoured place in a future supplement to Rose Macaulay's *They went to Portugal*, with their evocations of a Coimbra which has already vanished, and their descriptions of how wartime shortages affected even neutral Portugal. The train to Lisbon took up to seven hours. The decorated cars and lorries of the *Queima das Fitas* were replaced by ox-waggons and donkey-carts.

The letters tell, too, of his ever-increasing involvement with and love for the land where he was working. Immersed in a Portuguese milieu, away from the commerce and easy communications with 'home' which have so insulated the English colonies of Oporto, Lisbon, and now the Algarve, the influence of his thirty years' work is as incalculable as the number of his friends throughout Portugal is legion. Though in due course he became Director of the *Casa da Inglaterra*, this failed to satisfy his need for total integration. Today he is Professor Witcomb of Coimbra University.

He is one of the more recent of those foreigners who down the years not merely 'went to Portugal', but stayed there. The great majority, naturally, went to make a living, even when, like Kenneth Witcomb or Nicolas Chantarène, they acted as living links with the academic or artistic worlds outside. But in 1955 there died in Lisbon a foreigner whose legacy to his adopted country equalled the immensity of his affection for it.

Calouste Sarkis Gulbenkian was born in 1869 at Scutari, the town opposite Constantinople where a dozen years earlier

Florence Nightingale had set up her military hospital during the Crimean War. He grew up therefore as an Armenian in the old Ottoman Empire, a member of a persecuted Christian minority whose religion and culture were alike under attack from the Moslem majority who for centuries had occupied their homeland.

Such minorities, by a natural reaction, have often found at once self-expression and self-protection in commercial skills. Thus did 'Mr. Five Per Cent', that prince of honest brokers, use his knowledge of the oil industry and of Middle Eastern affairs to negotiate satisfactory and lasting agreements between those two opposites: the giant international oil companies, and Turkey's successor states.

The story of those negotiations, and of the fortune which accrued to him as a result, has often been told. And many readers are probably vaguely aware, as I was myself, that he left the main part of this fortune to a foundation which he had set up in Portugal.

However, it was only when I made a prolonged visit there to prepare this book that I realised the scale of his concept. I found the activity of the *Fundação Calouste Gulbenkian* omnipresent. Camped in Beira pinewood or by Algarve shore I have switched on my *Segunda Programa*—that admirable institution of Portuguese Radio which is all the BBC's Third Programme might have been —to hear yet another exquisite concert given by the Gulbenkian Chamber Orchestra. Driving in country lanes of Alentejo or Trás-os-Montes I have passed the mobile library vans of the Foundation, which take to remotest villages the widest choice of books (an expensive commodity in a country whose small population makes for tiny, uneconomic editions).

The casual visitor, hearing of the Foundation's choir and ballet company, as well as of its orchestra, and of the music festival it organises each spring with the participation of visiting foreign companies in Lisbon and fourteen other centres, may get the impression that its orientation is above all towards music. But at any one time scores of postgraduates in Portugal and overseas are being supported in every variety of artistic and scientific research by Gulbenkian funds. And a visit to the Foundation's headquarters at the Praça de Espanha in Lisbon will soon convince him that its interests are as catholic as those of its founder. These are reflected in his private art collection on display there.

Vast though its value, this does not overwhelm. Partly this is due to the manner of its display, which profits from the use of the most modern museum techniques in a specially-designed building. But partly, too, it is because the collector was not only catholic, but selective. He purchased only the best, so that we are not forced to walk past acres of the second-rate. And wide-ranging though his tastes, he clearly had a predilection for certain areas.

One, obviously, was the Middle East: Armenia itself, Assyria and so on. Another was England: the nineteenth-century English landscapes recall his cordial relations with the mandatory power in Iraq when his most momentous deal was concluded. And there was Portugal, and Portugal's relations overseas: here is one of the best examples of those seventeenth-century Persian carpets whose designs owe so much to the Portuguese presence at Ormuz.

These preferences reappear in the administrative machinery of the Foundation. There is a 'Middle Eastern Section', specially concerned with its functions in the lands where Gulbenkian himself once lived and worked. In Britain it is so active that it has a separate branch in London. And in Portugal, as we have indicated, it is at work everywhere.

It is worth noting that its 'International Section', following the long tradition of Portuguese cultural patronage, has brought hundreds of foreigners from all over the world to undertake research projects at Portuguese universities, or simply to study Portuguese language and culture. I met several Japanese who had thus been able to acquire a deeper knowledge of the land whose inhabitants were the first Europeans to visit them.

Why should Calouste Gulbenkian have had this interest in Portugal, and why should he have chosen it as the seat of his Foundation? Reasons often given are its financial stability, and its government, with whose policies he was in profound sympathy. I wonder whether he may not also have been influenced by its tradition of cultural patronage, through which for so long artists and scholars have been introduced from abroad without provoking xenophobic reactions. And surely allowance should be made for the understanding any Armenian must feel for the motives which sent King Sebastian on his disastrous but chivalrous expedition?

8

PORTUCALE

Portugal is such an unusual name for a country that most languages leave it in its original; though it is italianised as *Portogallo*, and at one time used to be 'englished' as Portingale. Porto, on the other hand, is so straightforward a name for a city that the English and Germans have had to deform it into Oporto, though with the excellent excuse that the Portuguese always speak of it with the definite article: *o Porto*.

The port which gave the dominant syllable to both words was the same: the mouth of the Douro, the only combination of a safe anchorage with an accessible hinterland between the Tagus and the Minho. There are anchorages on both sides of the mouth. It was the more important one on the northern bank to which the Romans gave the name of Portus, while that on the southern, now Vila Nova de Gaia, was called Cale. The combination of the two names, Buda-Pest fashion, gave Portucale a designation extended to the surrounding county when this was won back from the Moslems, and adopted by the kingdom when in the twelfth century this county became independent.

The present province of the Douro Litoral is a good deal less extensive than that ancient county. Entering it from the direction of Coimbra or Aveiro we have only a small bridgehead of land to cross before we reach the river. The roofs of many houses, as in the Beira Litoral, bear curious 'fretwork' designs, baked in brick: here a monogram, there a cock.

At Grijó stands a convent, where in the beautiful double cloister with its unusual seventeenth-century *azulejos* lies a brother of the princesses of Lorvão and Arouca. This cloister was in need of repair, but some officials from Oporto who were there at the time of my visit assured me that it would soon be getting it. And for the other conventional buildings dissolution has not spelt disintegration, but simply a sea-change. The chapel has become the parish church; the porter's lodge is now the meeting place for the parish council; and the rest have been adapted to form a charming private *quinta*, with a stone fountain in its trim, planted court.

It is only a short drive from quiet Grijó to the main N1. This is duplicated for its last ten miles by a motorway which crosses the Douro by a fine new bridge some distance downstream from the heart of the city. But the older route should be followed by those wishing to visit the only circular cloister in Portugal, at the Renaissance Serra do Pilar Convent, and then to enjoy the classic view from Vila Nova de Gaia.

The monuments of Oporto spread up the steep banks opposite. The lodges of the great wine shippers stand four-square beside the river immediately below. Although this is here crossed at a height of two hundred and twenty-five feet, another road connects these lodges to the quays of the northern bank across the same bridge but at a lower level. The dark steel tracery of this essential and unusual bridge, like that of the railway bridge built by Eiffel himself a quarter of a mile upstream, is a fitting introduction to the capital of the north, in whose make-up the Mediterranean is wholly subordinate to the Atlantic.

Not that the Mediterranean is entirely absent. Whatever they may say in Lisbon, the sun does often shine on the *tripeiros*'* un-northern red-tiled roofs and white façades. And the Italian architect Nazzoni, who settled here in the mid-eighteenth century, ensured that their skyline would recall southern Baroque. For though his work includes the Misericordia, and the *loggia* on one side of the cathedral, his masterpiece was the church of the Clérigos with its tower, at two hundred and fifty feet the highest in the country.

* The inhabitants of Oporto have answered proudly to the name of *tripeiros*, eaters of tripe, since their self-denial in sending all their meat to feed the expedition against Ceuta of 1415, while they subsisted on the offal. Anyone who has enjoyed '*tripe à la mode de Porto*' will agree that they made a virtue of necessity.

Slender yet massive in appearance, its six storeys stand well where two of Oporto's steep streets meet after climbing round to leave it as an island amidst the traffic. Neither its height, nor the oval shape of the body of the church, belong to any Portuguese tradition, which is better represented by the tower of Coimbra University. Nor, according to the brilliant young art historian Professor Pais da Silva, did Nazzoni have any profound influence on the art of northern Portugal, as has so often been imagined.

It required, indeed, a genius to coax the conceits of the Clérigos from the untreated dark granite of the north. Nazzoni's successors in the Rococo style were to find another way of dealing with this intractable material.

It was a stone better suited to the simpler demands of Romanesque, a style still evident in the fortress-like façade of the Cathedral. Within, these Romanesque origins are better concealed: we are a long way from the age of Afonso Henriques in a sacristy which Sacheverell Sitwell can describe as one of the best clubs in Europe. For as we noted when visiting Lisbon cathedral, Portuguese Baroque reached its height in the decorative arts here exemplified, rather than in architecture itself.

It attained its two peaks here in Oporto. They are the gilded interiors of S. Francisco and of S. Clara. Gilded means what it says. Sculpted wood was treated not merely with a coat of gold paint, but with a wafer-thin *lamina* of beaten gold, applied with consummate skill to cover every carved contour. The fashion for this art lasted in Portugal from the late sixteenth to the early nineteenth century, and the example of it within S. Clara dates from the very beginning of this period. The Gothic doorway of the church has had a Renaissance face-lift, but that of the adjoining convent is frankly Baroque, though of a century later than the gleaming gilt where the nuns once worshipped behind their grille.

The interior of the Gothic church of S. Francisco, on the other hand, received its baptism of gold much later, in 1753. As a result it has less of the 'old gold' lustre and feminine mystery of S. Clara. There is indeed an almost Joanine splendour, not to say ostentation, about these overgrown columns and overloaded festoons, evidence of the prosperity of Oporto when it was the principal entrepôt of Anglo-Portuguese commerce at its busiest.

The secular symbol of that prosperity, erected in 1785 by and for its beneficiaries of the 'British Association' of merchants or 'factors', was their Factory House, which stands in the same street. It was paid for by levies not only on port, but on oil, wood, fruit, cork and tartar exported in English ships. But from the start it was the great port shippers who effectively controlled, and still control, this last of the British Factories: at once exchanges, coffee-houses, and clubs, which once marked the nerve-centres of Britain's commercial empire (Lisbon, too, once had its 'jolly free factory').

Austere neo-Classical without, and chaste Adam within, it makes us thankful that Oporto's thirteen-month siege by the Miguelists in the civil war of 1832–34 caused so much less damage than the brief seconds of Lisbon's earthquake. Chippendale furniture, crystal chandeliers, dinner and tea services from the first English porcelain factories survive intact. So, too, does something of the flavour of an age when good design was not incompatible with good business.

Today they may have come together again. And there are apologists for the neo-Gothic and other manifestations of nineteenth-century taste who claim that their ways never parted. A good monument where the visitor can form his own judgement on this question lies close at hand in the Bolsa, or Exchange, next door to S. Francisco. An altogether more ornate temple of commerce, it would twenty years ago have been written off as a hideous joke. Today . . . well, these painstaking imitators of the Alhambra and the French Renaissance were at least superb craftsmen.

The street in which these last three monuments stand was once called the Rua Nova dos Ingleses. If today it has been renamed after Oporto's greatest son, the Infante Dom Henrique, we can reflect that he, too, was half English. His statue dominates a square (also called after him) opposite the Rua da Alfândega, where the Casa do Infante in which Queen Philippa in 1394 gave birth to Prince Henry has been turned into a museum for the city archives.

Two of Oporto's other museums also bear the names of famous citizens. That of Guerra Junqueiro is installed in the home of this anti-clerical poet. His private collection of art and furniture, here on view, is perhaps as valuable a bequest to posterity as his literary legacy.

The Museo Nacional Soares dos Reis is named after a sculptor and artist whose work we shall have seen though perhaps not noticed in the Bolsa. Its paintings, ceramics, coins and religious art are of the high quality and the provenance implied by the epithet *nacional*. For the regional museum of the Douro Litoral is elsewhere, in a palace ascribed to Nazzoni.

As indicated earlier, the Douro Litoral is not an extensive province. Its towns and villages within a ten-mile radius of Oporto have become to all intents and purposes suburbs of the city, even when they are not actually joined to it. Yet the country-side once lapped right up to the hills on which lie the monuments we have just visited.

The Romanesque church of Cedoféita, away up beyond the Clérigos and the various teaching institutes which have been federated to form the country's third university, was therefore 'quickly built' (which is what its name means) amidst what then were fields. Though it is six hundred years younger than once believed, it probably dates, even so, from when 'Portucale' was a county rather than a kingdom.

An interesting example of religious architecture from the other end of the time-scale is the church of the Immaculada Conceição, erected in the 1940s amidst the new districts to the north, in an almost white granite reminiscent of that of Aberdeen, rather than in the dark stone commonly used hereabouts.

This dark granite adds a grim note to the already forbidding fortress-church of Leça do Balio, three miles farther north, in a still-countrified valley between two main roads. But it is softened by the Manueline calvary close at hand; and the well-lighted and beautifully proportioned interior of 1336 is inspiring, if austere. *Balio* means bailiff, the title given to the senior knights of St.

25. Oporto: the gilded interior of S. Francisco

26. Pinhão on the Douro, at the heart of the port wine vineyards

John, several of whom are buried here. Leça was the property of these knights, who during their centuries-long defence of Rhodes and later Malta against the Turks were always supported by a '*langue*' of Portuguese knights, and were ruled by several Portuguese Grand Masters.

The quays along the Douro are no longer able to cope with all the modern shipping which now visits '*o Porto*'. As long ago as 1884 an artificial harbour was created beyond the river mouth at Leixões. This lies in the municipal district of Matosinhos, which boasts the highest *per capita* income in the whole of Portugal. For it contains not only Leixões, and the fish-canning and other industries which have been established there, but the nearest seaside resorts to Oporto. It is also the residential district favoured by the wealthier *portuenses* and British. On this side of the city, too, lies the airport, which has revolutionised the psychology of these British residents by enabling them to contemplate returning 'home' for a mere weekend.

The main road north runs farther inland than Matosinhos or the airport. It does not approach the sea until Azurara, with a rustic Manueline church gazing towards the beach of Mindelo where the liberal army landed to take Oporto in 1832. Only the little river Ave separates Azurara from the much larger Vila do Conde, dominated by the massive eighteenth-century façade of the Convent of S. Clara.

The climb up there, though even steeper than it appears from the river, is amply rewarded. For behind the convent stands its church, built in 1318 by the founder, a bastard son of King Dennis, who lies within beside his wife in a Manueline funerary chapel of two centuries later. Amongst other tombs is that of the daughter of the Holy Constable, whose marriage to an illegitimate son of John I was the origin of the House of Bragança. The Dukes of Bragança were also Counts of Barcelos, whose inheritance gave them their real power-base in the north: the Count of Barcelos was the 'Conde' remembered in Vila do Conde.

Despite the Manueline tombs of the founders, and some beautiful seventeenth-century woodwork and ceilings in the upper and lower choirs behind the grille, the church's Gothic origins are not concealed as were those of the gilded interiors of Oporto. It is a harmonious marriage of all the styles in which Portugal has excelled, completed outside by a monumental aqueduct of the rich days of John V, built to supply the convent from springs three miles away.

As at Aveiro the nuns are better remembered for their pastries than their prayers, in the *pasteis de S. Clara* still sold by confectioners in the little market town beneath the convent. In its main square stands the parish church with a Manueline doorway by João de Castilho, and a town hall and pillory from later in the sixteenth century. Vila do Conde is also a seaside resort, with a long promenade leading out to a seventeenth-century fortress at the river's mouth.

In this last capacity, however, it is eclipsed by Póvoa de Varzim, a couple of miles up the coast. The outstanding realist novelist Eça de Queiroz was born here in 1845, and is suitably honoured by his native place.

It is a rather flat, monotonous coast, though exciting things can be discovered only a few miles inland, such as the exquisite little Romanesque churches of Rates and Rio Mau, with their carved doorways. But the province has narrowed here, and we are soon over into the Minho. The true glories of the Douro Litoral lie east of Oporto.

A route close to the Minho border takes in a number of places of interest. Roads either from Vila do Conde or from Oporto lead to S. Tirso, one of the little textile towns of northern Portugal which, thanks to EFTA, are sending manufactures in a direction undreamt of by Methuen. Its vast Convent of S. Bento, although so white and clean, dates from the seventeenth century. The lower half of the cloister is three hundred years older still; and there are a few ancient relics in the church itself.

There is no mistaking the antiquity of the Citânia of Sanfins, on a hill a few miles east. We shall be seeing several more of these ruined prehistoric townships in the Minho, where we shall discuss them at greater length. Although descriptions of their thick fortifications, and of the round roofless huts these surround, make them all sound very much alike, each in fact still has its own personality, just as it did when inhabited by its Celtic or pre-Celtic builders.

The remoteness of these townships, and the immense views of unspoilt country which they command, have the power to render us sympathetic to those earlier inhabitants, whose memory has never been quite forgotten by their successors. Thus many have been christianised, with or without the erection of a chapel. Sanfins is none other than Saint Felix, who has reached this unrecognisable form by an extreme example of the Portuguese habit of contraction.

The quickest way from S. Tirso to Sanfins is by Roriz, where a rewarding Romanesque church survives from a Benedictine monastery. I found Roriz more satisfying than the much more extensive convent of Pombeiro, off the road to Felgueiras. Its Romanesque origins have been overlaid by eighteenth-century rebuilding without, and by Rococo decorations within. The Renaissance cloister is depressing in its decay.

Should you be unable to waken the old crone who guards Pombeiro, or should you even fail to find the steep side road leading down to the valley where it lies, you will be compensated by the countryside and the views. Drawing up in a pinewood to sleep in what I imagined to be deep rural seclusion, I was knocked up by the uniformed guard of a private forest, who suggested that I should camp near his cottage. I accepted his kindly invitation, for I felt sure that he wanted company. But I could not help smiling at his warning that the deserted road was the unlikely haunt of '*ladrões e mulherzinhas*' (thieves and prostitutes).

Soon after Felgueiras the route joins the main road east from Oporto, which on its way has passed within a mile or two of three interesting monastic churches. Those of Cete and of Paço de Sousa can be visited on the same detour. Cete mingles Romanesque with Manueline. Paço de Sousa, in a delightful position by a stream and between two eighteenth-century *quintas*, is more purely Romanesque, and shelters a famous tomb in this style.

Romanesque tombs are few. Few of them received the decoration lavished on cloister capitals or on west doors. Few are of non-royal personages. This exception to all three generalisations is of Egas Moniz, the honest counsellor of Afonso Henriques; and the carvings on its sides represent the events which made him the best-loved character of early Portuguese history.

In fact I had some difficulty in reading into them the traditional story: how, having given his word to the king of Leon for the submission of Afonso Henriques in return for the withdrawal of the Leonese army, like a burgher of Calais he voluntarily surrendered himself and his family when Afonso Henriques again broke out in rebellion. (Like the burghers of Calais he, too, was magnanimously spared.) Admittedly, I am a poor interpreter of Romanesque relief. But it is also possible that this document in stone, carved soon after the death of Egas Moniz in 1144, tells a slightly different story to that of later written accounts.

The third church, Travanca, is again Romanesque, with two carved doorways. The buildings of the former monastery, like those of several others in the north, now serve as a lunatic asylum.

After the main road has been joined by the route we were following earlier, it descends towards the Douro's biggest affluent, the Tâmega, which it crosses at Amarante by a bridge of the 1780s—a good period for bridge design throughout Europe. And the bridge is perhaps the best spot from which to take in this well-loved little town.

With under four thousand inhabitants it is smaller than it looks, for it extends to both sides of the river, and has three churches. That of the former Convent of S. Gonçalo faces the bridge, dominating the town and drawing a very special type of pilgrim. For at one end of the lofty church, with its asymmetrical yet beautifully balanced Renaissance façade, the recumbent effigy of a saint lies behind the grille. Single women who rub their naked bodies against this tomb of S. Gonçalo (a thirteenth-century churchman) will be married within the year.

Unfortunately there were no husband-hunters about on my own visit. Nor did I dare to ask at any of the well-stocked pastry shops for *testículos de S. Gonçalo*, the phallic cakes said to be given to each other by the young people of Amarante on the first Sunday in June, the *romaria* of S. Gonçalo. For I was with a party of students from Lisbon University, more than half of whom were girls. Had our tour been in the reverse direction I would have had less fear of hurting their susceptibilities. For two nights later, in the courtyard of Bragança castle, I watched them screaming with laughter as a witty don lit a match to find out if the prehistoric stone pig there was a sow or a boar!

After Amarante the road climbs the Serra do Marão, and runs over into Trás-os-Montes. All this end of the Douro Litoral is distinctly hilly, and the beautiful valley of the Tâmega is therefore steep. Although for much of its length it is followed by roads on one or both banks, these run high above the river, giving magnificent views.

Exactly the same is true of the Douro itself, though as might be expected the views here are more sweeping still. Yet no guide that I have read describes the route from Oporto up the Douro, presumably because it passes no monuments of great architectural of archaeological significance. Yet it is an historic route. It marks the effective southern boundary of the kingdom of the Suevi, the effective northern limit of Moslem penetration, the early frontier of the county of Portucale. And it was, and still is, the link between the vineyards of the high Douro, and the 'port' where their wines are blended and shipped around the world.

The Douro continues to act as a frontier today, dividing the Douro Litoral and Trás-os-Montes from the Beiras, and then for seventy miles separating Portugal from Spain. Indeed it is almost a *cordon sanitaire*, so few are the bridges, so steep and winding the roads which lead down to them. Yet the two facing banks, though deprived of easy contact, have more in common with each other than with the country to north and south. A description of the Douro valley belongs therefore neither to the pages on the Beiras nor to the pages on Trás-os-Montes, but here, following our visit to the city at its mouth.

The first bridge upstream from that by Eiffel is twenty-five miles away. The road, surprisingly hard to follow as it leaves Oporto, runs directly above the precipitous north bank. One of the many fine viewpoints it passes is at Foz de Sousa, where a well-designed modern bridge straddles the Sousa as it enters the Douro.

The junction with the Tâmega is even more impressive. This occurs just above the first bridge after Oporto, which I crossed to follow the road along the southern bank. I had a good reason for doing so, as a friend was staying in a remote mountain hamlet behind Resende. But the road on the opposite side of the valley, from what I have been told, is equally breath-taking.

It is hard to say what I remember best of the day spent following that fantastic road up and down along the northern flanks of Montemuro.

The little-known Romanesque churches? Amongst these the palm goes to S. Martinho de Mouros, at the far end of a rather unfriendly village. Its very early construction shows in capitals and columns, while later centuries have left a painted panelled ceiling, and altars and other decorations recalling S. Clara in Oporto.

Or stopping at the tiny spa of Caldas de Aregos, and speaking from the Heath Robinson telephone exchange to my friend's sister, twelve miles (the last three by mule) behind, and fifteen hundred feet above, only to learn that she had left for Póvoa de Varzim that morning?

Or the ever-changing view, as I was now close to the deep, swift river, now far out of sight of it in the back hills? Much of the time it consists simply of the hills of the opposite bank, so near and yet so far.

Or stopping at Cinfães—an even more deformed version of poor St. Felix—to buy the best *broa* I ever tasted? This doughy *pão de milho*, maize-bread with a superb crust, is typical above all of the Minho. The frontiers which divide the *broa* country from the regions of *pao de centeio* or rye-bread of Trás-os-Montes and Beira Alta, and from the wheaten flour territories of the south are invisible. But on crossing them there is a change in the whole flavour of the countryside, and of one's memories.

Of the road's many deviations inland, the longest comes when it swings almost ten miles south to join the N2 which we have already used at various points between Castro Daire and Luso. The point of intersection is Lamêgo, a little town of ten thousand souls which somehow resumes all that is best in northern Portugal. One evidence of this was that I was able to purchase both *broa* and rye-bread in its bakeries. Another is its unofficial title of 'capital of Portuguese Baroque'. Here we first meet *en masse* what Sacheverell Sitwell has called 'the granite and whitewash that is the vernacular of Northern Portugal'.

It is not wholly Baroque. The cathedral, though heavily restored in that style both outside and inside (the nave and its chapels by Nazzoni of the Clérigos), has a Renaissance cloister. And it still bears traces of its twelfth-century origins, whilst other churches—notably the Romanesque S. Maria de Almacave at the top of the town—remain frankly medieval. But the passing motorist driving through Lamêgo along the main road certainly gets the impression that it was built of a piece between about 1730 and 1760.

To this period belong most of the private palaces—town houses of the country nobility—which line the main road, and above all the central square. Pre-eminent amongst them, as no doubt was its tenant in provincial society under Pombal and Maria I, stands the episcopal palace. This is now an exceptionally well-arranged regional museum, rich with the treasures from dissolved convents and monasteries. Whole chapels in the gilded carving of the Oporto interiors have been re-installed here, showing that before 1834 Lamêgo was as Baroque within as without.

It was in this museum, under the guidance of the curator—artist himself, and son of a well-known painter and caricaturist—that I first realised the full power of Grão Vasco. The greatest concentration of his work, of course, is at Viseu, in the museum named after him. But the paintings here, taken from the cathedral altar, come after several galleries of pleasant but second-rate religious art of the seventeenth and eighteenth centuries. After this preparation the strength and sureness of touch of the sixteenth-century master overwhelm one like a conversion.

On my first visit to Lamêgo a fair was taking place all over an uneven field adjoining the tree-lined avenue which runs for half a mile south from the main square. There were stalls selling the famous hams of Lamêgo, equally as appetising as the even better-known hams of Chaves. And just as tasty were the cheeses, which are not famous at all.

I descended into the redolent country crowd from the silent height on which I had spent the night beside the pilgrimage church of Nossa Senhora dos Remédios. For its staircase of six hundred steps is a continuation at a steeper gradient of the tree-lined avenue. Although it was a wonderful way to arrive in the town, in due course I had to climb six hundred steps back to where my motor caravan was parked. Visitors with less time and energy at their disposal can save both by taking a good look up at the church from below, and later exploring the first flights of the staircase from the top.

In this way they will avoid the modern extension to the base of the staircase, yet enjoy the unspoiled Baroque crown of this 'capital of Baroque'. Its jewel is not so much the church itself, as the so-called 'Court of the kings', the topmost of the staircase's nine 'landings'. The other eight have each their chapel or fountain to interest the pilgrim. But this, surrounded by granite columns bearing statues, is cunningly concealed from view until he is standing in it, compassed about by the anonymous figures to whose features lichen has added a deeper imprecision and mystery. It is a relief for him to climb the last flight of steps back into the real world, slaking his authentic thirst from the clear spring beside a huge chestnut tree.

The view from Nossa Senhora dos Remédios cuts right down towards the Douro eight miles away. But these sweeping panoramas of the upper Douro hide many deep, narrow, subsidiary valleys: it is their depth and narrowness which permit that building up of heat to which we owe port. At the bottom of such a valley, only a couple of miles out of Lamêgo, lies Balsemão. There is a steep road of sorts for part of the way. But the last half mile is by a mule track over an ancient bridge to a hamlet whose inaccessibility is typical of thousands we have no reason to visit.

Our reason for visiting Balsemão is its church: a tiny seventh-century basilica with an inscription in Visigothic characters set in the wall, and with Visigothic horse-shoe arches within. It is probably nearer its original condition than the larger seventh-century church of S. Frutuoso at Braga. And although Balsemão, too, underwent a restoration, the seventeenth-century painted ceiling and chancel furniture which date from then simply add a further note of archaic *naïveté* to this remote survival from Iberia's least-documented era.

We have already noticed the infrequency of the bridges over the Douro, and the consequent importance of those which do exist. Above Oporto there are only six; and of these by far the most important is that on the road between Lamêgo and Vila Real, our old friend the N2 on its way up to the northern frontier at Chaves. Immediately across it lies the nondescript little town of Peso da Régua, the administrative centre for the port vineyards.

The only easily negotiable road which cuts through the heart of these vineyards, passing many of the *quintas* from which the *vindima* is directed each autumn, is that running from the southern end of this bridge close beside the river to the next bridge at Pinhão. But upstream from Pinhão the Douro flows deep, unaccompanied by a road, crossed only by a bridge at Pocinho, and another at the frontier amidst the almond orchards of Barca de Alva.

The road joining Pinhão to Pocinho climbs far away from the river through bare brown countryside relieved by patches of wild lavender and golden broom. The two villages of any size: S. João da Pesqueira and Vila Nova de Fozcoa, are both worth exploring. S. João da Pesqueira has a first-floor prison, where the only prisoner incarcerated at the time of my visit was able to stroll out on to the balcony to gaze at and chat with the world below. The church of Vila Nova de Fozcoa has a Manueline doorway: its columns within lean curiously outwards due to an earthquake tremor.

Deserted though it is by the road, the upper Douro is well served by the railway, which shadows it almost all the way from Barca de Alva to opposite Cinfães. For remote hamlets on both sides of the river, connected with tiny stations by tracks and ferries, it is the main link with the outer world. As such it played a major part in *I gathered no moss*, the travelogue-cum-meditation of John Gibbons, which won him a Camoens Prize. The anonymous village where this fifty-six-year-old 'drop out' from banking spent four happy months in the winter of 1938-9 was in fact

Culeja. And the station on the other side of the river, at which its mail arrived together with the few other requirements it could not produce for itself, was Vezuvio.

We have trespassed on to territory which for the English-speaking world will belong to Gibbons for ever. It is time for us to leave the lands dependent on Portucale.

TAILPIECE: VINHO GENEROSO

It would be ungenerous indeed to write a book about Portugal without mentioning the 'generous wine' which is its most famous export, and all the generous people who organise and carry out its production. But this is very well-trodden ground. Those really interested should consult the many books which deal with nothing else. Some of them are written by people who have spent a lifetime in the port wine trade. Others are by writers who have at least devoted many months to mastering their subject. This brief account is as cursory as my own acquaintance with the world of port.

For a world it is, from the small farms where the vines are cultivated to the central *quintas* where the grapes are processed, to the lodges of Vila Nova de Gaia where the wine is matured, and on to their agents and customers around the five continents.

A changing world, too, at every point along this line. Though the grapes can only be picked by hand, the 'treading' is now largely carried out by automatic crushing and vinification plants. Mechanisation has been speeded up by the rise in wages and shortage of labour caused by emigration. But it is also more efficient. For although the pressure of the naked foot on the stone *lagar* was exactly calculated to break the grapeskins without crushing the pips, it allowed a crust of these solids to form, from which further extraction—essential for colouring—was difficult.

This mechanisation has proceeded throughout the 1960s. Similar changes in transport had taken place earlier, as more and more wine was sent down river first by railway, and then by road in tanker lorries. Four of the beautiful *rabelo* shallow sailing boats, which used to ply up and down the Douro, and which still figure in advertisements, can sometimes be seen between Vila Nova and Oporto. But they are mascots from a past age, like the horse-drawn drays of a well-known London brewery.

The principal changes at Vila Nova de Gaia are in management. As in many less ancient and traditional industries, there has been a certain amount of rationalisation since the war. One result of this is that Portuguese capital now plays a larger part in financing the industry. This has further accentuated a tendency to employ Portuguese staff initiated by labour laws which naturally favour nationals. A member of one of the leading British shipping families told me that today the total number of his compatriots actively employed in port in Portugal was no more than twenty-five. Some consequences of this decline for the British colony in Oporto were remarked on in the Tailpiece to Chapter 3.

An equally dramatic change has occurred in markets, where it comes as a shock to learn that France has overtaken Britain. I had several times been surprised in French homes on being offered '*un porto*' as an *apéritif*, or with a mid-morning biscuit. But it seems almost incredible that the French, after trebling their port imports during the decade of the 1960s, should now consume twice as much of the wine deliberately developed to damage their commerce, as their eighteenth-century enemy.

The fact that port's popularity in France is as an *apéritif* points to changes at the very end of the line: in consumer habits. For *apéritifs* call for drier wines than those served after dinner. There has, therefore, been an increase in the production of the drier tawny and white ports. Not that any type of port is necessarily 'sweet' or 'dry', or for that matter more or less 'strong'. White port has just as many degrees of alcohol as red, but tends to be drier because it contains less sugar. But sweet white ports do exist, and are particularly popular in Switzerland and Norway.

But then the whole history of this apparently timeless industry is one of change. The greatest changes were perhaps those originated by the Marquis of Pombal in 1756, with the establishment of the Wine Company of the Upper Douro. Then as now port was the one Portuguese product universally recognised as such on the world market. It was essential that this standard-bearer of the country's commerce should be protected as to price and quality. Both had suffered together, when adulteration by shippers had caused a precipitous fall in the price per pipe (this measure, still in regular use, is equivalent to five hundred and fifty litres).

Pombal's formula: demarcation of the area outside which no port could be grown, and insistence on standards in the wine exported, still holds today. Following a reorganisation in 1932, the machinery for carrying it out consists of the government's Port Wine Institute (of which we visited the Lisbon limb in Chapter 1), the *grémio* or corporation of Port Wine Exporters who themselves guarantee the quality of port shipped from Oporto, and the Casa do Douro up at Régua.

Régua, situated just where granite gives place to the looser schistose soils in which the vines flourish, is the natural 'capital' of the delimited area. A visit to the Casa do Douro soon shows us that this delimitation is more than merely territorial. There is a wide hierarchy even within the charmed boundaries winding round the rivers Douro and Corgo and Tua. Depending upon such factors as altitude, exposure to the sun, quality of the soil, and weather in any particular year, one farm may be allowed to produce as much as eighty pipes of port where another, of exactly the same size, may be allowed only fifteen. This is not the ceiling to their production. But everything in excess will be common or garden wine such as is produced outside the boundaries (not unlike what I purchased at Moimenta da Beira, only a few miles south of the boundary, in Chapter 6). Because the grapes for port will fetch a far higher price than the rest, they are naturally the best that any particular farm has grown.

The Casa do Douro governs the activities not only of the growers, but of the shippers and their agents on the upper Douro. In particular it exercises a strict control over the brandy which these supply for blending, in the proportion of two parts brandy to nine parts wine. So hot are the Douro summers that port is almost strong enough to be classed as a 'fortified' wine even without this addition. Brandy was first mixed with it simply to keep it in good condition on the high seas. But it was discovered that adding the spirit earlier halted fermentation and gave port an uncloying sweetness in which the palate delights. Art had been joined to utility.

So there is forever a to-ing and fro-ing through the doors of the Casa do Douro, with a report on the vines here, and a request to sanction the use of so much brandy there, and the delivery of one or other of all the necessary chits and certificates which regulate the production each year of some sixty thousand pipes.

Régua is well served by roads, and is the nearest point within the delimited region to Oporto. But when the shippers down at Vila Nova de Gaia spend their pleasant but busy busmen's holidays, personally supervising the *vendima* or grape-harvest, they generally stay nearer Pinhão, fifteen miles up the river. This tiny place has only one permanent English resident; and it is a curious experience to sit amidst the lovely old furniture in her home above the Douro, or to find rows of *Penguins* between the homely chintz of the other *quintas* which only awake once a year.

Until not so long ago Pinhão itself, deep in its suntrap beside the river, suffered from malaria. The delimited area is not naturally an ideal one for human habitation, and has always had to call on Trás-os-Montes and the Beiras for the extra workers necessary at the *vendima*. This partly explains the famous festivities: these grape pickers are enjoying an excursion, as well as making a useful addition to their earnings.

Indeed, before British demand, and the development of port as we know it, led to the planting of these furnace-like slopes, they were almost uninhabited. This is why we passed so few monuments of interest as we travelled up the Douro in the last chapter. Yet this, first of all the changes in the history of port, made the upper Douro the only centre of a 'Portuguese rural capitalism'. It is in every sense a *vinho generoso*.

9

THE ANCIENT PLACES

Many countries have a region which its citizens, for no immediately apparent reason, regard as typical, as in some way resuming the essence of the national character. Such regions are often anything but central, and of little economic importance.

Thus do the French regard the valley of the Loire, the Swedes Dalecarlia, and the English Devon. In each of these cases the region concerned does have certain qualities—of architecture, of folklore, of landscape—to inspire affection. But in each case there is a profounder, historical reason why it has been adopted, mascot-like, as a national symbol.

This is its intimate connexion with the idea of national independence. The valley of the Loire was the focus of French resistance to the English invaders who occupied more than half the country, Paris included. At Chinon on the Loire the uncrowned Charles VII received Joan of Arc; and her first victory was the relief of Orléans on the Loire.

It was to Dalecarlia that Gustavus Vasa fled to raise an army, having alone escaped from the Danish king's murder by explosion of the entire Swedish nobility, and from there raised an army, and launched the war of freedom against the treacherous sovereign in Copenhagen.

And what does Devon evoke, before even thatched cottages or clotted cream? Why, Drake and Hawkins and Raleigh, the singeing of the king of Spain's beard, and the confident words of defiance on Plymouth Hoe!

The Portuguese, too, have such a region, on whose charms they dwell with a nostalgia exaggerated even in this land of *saudade.* The feeling which goes into these encomiums of *o Minho* springs not only from the white-and-dark-grey Baroque churches, the *espigueiros* where the golden maize dries in safety, the gentle valleys, the neat vineyards yielding *vinho verde*. It owes an unquantifiable measure of its emotive force to the fact that here Portugal first gained independence.

'The cradle of nationality' is the phrase often used, frequently in association with a photograph of the sturdy, determined-looking castle of Guimarães, where the sturdy, determined Afonso Henriques was born in 1109. The Minho was the theatre for the young count's first steps towards becoming king, and towards being acknowledged as such. At Guimarães itself he defied his mother, and later his sovereign—on the occasion when Egas Moniz went surety for his future obedience. At Arcos de Valdevez he withstood that sovereign in a combat with many of the features of a tourney. And one of his firmest supporters was always the Archbishop of the Minho's cathedral city, Braga, who saw in political independence the opportunity for his ancient metropolitan see to assert its ecclesiastical independence from the pretensions of Santiago de Compostela.

Mention of the Archbishop of Braga gives us clues as to why Portugal achieved independence, and why it was the Minho where that independence was born. The little county became independent because it wanted to be. The ambition of Afonso Henriques, sturdy and determined though he was, only achieved fulfilment because it was shared by the entire ruling class: by everyone who mattered from the Archbishop downwards.

The idea of independence was born in the Minho from the mingling there of certain ancient traditions of separatism with these new stirrings of individuality. From the earliest times the north-west corner of the peninsula had led a life of its own whenever given the opportunity. The pre-Roman tribe of Gallaici have left their name in the modern Galicia. And when the Suevi, one of the first German peoples to cross the Pyrenees, were driven by the later-arriving Visigoths into this north-west corner, it formed an independent kingdom for a hundred and fifty years.

It formed, indeed, a separate entity within the Visigothic realm right down to the Arab conquest, although these three hundred years of the 'kingdom of the Suevi' have left almost no trace. The only two Portuguese words of indisputably Suevic origin are *britar*, to smash, and *laverca*, a bird. And in the national memory the Dark Ages belong to the Visigoths—who, it is true, controlled everywhere south of the Douro.

Yet the Suevi were not identical with the Visigoths. The Visigoths were a nomadic East German tribe, who in barely two centuries travelled from the Baltic to Spain via the Ukraine and the Balkans. The Suevi on the other hand were a settled West German people who had been in contact with Rome as long ago as Caesar's time. Some of them stayed in Germany, to give their name to Suabia, the modern Schwaben. They brought with them to northern Portugal a heavy plough, just as the equally settled Anglo-Saxons brought a heavy plough to England, making possible the cultivation of the heavier and potentially more fertile soils. Could they be in part responsible for the intense cultivation and dense population of the Minho and Galicia?

They became Catholic long before the Visigoths at last abandoned the Aryan heresy. And the seat of their bishop, and capital of their king, was not in the modern Galicia, but at Braga. The Minho was indeed the heart of this ancient forgotten kingdom. From Braga, as from other unlikely centres like Tours and Seville, confused and ambiguous signals reach us from amidst the rising barbarism of the Dark Ages. St. Martin of Braga, like Gregory of Tours and St. Isidore of Seville, was one of the giants of that fallen world.

The Archbishop of Braga still bears the title of Primate, giving the city something of the role of Canterbury in England or of Toledo in Spain. And Braga remains the capital of the Minho, and is the natural centre from which to explore the province.

I approached it myself with all the misplaced reverence due to a remote and ancient centre of culture, forgetting the fourteen well-filled centuries which separated St. Martin and the Suevic kings from 1970. I was therefore a little bewildered to arrive in a busy modern city an easy thirty miles drive north-east of Oporto. There was more immediate evidence of new residential suburbs, and of thriving industrial activity, than anywhere else except Lisbon itself. Even in the centre antiquity only intruded in the shape of a medieval keep of King Dennis, which might have belonged anywhere in Portugal.

But although seventeenth- and eighteenth-century restoration reduced the Romanesque and Renaissance architectural patrimony which once made Braga 'the Portuguese Rome', much of that patrimony remains in its narrower streets and quieter squares. Nor are the replacements and additions of those centuries to be dismissed.

A walk down the Rua do Raio, for example, which leads off from the wide Avenida Central, brings one face to face with an extraordinary Rococo palace covered with *azulejos*, which curiously relieve its rather heavy decoration by statues. A quiet square just round the corner—Braga has a number of such pleasant *largos*—is dominated by the neo-Classical hospital of S. Marcos, whose statues are unrelieved by wanton *azulejos*, and by the early Baroque church of S. Cruz. And only a few yards on stands S. João do Souto, of 1772, where *azulejos* have been brought in to enliven an ecclesiastical façade.

This walk will already have taken us past survivals from an even older Braga. Adjoining Number 389 of the Rua do Raio is a sunken spring, presided over by a roughly carved female bust and some slightly more sophisticated figures and inscriptions. It seems probable that this 'Fountain of the Idol' was dedicated to a prehistoric tutelary deity whom the Romans in their pantheistic way adopted. And alongside S. João do Souto can be seen the Manueline windows which once belonged to the town house of the Coimbra family. Their private chapel is also of the early sixteenth century, but in a style nearer to our own ideas of late Gothic. Within it are several tableaux in Ança stone by the French school of John III's reign.

This walk is also a satisfactory if unusual approach to the cathedral itself, a corner of which can be seen from S. João do Souto, at the end of the street of the same name. It is probably the corner we shall remember the best, for there on the outside wall stands the statue—attributed to Nicolas Chantarène—of the breast-feeding Nossa Senhora do Leite: Our Lady of the Milk, a great favourite with the *bracarenses*.

She offers a happier first view of the primatial church than the main façade, a Baroque caricature of the Romanesque original. The south doorway remains, however, to give us a glimpse of the building raised by S. Geraldo, the first Archbishop, soon after the year 1100; and his plan has been adhered to in its broad lines by subsequent restorers.

Much though these have been criticised, it was only natural that a monument of such national importance should enjoy—or suffer—embellishment during periods of national prosperity. Thus Diogo de Sousa, Archbishop during the 'fortunate' reign of Manuel I, added the porch and transformed the apse. And to the eighteenth century we owe not only the unhappy reconstruction of the main façade, and of much else, but also the superb Baroque organ, gilded with the gold which flowed in under John V, beside which that of Lisbon cathedral seems provincial.

The earliest period of national prosperity to affect the cathedral was that of its very foundation. Thus its treasury contains a priceless collection of religious art of every period from the tenth to the eighteenth century. But Braga's proudest possession is elsewhere. It is the tombs of the founders, who are none other than Count Henry of Burgundy and his wife Teresa, on whom in 1095 her father Afonso VI of Leon bestowed the County of Portugal, which their son, Afonso Henriques, was to make into an independent kingdom.

Their present tombs are of the Manueline period, as is that of their contemporary, S. Geraldo. But two other important tombs belong to the same period as their occupants. That of Archbishop Gonçalo Pereira, a close relation of the Holy Constable, was carved in Ança stone while he was still alive. That of Prince Afonso, a work of gilded copper made in Brussels on the orders of his sister the Duchess of Burgundy, is particularly poignant. For had he not died at the age of only ten in 1400 he might be lying, covered with years and fame, beside his younger brothers, those *altos infantes* who surround his parents John of Avis and Philippa of Lancaster, in the founders' chapel at Batalha.

One pride of the cathedral I was unable to investigate: the Rite of Braga, one of the handful of local liturgies licensed by the Roman Catholic Church between the Councils of Trent (1545–63) and Vatican II (1962–65). Having attended a Mozarabic mass at Toledo cathedral, I would dearly have loved to be present at the corresponding office in Portugal. Both are survivals of the masses heard by the Christians during the centuries under Moslem rule, when they were out of touch with liturgical developments elsewhere in the West. That of Toledo is often called the *misa visigoda*, because it is a fossilised survival from the Visigothic church which, like the realm, had its capital at Toledo. And in the same way that of Braga may enshrine some elements of the mass once followed by the church of the Suevi.

The Tourist Office had never heard of it. The sacristan when I approached returned a blank stare. Even the highly cultivated lady at whose home I lunched off what must surely be the best of all the hundred and one recipes for *bacalhau* (cod) was unaware of its existence. With more time at my disposal I would have approached one of the canons—or even bearded the Archbishop himself.

My disappointment, however, was made up for by the library and archives which occupy the former archiepiscopal palace, a group of buildings of different periods which marry harmoniously round a Joanine fountain at the centre of a precinct giving on to the main street. For me it remains the most memorable library in the country. Not only are its contents on the same level as those of Évora and Ajuda, but it is shown to visitors without formality and with the greatest courtesy. When, after visiting countless rooms full of manuscripts relating to the history of the city, and to every parish of the huge diocese, I asked to see those famous documents which relate to the very earliest days of the monarchy, I was at once hurried back up staircases and along corridors to where they were kept under glass cases and shaded from the light.

As a general rule the older manuscripts seemed to have been housed in the older, fourteenth-century wing of the palace. Here, too, I was shown a beautiful room prepared for lecturers visiting Braga, or for other cultural events. It must have made an ideal setting for the Chamber Orchestra of the Gulbenkian Foundation, which had given a performance there the previous week.

On the other side of the library the formal garden of S. Barbara is set off by some Gothic ruins which have been tidied up, but otherwise left untouched.

Even better, however, are the gardens of the Casa dos Biscainhos, a seventeenth-century private palace which on my visit was in process of restoration to form a civic museum. All I could see of the house was a charming interior courtyard supported by statues in caryatid fashion. But the garden, though untidy, entranced me. It was the quintessence of all those gardens of infancy: enclosed, other-worldly, with secret corners, with fruit-trees and hedges as well as merely lawns and borders, which colour for ever the minds of those of us who were lucky enough to play in them.

The Casa dos Biscainhos lies in the northern sector of the older, central part of the city, facing up the vast Praça do Conde d'Agrolongo. This is dominated by the church of Nossa Senhora do Popolo: its design, like that of the Sé Nova of Coimbra, was inspired by the Jesuit church in Rome.

Time would never drag during a long visit to Braga. It is a friendly city, as I have good reason to know. Both the older and the younger generations have their cafés, with appropriate Victorian or psychedelic *décor*, where in their different ways they express their widely-differing views. When the visitor has at last seen all its monuments—many of which, for reasons of space, I have been unable to mention—he will find others of almost greater interest within walking distance.

Pride of place amongst these will probably be given to the Bom Jesus, most famous of all the staircase-approached sanctuaries of northern Portugal. Rebuilt in its present form at the very end of the eighteenth century by Braga's great Baroque architect, Carlos Amarante, this 'minuet', as David Wright has described its 'parting and meeting' in a beautiful poem, has been criticised in detail. But its overall effect is overwhelming.

Emotionally or aesthetically, even if not theologically, everyone will find something addressed to himself in the Bom Jesus. The nine-year-old Castelo Branco was never to forget the statue of a lad his own size, who hands the nails to the soldiers carrying out the crucifixion, in one of the tableaux of the *via sacra*. And the disappointing church itself is backed by many acres of exotic trees, filled with more chapels, grottoes, a pleasure lake, and three good hotels for the many people who take summer holidays here.

The Bom Jesus forms the first angle of a '*triângulo turístico*' of unequal parts. A road along the range of hills continuing from the Bom Jesus takes one in barely two miles to its bathetic sister-sanctuary, the Sameiro. This offers an even better view, but nothing else. Its existence is explained by the need for a centre to express that devotion to Our Lady which swept the Roman Catholic world in the later nineteenth century. Until the Virgin had herself appeared at Fátima in 1917 this group of buildings, built between 1876 and 1904, provided the devout of Portugal with the necessary outlet.

Mercifully the third angle of the 'touristic triangle' is in better taste. S. Marta de Falperra, a perfect Rococo shrine which almost recalls Manueline in its carved granite, is architecturally more satisfying than the Bom Jesus itself. Though it lies below the Sameiro, the *serra* of Falperra from which it gets its name is wild enough, if only three miles out from Braga.

But then the mountains are never very far away from the tidy Arcadian farmsteads of the Minho. They cover much of the eastern half of the province. Travelling east from Braga one has soon climbed to the *miradoiro* of Lanhoso, from which I was lucky enough, like Napoleon's Marshal Soult a hundred and sixty years before me, to have my first view of the Minho lowlands.

The road I had then followed coming from the opposite direction, from Trás-os-Montes, runs high above the left bank of the River Cávado. It offers almost continuous views across the deep, narrow reservoirs which have been created in the valley, towards the serrated Gerez range which marks the frontier. This is as wild as it looks. Its highest point within Portugal, at a little over five thousand feet, makes it second only to the Serra da

Estrêla itself. The subsidiary valley running up into it, through the spa of Gerez, has the highest rainfall in the country.

From opposite this subsidiary valley it is possible to cross the Cávado and to return to Braga along the other bank. This road passes Bouro, one of those deserted and disintegrating monasteries which rightly made a strong appeal to the authors of *The Selective Traveller in Portugal*. I was particularly interested by the eighteenth-century *azulejos* covering the walls of the sacristy. They show monks being tempted by devils against a contemporary background which includes such artefacts as coaches.

I slept high above Bouro, at the sanctuary of Nossa Senhora da Abadia, which I suspect occupies an ancient site. It is approached by a track up the foothills of the Serra do Gerez, lined by chapels of a *via sacra* which are certainly a hundred years older than the nineteenth-century church itself.

On the other side of Braga, and even nearer than the Bom Jesus, is the only church in the whole peninsula to have been built on the design of a Greek cross. It no longer follows this plan exactly. For when the Franciscans built a convent alongside, they destroyed one arm of the cross in order to annex it as a chapel of their church. It is through this eighteenth-century church that the visitor now approaches S. Frutuoso.

Let him decide for himself whether it stands today much as it was built by S. Frutuoso in the mid-seventh century, or whether, as many experts believe, it was rebuilt in the eleventh, after being destroyed by the Moslems. For me the strongest argument in favour of this rebuilding is less the incomplete roughly-repaired columns, lacking their plinths, than the dedication itself. It would have required a fairly drastic restoration for the dedication to be changed from the original one to S. Salvador, given it by S. Frutuoso, who was Bishop of Dume, as the Suevic see was called. Dume stood a mile or two farther on this side of Braga.

But a great deal of the original must have survived intact for the restorers to have caught so well the spirit of Byzantine architecture. I was reminded strongly of that survival of the Exarchs' rule, the Cattolica at Stilo in Calabria, allowance being made for granite at S. Frutuoso instead of brick, and the proximity of the Atlantic instead of the Mediterranean.

A visit to S. Frutuoso can be extended to include the monasteries of Tibães and Vilar de Frades in the Cávado valley. Tibães stands on an eminence. Though generally classified as Rococo, I felt this was a more appropriate description for the decoration of the church and chapter house, than for the immense mass of the convent as a whole.

Vilar de Frades, five miles east, lies nearer the river level, down an enchanting road between walled gardens and tree-shaded greensward: a therapy in themselves for the mentally ill who now occupy the conventual buildings. The church, with a Baroque interior, has a blocked-up Romanesque doorway alongside the Manueline one now used as the entrance.

We have ventured to within a few miles of Barcelos. But before proceeding there we must turn back to explore the corner of the province around Guimarães. This can be reached on a main road from Braga, or better still by continuing along the ridge road which connects the Bom Jesus and the Sameiro.

This has the advantage of leading us directly past the Citânia de Briteiros, a prehistoric hill fort not merely better preserved than that of Sanfins, but even slightly restored. The few huts which have thus been built up and thatched give a glimpse of life among the Lusitanians, and indicate the size of the leap forward represented by the move down to Bracara and Conimbriga. They have been skilfully selected from amongst the minority of huts over the brow of the hill from the main entrance, leaving the greater part of the street plan just as it was uncovered by the devoted archaeologist Martins Sarmento and his successors.

'Streets' they certainly were, cobbled, well-worn, sometimes even drained; and with at least as much 'plan' as the present-day hamlets of *serra* or *sierra* they so much resemble. The *Guide Bleu* conservatively estimates the number of huts at more than a hundred and fifty. Even if the total number was twice this, plenty of open space was left within the triple line of fortifications for the refugees and cattle who would have sought protection here when under attack.

Like many prehistoric sites in Britain, Briteiros continued in occupation under the Romans. The Mediterranean, city-based civilisation introduced by the latter to western Europe became a progressively thinner veneer in proportion to the distance from the inland sea. In predominantly Atlantic regions like northern Lusitania, northern Gaul, and Britain, the straight highways between the tiny, artificial cities crossed countryside whose inhabitants' pre-Roman culture continued almost unchanged.

This can be regarded in two ways. The first is that their level of technical accomplishment was already high before the Romans came on the scene. Though few Celts may have moved so far west—the claim that the Galicians are blood-brothers of the Bretons, Welsh and Irish is unproven—the introduction of Celtic iron metallurgy was a revolution. By giving weapons to every man it destroyed the Bronze Age aristocracy, and gave rise to this *civilização castreja* of *citânias* and their near-relatives the smaller *castros*.

The second way of looking at the matter is to note that the purely technical achievements of the Romans, other than architectural, were little higher than those of many of the peoples they conquered. The techniques in which they did excel were those of administration. It was the legions' organisation, rather than any superiority in weaponry, which eventually enabled them, fighting in part as the representatives of southern Mediterranean Lusitania, to pacify the tribes of the Atlantic north who had so often raided beyond the Tagus. Rome's greatest achievement was the imposition of her language, a slow process only accomplished in Gaul as late as the fourth century. It would be interesting to know until when the inhabitants of the Citânia de Briteiros were still speaking the local dialect.

Objects discovered during excavations at Briteiros and the nearby Sabroso (a smaller *citânia* probably deserted before the Roman conquest) are housed in the museum named after Martins Sarmento at Guimarães ten miles away. After visiting it one is less surprised that the methods of making animals in metal introduced by the Celts are still those preferred by modern artists.

Guimarães has two other museums. The regional museum of Alberto Sampaio is equally important for its contents—notably some exquisite medieval religious ornaments from the twelfth century onwards—as for its home. This is Nossa Senhora da Oliveira, an abbey established by the Countess Mumadona, the tenth-century foundress of Guimarães, which was subsequently raised to the rank of a Royal Collegiate church by Afonso Henriques. The oldest parts are now his twelfth-century cloister and chapter house, which house the museum's sculpture. The church itself, an enormous mixture of styles, has already been restored once in this century, and was undergoing another at the time of my visit.

The other museum is in the palace of the Dukes of Bragança (who were also Dukes of Guimarães) on the hill above the town. My visit there was one of the least satisfactory of all those I made to monuments throughout Portugal. The palace, for long neglected, has been completely rebuilt—admittedly in the best materials, and with loving craftsmanship—and filled with borrowed cast-offs of minimal interest from museums elsewhere. But then its main function is to provide a suitable setting for the visiting dignitaries who from time to time are welcomed to this 'cradle of nationality' by the President of the Republic.

A far more lasting impression is made by the castle itself, on the same hill. This has simply been tidied up. The keep built by Countess Mumadona looks much as it might have appeared to the Moslems of Almansur on their way to sack Santiago de Compostela in 997. And the wall added by Henry of Burgundy a century later could still be recognised by Afonso Henriques, even if the living quarters, including the room where he was born, have fallen into ruins. The little Romanesque chapel of S. Miguel just below, where a font is still pointed out as having served for his baptism, is just as impressive in its simplicity.

Down in the town are other churches of interest, including the fifteenth-century S. Francisco, and the Rococo Santos Passos, the granite of whose narrow façade has been set off by *azulejos* instead of whitewash. All these monuments contrast strongly with the reputation Guimarães enjoys on Portuguese radio, where its name is always linked with the fortunes either of the linen industry (of which it is the centre), or of its football team.

Penha, a modern pilgrimage sanctuary and summer holiday resort rising to over two thousand feet immediately to the south of Guimarães, was wreathed in mist on my visit. So I drove instead the five miles out to S. Torcato, centre of the cult of a Moslem-martyred prelate whose ankle-bone in a reliquary had caught my attention in the Alberto Sampaio museum.

Unfortunately, I approached S. Torcato in a rather frivolous mood. This was increased by the sight of his incorrupt body (less ankle-bone) looking like baked mud behind a glass case in an unattractive nineteenth-century basilica; though I liked the little Romanesque church in the hamlet above, where it originally lay. But I had reckoned without the Saint's very real powers. I was persecuted by a whole series of misfortunes, culminating in a leak in my petrol tank, until I was well beyond the Douro. It is not merely in jest that I ask for S. Torcato's blessing in my present venture—albeit merely literary—back into the Minho.

Before turning south to Guimarães we were travelling from Braga towards Barcelos, through the stretch of countryside which gave birth to the oldest surviving written document in Portuguese: the *Noticia de Torto* of before 1211. Barcelos is at once the meeting-place and the show-place of the rural Minho, where all those quiet farms and cottage industries find at once a voice and a market in the great fair each Thursday.

Oranges, lemons, vegetables, cheeses, carved wooden ox-yokes, modern farm machinery alongside serviceable implements of a type the people of the *citânias* might have used, tinkers' ware in unpolished metal, and at least half an acre of pottery, are then displayed on a vast irregular quadrilateral on one side of the little town. It is as if the Minho gallery of Belem's museum of Popular Art were brought to life.

When our feet at last tire, we can rest without leaving this charmed rural world in one of half a dozen taverns along the south side of the square. These serve, at long trestle tables on their sawdust-strewn floors, a *minhoto* version of the 'farmer's ordinary' of English market towns. And there is no need to remind them to provide the half litre of wine which by law is included in every table d'hôte purchased in Portugal. The serving wench—the phrase comes unprompted—brings it naturally with the steaming plates of chicken, brawn, kidneys or cod.

The churches on the three other sides of the square: the Misericordia, the Terço, and the Bom Jesus da Cruz, all belong to the seventy years after the Restoration. That of the Bom Jesus da Cruz, of 1705, is the most unusual: a Baroque compromise between a cross and a rotunda, with a granite dome rising above its white walls. The fifteenth-century keep nearby shelters a most helpful tourist office and a handicraft exhibition.

The centre of Barcelos, however, lies down one of several narrow streets leading to a cluster of old buildings above the bridge over the Cávado. This bridge, like the keep, the ruined Ducal palace (now a free museum of medieval sculpture), the house of the Pinheiros, and a fine pillory, are of the fifteenth century, when Barcelos was the principal seat of the powerful Dukes of Bragança, who were in due course to ascend the throne. But a more humble house of the previous century is pointed out with greater pride: it was used by the Holy Constable, who transmitted his huge estate, along with his title of Count of Barcelos, to his daughter who married the first Duke.

To the fourteenth century, too, belongs the most dearly-loved and best-known monument of all: the calvary of *o Senhor do Galo*, Our Lord of the Cock. It was erected, according to legend, by a Galician pilgrim who on his way to Compostela was arrested at Barcelos and sentenced to death for a crime for which he was not responsible. Making a last appeal to the judge, who was seated at a banquet, he called on the roast cockerel which had just been brought in to crow in proof of his innocence. When this miracle occurred just as he was about to be hanged, he was released.

Now St. James of Compostela can be seen on the calvary beneath the innocent victim on the gallows. Above him and beneath the cross stands the miraculous bird, the cock of Barcelos, which is on sale in every size and combination of colours in the pottery section of the fair, and which has become one of the national symbols.

The valley of the Cávado, which we have followed from the narrow reservoirs which contained it up on the mountainous borders with Trás-os-Montes, is just as pleasing, if less spectacular, in the ten miles from Barcelos to its mouth at the fishing village of Esposende. It is dominated by the ancient pilgrimage centre of Franqueira, with a medieval church and castle, and remains of a *citânia*. But even those who love the Cávado must agree that the essence of the Minho belongs rather to the next valley north (forgetting the tiny Neiva): that of the Lima.

If the Lima did not run half its course in the mountains of Galicia, it might well have been adopted instead of the Mondego as the most Portuguese of rivers. Certainly I soon found myself coming under the enchantment it has exercised on everyone since the Roman troops who refused to cross it in 135 B.C., in the belief that it was the Lethe, which induced oblivion. Why the Lethe? Because it flowed through the Elysian fields!

The Lima's early course in Portugal, between the *serras* of Gerez and Soajo, runs through a mountain Arcady rather than an Elysium. Almost at the frontier the Romanesque Convent of Ermelo has stood on the right bank since before that frontier existed, for it was founded by Afonso Henriques's mother. But these mountain fastnesses of the Minho have recently been well explored and well described by David Wright and Patrick Swift; and I would prefer to make my own little contribution to the survey of lost hamlets of northern Portugal in Trás-os-Montes. Even in these fastnesses, life is changing. A priest in Ponte da Barca with whom I struck up a friendship told me that there were now very few shepherds left on the green *massif* of the Serra do Soajo.

Ponte da Barca stands where the Lima leaves the mountains. Though no more than a big village, it has a certain sophistication, due perhaps to the firework factory which is its biggest employer. Its most charming corner, as might be expected, is down by the river, where a beautifully-proportioned stoa-like building and a Manueline pillory stand beside a bridge of 1543, whose harmonious lines somehow echo the unhurried clarity of the water beneath.

An important road from Braga crosses this bridge on its way to Monção and the frontier at Valença. It follows tributaries of the Lima on both sides. That to the north, the Vez, is the more important. It has given its name to Arcos de Valdevez, three miles north of Ponte da Barca and more than twice the size, though without any outstanding monuments. A side road from there runs up into the Serra do Soajo and to the village called after it; while the main road follows the Vez until it climbs magnificently the Serra do Extremo where the stream rises.

From Ponte da Barca onwards there are roads down both sides of the Lima, and it is hard to know which to recommend. The southern should be followed for at least the three miles to Bravães, whose church is the epitome of all the small Romanesque churches of early Portugal. The intractability of its granite gives to its many carvings an even greater charm and *naïveté* than one expects from this period.

Along the northern bank, the most attractive features architecturally belong to six centuries later. Near Soto I came across a Rococo shrine at the top of a *via sacra*, unmentioned by any guide. Soon afterwards I saw at the end of a driveway the lovely Solar da Gloria, an eighteenth-century crenellated mansion which is the home of a lucky English bachelor. As I lunched near the river on that March 19th, the sun was strong enough for me to remove my shirt.

'You should see how it can flood,' said an old man whose view of the Lima was a little less Elysian than my own. 'If it wasn't for my age I'd go to work in France like the younger ones.'

I had been looking forward to the monastery of Refoios, a few miles on; and this Rococo study in granite and whitewash proved no disappointment. Precisely because the 'anti-Classical', 'bat's wing' decoration of the church's façade appears beyond a level terrace in deep rural solitude, one is able to adjust to this phenomenon better than in a busy square of Viana do Castelo, or a narrow street junction in Vila Real. The woodwork within is amongst the richest I saw anywhere.

Ponte do Lima is just what it says. As at Ponte da Barca it is the bridge—in this case of the fourteenth and fifteenth centuries—

and the views from the bridge, which we shall most remember. Naturally the river is wider here, but just as clear, just as unhurried: its essence is somehow reflected by the Rococo church of S. António de Torre Velha, standing alone beside a waterfront piazza at the northern end of the bridge. But the town also holds, within what is left of its fortifications, as many as four churches, several old houses, and the palace of the Marquises of Ponte do Lima, with Manueline windows.

The journey on down the Lima again presents us with the choice between the left and right banks. Both are delightful. Both pass Romanesque churches. And both lead to Viana do Castelo.

The southern route joins the main road up the coast from Oporto two miles before the town, of which it offers a splendid view, spread below the *serra* of S. Luzia. Concentrated thus between hill and river, we can embrace it in a single glance, and understand that this northernmost district capital—it shares the Minho with Braga—numbers less than twenty thousand inhabitants. But to the charms general to the province, and to the more particular pleasures of the Lima, Viana adds delights of its own. They are all due in part to this human, comprehensible size.

The first of these is the opposite bank, from which we have surveyed it. Because the city has not spread over there, this remains a deep pine forest, stretching right up to the river's edge, and to the wide arc of golden sand bordering the ocean. It forms a literally natural playground not only within easy reach, but within constant view.

The second is the city itself, which because it is retained within its ancient limits, retains too its ancient spell. It centres on the narrow triangle of the Praça da República, where from the usual mosaic pavement we can contemplate a far from usual sixteenth-century ensemble of town hall, fountain, and Misericordia.

The former town hall, though Manueline in date, belongs to a more austere tradition. The crenellated roof of the façade, which was left standing when the rest of the building was pulled down fifteen years ago, emphasises how far we are from Lisbon. But by 1554 more decorative fashions had penetrated here, as testified by the elegant 'three-storeyed' fountain by João Lopes. His son had by the end of the century evolved a Renaissance style as elaborate as any in the country: his Misericordia has a 'three-storeyed' arcade, of which the two upper rows of columns are in female, caryatid form.

The streets behind this square contain two fine eighteenth-century palaces (of the Malheiras and of the Távoras). The frankly medieval lanes between it and the river contain some far more ancient houses. The river front, apart from the pleasant gardens now planted there, can have changed little since Viana, three hundred years ago, was at least as important an entrepôt for English merchants as Oporto itself.

There are a good museum, and a number of interesting churches, amongst which Nossa Senhora da Agonia must be seen even by anyone in a hurry. Though small, it compels attention by its raised position at the end of a long open space, and by the same 'anti-Classical' effect we saw at Refoios, of reversed and broken lines in black granite splaying out above the door. It has been said with truth that whatever Rococo may have lost in Portugal in delicacy, it has gained in force.

The third delight owed by Viana to its human size is that S. Luzia remains unspoilt. One can be climbing its green, wooded slopes within three minutes of leaving the Praça da República. If lucky in one's timing one can even be at the top in only three minutes more, deposited by the funicular beneath a modern basilica. This and a luxury hotel in lovely grounds are the only buildings on this splendid belvedere, which was more densely populated in the time of the *citânia* whose ruins still cluster between the hotel and the actual summit (this can be reached by road).

S. Luzia owes its impressiveness to its isolation. Even this western, coastal half of the Minho is full of *serras* two or three times its mere six hundred and fifty feet. One wonders how the province is so densely populated, for the sparsely peopled Alentejo and Trás-os-Montes are both flatter, and less broken up.

The answer lies partly in its climate. This is an Atlantic, well-watered region, just far enough south to be able to grow such Mediterranean fruits as grapes, oranges and lemons. It is as if the products of Connemara and Provence met invitingly on the stalls of Barcelos fair.

The answer also lies partly in the tiny size of its farms, '*minifundia*' just large enough to support a family, so long as they are given the care normally reserved for gardens. It is this contrast between the deserted pinewoods of the *serras*, and the intensively-worked valleys, which forms one of the Minho's charms. Often a second crop is growing beneath the granite 'pergolas' which bear the vines. Sometimes these are even trained up the branches of other fruit trees.

In an earlier chapter we spoke of the Minho as the land of *broa*, maize-bread, in contrast to the cornlands of the south. We can continue the opposition by describing it as the land of oxen, of intense religious devotion, and—for no good economic reason—of bare feet, by contrast with the southern regions of horses, of a certain apathy in matters ecclesiastical, and of shoes.

Fifteen miles north of Viana the coast curves round into the mouth of the River Minho, which is guarded by the little port of Caminha. The frontier river (the old name of the province was not the misnomer Minho, but Entre-Minho-e-Douro) swells out into a wide estuary for its last few miles. The protection this affords gave Caminha the excuse not to rebuild its low medieval walls, from which a fifteenth-century clock tower looks down on the square where a lively market was in progress on my visit. Several of the customers were from La Guardia over in Spain: I had seen them landing from the ferry on the other side of the town, beyond the parish church. This is something of a fortress despite its rustic Renaissance façade.

But then so many buildings have been built to double as fortresses along the river, which soon narrows to little more than a hundred and fifty yards: a fortified manor at Lanhelas, a twelfth-century castle up at Melgaço, and solid little Romanesque churches there as at Ganfei and Friestas. And whereas Vila Nova de Cerveira, like Caminha, preserves much of its medieval walls, more elaborate fortifications were erected in the seventeenth century at Valença and Monção.

The French were then allies of the Portuguese in their war of

27. *Vindima* above the Douro: the gathering of the port wine grapes

28. Ponte da Barca
(Minho)

independence, and Vauban's techniques were employed here, as at Elvas and Almeida. Monção is the larger place, but its fortifications are smaller, so that it occupies all the area within them. Every guide tells how lampreys, that medieval-sounding delicacy which killed an English king, can be enjoyed in springtime at the *Chave d'Ouro*. It is true: watch out for a scrap of paper inscribed with almost medieval illegibility '*há lampreias*'.

My memories of Monção include a walk by moonlight in the park beside the Minho, here narrower still; and later coming, by the earliest light of dawn, upon the vast palace of Brejoeira. 'The last of the great country houses to be built in Portugal,' reads a caption from *The Selective Traveller*; for this copy of the Ajuda Palace was almost completed when the separation of Brazil in 1822 ended, perhaps at just the right moment, the great era of building in the north.

Valença is smaller, and nestles in a corner of its huge network of salients and bulwarks. Built into these is its *pousada*, named after S. Teotónio, a right-hand man of Afonso Henriques, and the first Portuguese saint. Though the village stands immediately above the river, it is necessary to go about a mile out of one's way, and through two separate systems of defence, in order to reach it from the international bridge which links it to Tuy in Spain.

This bridge forms the gateway between Portugal and Galicia, although there also exist ferries such as at Caminha, and less important frontier posts near Chaves in Trás-os-Montes, and up at S. Gregorio where the river ceases to be even half Portuguese. Let us leave the Minho gazing across the water at this Spanish region, which shares with Portugal so much more than a common frontier.

Originally they had everything in common. A common history under the Suevi, and later in the 'Kingdom of Galicia' which reappeared so often amongst the Christian states of northern Iberia. A common tongue in that Galaico-Portuguese which was the earliest literary language of the peninsula. A common architecture, when all roads led to St. James of Compostela, and the cathedral of Tuy directly inspired Romanesque churches south of the river such as Bravães, Ganfei and Friestas. A common social system, with the *minhoto*'s tiny farm resembling in size, if not always in crops, the smallholding of the *gallego*.

What they do not have in common, however, is the shared experience of nationhood. History, and history alone, can bind together the most diverse, and sunder the closest. When in 1095 Alfonso VI of Leon settled Galicia on his legitimate daughter Urraca, and Portugal on his illegitimate daughter Teresa, he gave the barons beyond the Minho the opportunity they yearned for to establish their independence from Galician overlordship. For close on nine centuries now the two peoples have led separate lives, looking in different directions.

Though *gallego* is still the same language as Portuguese, sharing pronunciations if not always vocabulary with *minhoto* and *trasmontano*, to a greater extent than these share them with *alentejano* and *algarvio*, it is used less and less in the busy coastal provinces of Vigo and La Coruña. I found no one who spoke it in Tuy, for example. As an example of disinterest on the other side of the frontier, I gave a lift to a middle-aged woman who lived overlooking the Minho near Caminha, who had never in her life been to Spain.

English newspapers are very fond of talking, all in the same breath, about Galician, Basque, and Catalan separatists. I have yet to meet such an animal from Galicia, although I have known plenty in the Basque country and in Catalonia. Like the Scots from James VI and I to Harold Macmillan, the *gallegos* have found a better way of expressing their nationalism. For on the 4th December 1892, a baby was born at the town near La Coruña now called El Ferrol del Caudillo, and baptised as Francisco Franco.

He is an outstanding example of yet another feature common to Galicia and to Portugal—and to the Minho, in particular. Both to north and south of the frontier, a high proportion of the population leave their homes, to seek their living elsewhere.

TAILPIECE: OS EMIGRANTES

Emigration is nothing new in Portugal. Without emigration the empty marches could never have been repopulated, as the Christian orders and warlords drove beyond the Douro, beyond the Mondego, beyond the Tagus. Without emigration the Atlantic islands could never have been settled in the fifteenth century, the route to the East garrisoned in the sixteenth, the interior of Brazil colonised in the eighteenth.

Nor has it always been thought of as the social problem many authorities regard it today. Nineteenth-century finance ministers welcomed the allowances sent by settlers overseas to their families at home. For these remittances in American dollars or Brazilian cruzeiros enabled them to pay the interest on the loans they raised on the London and Paris money markets. (For this reason the financial instability in Brazil following the deposition of the last Bragança emperor in 1889 had serious repercussions in the brother-land.)

And only at two periods has the tide of emigration prevented a steady growth in the Portuguese population. The first was in the sixteenth century. 'The whole of Portugal embarks for India in Cabral's fleet.' A sizeable number literally did embark, and over half of them died: of scurvy, shipwreck, tropical diseases, and in warfare. Camoens was the exception rather than the rule in getting back alive—and he only just made it! From rather more than a million at the beginning of King Manuel's reign the population had dropped to a bare million when King Sebastian sailed to Morocco.

Thereafter, however, the figures take on a more Malthusian look, rising from about two million to about three million during the eighteenth century. Their acceleration in more recent years is better grasped by giving the number of inhabitants per square kilometre: 38 in 1841, 52 in 1890, 81 in 1940, 93 in 1960. At this last date the total including Madeira and the Azores had passed nine million.

But now this acceleration has been halted. For the second time in her history Portugal is no longer experiencing a steady rise in her population. Not even the most optimistic forecasts foresee the figure of eleven million being passed. Her present annual increase of 0·3 per cent, comparing with 4·5 per cent for the EFTA countries as a whole, is the smallest in Europe.

Emigration is not the sole explanation. A drop in fertility is also partly responsible. Although the 'Pill' is not a subject for jokes on television, or for small talk in mixed company, its existence is perfectly well known. When used, it seems to be taken with a sensible discipline. And while the war in Africa continues, the removal of young men of military age for three and a half years of their early twenties obviously gives the demographic graph a 'bulge' in the wrong direction.

But the 1960s brought not only that war, and the 'Pill'. They brought, too, a dramatic change in the direction of emigration. Just as variously-labelled nationalisms were closing the doors of former favourite destinations, such as Cuba and Venezuela, the message began to spread through *aldeia* and *vila* and *monte* of a new and far more accessible market for labour, just the other side of the *país vizinho*.

France has imported workers ever since the sag in her own demographic graph under the Third Republic. I know parishes in the south-west where half the farms are owned by Italians, and Monsieur le Curé is Dutch. But the prosperity which marked the opening years of the Common Market provided jobs for the Italians at home, just as de Gaulle's Fifth Republic needed more hands. French demand was nicely equated with Portuguese supply.

The working of this economic law was not entirely painless. The Portuguese government was by now worried about the implications of this blood-letting on the country's agriculture, on its own industrial development, and on its military sufficiency. So passports were granted less easily. Frontier control was tightened.

Attempts to deny economic laws, however, set up uncontrollable pressures. What could not be done legally was carried out clandestinely. Far away at Fuenterrabía, on the very threshold of the promised land of France, I remember hearing fantastic stories in the early 1960s from friends in the Spanish *Guardia Civil*. Tales of lorries stopped at emergency checkpoints, which proved to be carrying not potatoes, but Portuguese. Sad tales of bands of woebegone peasants, twenty or thirty strong, who until a few days before had never left their hamlets in Trás-os-Montes or

Beira Alta, and who had been fleeced and then deserted in lonely *sierras* by their self-appointed 'couriers'. Tales all too like those of illegal Commonwealth immigrants into Britain a few years later.

Nor did an undiluted paradise await these emigrants beyond the Pyrenees. Without documents and social security cards they were ready prey for exploitation. There was work for them, certainly, but at the hardest jobs, and at the lowest wages. And accommodation, especially for those who contrived to bring their families, was all too often in *bidonville* shanty-towns.

French public opinion was not unaware of what was going on. There were good-humoured radio jokes about communication difficulties with one's servant, grocer, bus conductor, doctor, and even priest, all of whom were Portuguese! And there was a notable and sympathetic semi-documentary film called *O Salto* (*Le Saut, The Jump*). This recounted the experience of a young Portuguese who decided to make the great leap into the dark of emigration: his adventures in travelling to France, his disappointments on arrival, and the help he received from the close-knit society of his poor but friendly fellow-countrymen already established there.

The situation is no longer so grim as described in *O Salto*. The government has wisely removed the artificial barriers to emigration. At the same time it has reached agreements with the French authorities, not only regularising the position of Portuguese immigrants, but even setting up an organisation in France to care for their physical and social welfare.

France is only too pleased to co-operate. She needs extra hands. The Portuguese often already possess those specific skills: quarrying, cork-bark stripping, or resin-tapping in the pine forests, which Frenchmen are no longer prepared to learn or to practise. And how much better these easily-integrated Latins, the quickest language learners of Europe, than unassimilable North Africans!

This brings us to the saddest aspect of emigration for Portugal itself. It is an aspect unknown to Britain, whose emigrants depart to an English-speaking culture stretching from Capetown to the Canterbury Plains to California. For just because the Portuguese emigrants—to Venezuela, to the United States, to France—integrate so well into their host-cultures, they are all too easily lost not only to Portugal, but to Lusitania. So often they take the boat from Leixões without ever seeing Lisbon, or even the train from Guarda without ever seeing Oporto. And immense though the *saudade* of the first generation, it is rare for later ones to feel the loyalty which prompted the late John Dos Passos to write a fine history of the land of his forefathers.

Fortunately, some straws in the wind suggest that the day may come when part of the national dish, cod, will no longer be imported from Germany after being caught off Newfoundland by emigrant Portuguese fishermen working for German trawling companies; and, more important, when Portuguese emigrants will retain their Portuguese culture.

One is that the wages of skilled workers in the industrial zones round Lisbon and Oporto are already as high as anywhere else in western Europe. The trained craftsman no longer has any incentive to expatriate himself.

Another is that Brazil continues to take a certain proportion of emigrants and, her economic problems once mastered, could take far more. They are not lost to Lusitania, who settle in the *pais irmão*.

Lastly, and most encouraging, is the number of conscripts who, on demobilisation, elect to remain in the African territories where they have been stationed during military service. In the 1930s and 1940s opportunities here were perhaps missed, though some successful agricultural settlements were made in Angola. But now plans are going ahead, both in the healthy Angolan highlands around new cities like Nova Lisboa, and in Moçambique, especially in the area of the projected Zambezi dam at Cabora Bassa. This project, far more ambitious than Kariba, will benefit not only Moçambique itself, but all the neighbouring territories of southern Africa.

It may also bring those neighbouring territories an uncovenanted benefit: lessons in the great Lusitanian achievement of multi-racial living and assimilation. And in so far as these schemes attract emigrants who would otherwise have gone to France, they will save unnumbered Portuguese yet unborn for Portugal.

10

BEHIND THE MOUNTAINS

'Trás-os-Montes? Behind what mountains?' I used to wonder to myself somewhat scornfully, before that afternoon when we drove out of Amarante. 'If even the Estrêla doesn't touch two thousand metres, however can these lesser hills isolate a whole province, as they are supposed to do?'

Our switchback journey from Oporto to the Tâmega that morning had already made me begin to realise that other things besides altitude make mountains. But it was the ascent of the Serra do Marão which completed my conversion. The higher we went the steeper became the slopes into which the road was cut, and the more menacing the wooded heights above. When we paused at the well-placed *pousada* of S. Gonçalo (named after the marriage-minded saint of Amarante) it was hard to believe we stood at less than three thousand two hundred feet. Well might they say:

> '*Para cá do Marão,*
> *Mandam os que cá estão.*'

> 'On this side of the Marão
> It's those on the spot who give the orders.'

A couple of miles later came the pass, which is marginally higher, just topping the thousand metres. We were in Trás-os-Montes. The descent to Vila Real proved something of an anti-climax. It was more gradual. It was also less in absolute terms, for Vila Real, like the province as a whole, stands high. In a sense it lies not only behind the mountains but on the mountains; for much of it is a plateau resting on a series of ancient eroded *serras*. The names of these *serras*: Padrela, Vilarelho, Barroso, Roboredo, da Nogheira, evoke neither the Pyrenean freshness of the Estrêla, nor the serrated grandeur of the Gerez, but instead barer, drier, more desolate eminences in a countryside already bare, and dry, and desolate.

Trás-os-Montes is dry for the same reason that Beira Baixa is dry: because the Atlantic winds have deposited most of their moisture before they reach it. But it is too far north, and too high, to enjoy the lingering Mediterranean influences which transform the Cova da Beira. Some geographers therefore see in it a 'Continental' region of intensely cold winters and intensely hot summers, to add to the 'Atlantic' region and the 'Mediterranean' region which divide between them the rest of the country.

Some historians, likewise, see in it an essential economic unit of early Portugal, without whose wool and rye and chestnuts the young kingdom would never have achieved the basic self-sufficiency necessary for a medieval state.

Both are perhaps giving the province an importance it never possessed. In a similar way many foreigners—I was amongst them—develop an intense curiosity about Trás-os-Montes simply because it is so little visited. There are generally good reasons for places being little visited. There may be little to visit. There may be few facilities for visiting what little there is. It is possible to be at the same time inaccessible and uninspiring.

So be prepared for that sensation of anticlimax as you coast down the Marão, or climb up from the *terras quentes*, the hotlands of the Douro tributaries. You will meet a deep silence, and the monotony of a landscape whose undulations have something in common with those of the Alentejo without its fertility, and without the sparkling cleanliness of its human habitations.

For the *trasmontano* hamlets, lost amidst immense horizons, and built in local stone unrelieved by whitewash, so that they almost fade into their background, prove when we turn aside to visit them to be as earthy in atmosphere as in construction. Unmade streets of dust or mud are lined by low, irregular cottages through whose thatched or slated roofs escape wisps of smoke undirected by any chimney. There are five bent old women in black for every man under sixty, and ten scraggy chickens for every human of any age. The only shop consists of a few shelves of ancient merchandise behind a rude counter which doubles as bar. The visitor feels himself not only in an inhospitable landscape, but in an alien society. For even if he speaks Portuguese, how can he hope to communicate with these beings from a more primitive world?

Let him pause and take courage, however, before he turns tail and retreats to the bosky ruritania of the Minho, or to the more human landscape of Beira Alta. There is no need for him to expose himself to total alienation all at once. There are three towns of a certain size where he can accustom himself to Trás-os-Montes without altogether leaving the twentieth century.

First comes Vila Real, a district capital, and once the 'royal town' from which the whole province was governed. It therefore has a number of town houses of those members of the local nobility who could not aspire to the distant Lisbon. Its cathedral is a not unpleasing mixture of medieval styles. But its most interesting church is its Capela Nova, a small but elegant Rococo chapel, where the 'anti-Classical' techniques we saw at Refoios and at Nossa Senhora da Agonia at Viana, have been employed to fill and to distinguish an awkward narrow façade on the angle of two streets.

The most important members of the local nobility were—and are—the Counts of Vila Real. Their own seat stands a couple of miles outside the town, surrounded by beautifully maintained gardens. With its dependencies it provides offices and storerooms for the highly efficient commercial enterprise into which its surrounding estates have been organised. Even the visit to the inside of the house, with its somewhat second-division collections of furniture and family heirlooms, has been so skilfully promoted that the visitor feels he is honoured to be allowed to pay twenty-five escudos for the privilege.

I have no cause for bitterness myself. Not for the first nor the last time my enrolment at Lisbon University had given me a contact, and the door was opened. I need not describe the Baroque extravaganza facing me as I approached that door, nor the balustraded staircase I climbed to it. For thanks to the same skilful marketing the Solar Mateus is known to every browser in the English-speaking glossies, and to every purchaser of the so cleverly-packaged *Mateus Rosé*, my own least favourite Portuguese wine.

The most unexpected aspect of a visit to the Solar Mateus is coming upon it in austere Trás-os-Montes. But there are in fact, other, less publicised palaces in the region. In or not too far from the 'hotlands' of the Douro tributaries, they were built likewise by the older, richer nobility of the north during the good eighteenth-century years when the British drank port and the Brazilians mined gold.

The road from Vila Real to Chaves, the second of our three towns, runs through the spas of Pedras Salgadas and Vidago. Thermal activity where it occurs is rarely isolated. There is another spa up in the Serra de Barroso at Carvalhelos. Chaves itself has baths of its own, set in a park where beneath cunningly arranged little glass domes the mineral water can be seen reaching the surface at 73° Centigrade.

These springs helped to attract the Romans to the site, and account for the *Aquae* in its Latin name of Aquae Flaviae. Its present name is derived from *Flaviae*, by the same process that *chama*, a flame, is derived from the Latin *flamma*, and *not* from the word *chave*, meaning key, as stated by two otherwise well-informed guides.

But by coincidence Chaves, a larger town than Vila Real, the district capital, is also the defensive key of the north. Spaniards, French, and pretenders have all attempted this particular route. (The most recent such attack, under the early Republic, is commemorated in Lisbon by the long-winded Avenida dos Defensores de Chaves.) Hence it has a good medieval castle, as well as seventeenth-century fortifications. Down nearer the river two charming little interconnecting squares are distinguished by a fine pillory, the parish church with an eighteenth-century organ, the Renaissance chapel of S. Cabeça, and an unusual Baroque Misericordia.

But the great monument of Chaves is the Roman bridge, a vital link on the legions' road from Braga to Astorga, with inscribed milestones still standing to proclaim the fact. It is still in constant use, although it has recently been duplicated by a wider bridge some way downstream. The Tâmega, which it crosses, is a gentler, more civilised river than the fierce current we last saw above Amarante, for it is here flowing across a small but fertile plain. Chaves's not-to-be-missed market therefore acts as an exchange between the fruit and vegetables of this *veiga*, and the products of the surrounding *serras*. Outstanding among these are the hams, even better-known though no tastier than those of Lamêgo.

The road on to our third town, Bragança, runs a mere ten miles south of the mountainous frontier. It is therefore often steep and winding, especially near the remote Vinhais, where in the vast Convent of S. Francisco the seminarists of Bragança diocese lead a cloistered life indeed. Three miles before Bragança a side-road leads to Castro de Avelãs, with the only Romanesque brick church in Portugal.

As we noticed in the Tailpiece to Chapter 2, Bragança is one of the best-known Portuguese place-names. It owes little, however, to the dynasty to which it gave a title. Its small and simple cathedral has only been such since 1764. And it is an earlier dynasty which is recalled by the church of S. Vicente, rebuilt in the seventeenth century. For it was here that Pedro claimed to have gone through the marriage ceremony which made Inés de Castro his lawful wife.

It was under this first dynasty, too, that the great castle above the town was erected. Within its high walls, and in the shadow of its keep, is a whole village which includes the most interesting monuments of Bragança. These are the early Baroque church of S. Maria; a prehistoric carving of a boar, transfixed by the shaft of a Gothic pillory; and the Domus Municipalis.

This last, an irregular pentagon of twelfth-century construction, is even more impressive from within. It is easy to see why some authorities have imagined the grave counsellors seated round the bench which runs under the deep little unglazed Romanesque windows, and have seen in this 'oldest civil building' of Portugal all sorts of evidence of local self-government. But this is conjecture. It may after all have been no more than a cover for the invaluable cistern it still protects. Seen from the south, from the road past the *pousada* of S. Bartolomeu which gives the best view of Bragança as a whole, the Domus Municipalis seems altogether too dominated by the keep for it ever to have been a seedbed of twelfth-century democracy.

Had we travelled directly from Vila Real to Bragança we could have passed, at Murça, a larger and even finer survival from the prehistoric boar-cult once diffused over much of the central part of the peninsula. These statues can only have survived because they have continued to receive a certain veneration, or at least respect, throughout Roman and then Christian times.

They still do. The high-spirited Portuguese students with whom I was travelling executed an impromptu war-dance round *a porca de Murça*, 'to venerate the god of our Lusitanian ancestors'. But this horse-play was not to the taste of an old lady who emerged from a house on the square behind with its Baroque Misericordia. Seeing what she interpreted as impiety, she rushed towards us with her broomstick, and quite literally laid about her until our sacrilegious behaviour had ceased!

A little earlier we had gone a few miles out of our way to S. Martinho de Antas. This typically *trasmontano* hamlet is the birthplace of one of the giants of modern Portuguese literature, Miguel Torga. He still has a home there, where he spends summer holidays. A doctor by profession, he practises at Coimbra, and is married to a brilliant Belgian philologist.

Two young English graduates, studying in Portugal on Portuguese grants, told me how they called on him, hoping to elicit his sympathy for their own left-wing ideas. He was kind enough to receive them; and I was irritated beyond measure by their objection to his way of speaking to them 'as a superior', '*ex cathedra*'. How else is a man of his stature expected to address a couple of youths? And what right had they—and others like them every year from all over the world—to accept money from a government which they never cease to criticise?

What may at first seem political in Miguel Torga's own writing is simply a reaction to the inevitable harshness of life in his native province. He is not the only great literary figure to whom this has acted as a stimulant. Camilo Castelo Branco was brought up at Vilarinho de Samardã, eight miles north of Vila Real. And the prolific and best-selling Ferreira de Castro, the only living Portuguese to earn his living by his pen without recourse to journalism, sited his moving *Terra Fria* at 'Padornelos', deep in the *terras frias* of the Serra de Barroso, east of Chaves.

'Padornelos' is a thin disguise for Padronales, and conditions there were unchanged when I visited this grim, granite upland hamlet. It stands in a bare landscape with all the climatic disadvantages, but none of the grandeur of true mountain scenery. Though it was the very end of April, the wind was bitter beneath a superficially bright sun.

Watching with fascination as smoke permeated through a chimney-less thatched roof, I was invited by the housewife to see inside the first-storey living-room. Climbing the stone steps leading up to it, I had no sooner crossed the threshold than I was asphyxiated. Only after some minutes did I realise that the woman herself had bent double. She thus kept her head *below* the level of the thick smoke from the wood fire in the centre of the stone floor, which eddied round until it slowly found its way out through roof and door and window.

Following her example I was then able, my eyes smarting, to look about me. In one corner stood the cooking utensils. In another the bed. And from another came a proud cackling, as one of the family hens announced that it had laid another egg!

Later one of the men of the village was kind enough to put on one of the straw capes of these 'cold lands'. It gave him the appearance of something between a scarecrow and a small hay-rick. The rain runs off the overlapping rows of straws as off a bird's feathers. Like feathers, or thatch, they also provide warmth for the shepherds on their exposed vigils. The cape was almost falling to pieces, and took sometime to find in the storeroom-cum-stable which made up the ground floor of every house. I got the impression that plastic and nylon were rapidly taking over.

Elsewhere in Trás-os-Montes, however, I saw several of the tiny thatched huts on wheels—primitive caravans—in which shepherds sleep, trundling them like wheelbarrows as they transfer their flocks to fresh pastures. And all over the province I saw the curious white *pombais*, or dovecotes, looking like miniature, sail-less windmills.

Despite—perhaps because of—the rudeness of life at Padronales, I tasted there the best of all the delicious bread I ate in Portugal. The village oven, where women were bringing their individual loaves, was at least properly sheltered, unlike some of the kiln-like bakeries in the open air I have come across in warmer climates.

In some memorable lines of *Terra Fria* Ferreira de Castro describes the appearance from the village of the local 'capital', Montalegre, a remote township on the upper Cávado:

'In the hours of darkness, when only the wind howled, Montalegre, there far away, might seem a paradise. It consisted of half a dozen tiled houses, and the rest thatched, dirty, as wretched as those of the village. The castle alone with its noble silhouette, gave it, during daytime, a certain air of dignity. But, by night, the peopled eminence was lit up by electric lamps and, seen thus from a distance, from a dark hamlet, it fascinated like some wonderful city raised on the edge of a black desert'.

Today only some 15 per cent of Montalegre's houses are still thatched. The fourteenth-century castle has been tidied up, giving it, with its four towers and central keep, an even more 'noble silhouette' than ever. But the Terras de Barroso between the Tâmega and the frontier, of which it is the centre, and which a visiting Archbishop of Braga in the sixteenth century found hardly Christian, are even today as archaic as any part of the province. The Cávado has been dammed up here, just as lower down in the Minho. But once the construction gangs and engineers depart, the hydro-electric plants operate with skeleton staffs, and life goes on as before, with a few hundred acres submerged, and fine new lakes created. A friend who recently made a prolonged exploration of the province reported that the Terras de Barroso, besides producing their wonderful race of long-horned cattle, probably hide even more living folklore than the Terra de Miranda.

It is Miranda do Douro, however, which for several reasons has caught the imagination. As the seat of a bishopric from 1545 to 1782 it has the status of a city, though the number of people living in the 'city' itself hardly exceeds fifteen hundred. The region round about has its own dialect, and an active folklore movement which has attracted international interest. And it is remote: farther from other centres, and more deprived of normal communications, than even Beira Baixa or Terras de Barroso.

I found this out when, more than a year after my visit to Padronales, I determined to see Miranda for myself. My motor caravan had developed clutch trouble near Torre de Moncorvo, a pleasant little town with a Renaissance church and an unlikely industry of sugared almonds. A small but vital part had to be sent for from Oporto. It was the end of May, and a sudden heatwave had transformed the Douro valley and anywhere near it into a furnace. At last I understood why Trás-os-Montes has its *terras quentes*, its 'hotlands', as well as its *terras frias*. A journey over the *trasmontano* plateau to Miranda would get me out of the oven of Moncorvo, besides showing me the only corner of Portugal I had not yet visited.

A narrow-gauge railway runs from Pocinho on the Douro, through Moncorvo, to Duas Igrejas. But this is six miles short of Miranda, which it is supposed to serve. A friend I had made in Moncorvo was sure that I could get a lift all the way.

'And if you do have any trouble, here's my card for the *guarda nacional* at Carviçais, an old friend of mine. It's the first village on your road out, and he's quite capable of stopping a car and asking them if they'd mind giving you a lift.'

The Unilever representative for Trás-os-Montes took me as far as Carviçais, where he had some detergents to deliver. But the village policeman to whom I presented my card looked glum.

'There simply isn't much traffic,' he said, staring at the empty road. 'It's true that if there was anyone going all the way, I'd be the one who could help you. I was born at Sendim in the Terra de Miranda, and as a boy I was proud to dance as a *pauliteiro*. Yes, I speak *mirandés*', he replied in answer to a question of mine. A car came into view in the distance, even before we could hear the noise of its engine, carried away by the wind over the empty cornfields. 'That's a contractor who's only going as far as Mogadouro.'

There was another sound behind us as a diesel car pulled into the station of the narrow-gauge railway which here ran parallel to the road. Thanking the *guarda*, I ran to catch it.

This remotest branch of the *Caminhos de Ferro Portugueses* was as clean and efficient as the rest of the network. And even more courteous! The driver and ticket collector were delighted to find a foreigner amongst their few passengers. Presently they invited me to occupy the well-upholstered bench right at the front, reserved for first-class passengers, of whom none were travelling.

From the panoramic view thus afforded I was able to take in all the points of interest they indicated on their lonely run: the distant roofs of villages miles from the stations which bore their name: a glimpse of bare Spanish *sierra* when the line curved momentarily towards the Douro valley. Clearest in my memory is the country cleft by the narrow tracks: here brown, here gold with ripening corn, here blue with clover: sometimes flat, more often gently swelling, and once broken by the curious Cimos de Mogadouro, low hills crowned by rocky serrations, like the exposed backs of fossil dinosaurs.

The only passenger still aboard when we drew up at the terminus at Duas Igrejas, I emerged into silence and solitude. No bus for Miranda. No sign of life, although it is Duas Igrejas, thanks to the enthusiasm of its parish priest, which is the real centre of *mirandés* folklore. Thankfully I accepted a lift from a lorry which rumbled through the noonday silence past the older of the 'two churches'.

As other travellers, writers amongst them, have discovered, there is very little to see at Miranda when they finally get there. But we shall go on doing it just the same. Nor shall we regret our pilgrimage when we at last emerge before the Renaissance cathedral, built like those of Leiria and Portalegre by John III in the mid-sixteenth century. Within is some good woodwork, and

29. Romanesque doorway
of Bravães church
(Minho)

30 The castle of
Guimarães (Minho),
birthplace of the first
king of Portugal

31. *Espigueiro* for drying maize out of reach of rats and mice (Minho)

32. Bragança

a statue of the Christ child particularly loved by the *mirandeses*, in the clothes of about 1820, including a little top hat. The terrace outside is built directly over the gorge which holds the Douro and marks the frontier.

That frontier accounted for Miranda's past importance, and for its castle, whose ruins have never been repaired since it blew up in 1762, during Portugal's brief involvement in Britain's Seven Years War. Today the land across the Douro is less menacing. Recent excellent relations with the *pais vizinho* have allowed the joint construction of three dams on the seventy miles of the river which the two countries share. The highest, directly beneath Miranda, is in full view both from the cathedral terrace and from the *pousada* of S. Catarina, which offers civilised hospitality in an unlikely setting, as did the *paradores* of the unvisited Spain of only twenty years ago.

This dam, already providing electricity, may soon bring to Portugal's remotest region some of the twenty million tourists who now enter Spain each year. For it also acts as a bridge; and once the Spanish authorities have connected this to their own highway system, a frontier post can be set up and the invasion can begin.

In ending the Terra de Miranda's isolation, will it also destroy its individuality? In the case of Miranda itself, most certainly. It is no more than a large village. The decaying old houses of the Rua da Costavelha will soon be tarted up to serve as *boutiques* or restaurants, no doubt with sales girls in *mirandés* costume, and waiters attired as *pauliteiros*.

But then the Terra de Miranda is always a little doubtful about the cultural loyalty of Miranda itself. The *mirandés* dialect is rarely heard in the 'capital' from which it takes its name, and owes its preservation to the dozen surrounding parishes where it is still in daily use. It is the nearest surviving descendant of Leonese, the tongue of the old kingdom of Leon, from which the county of Portugal separated itself under Afonso Henriques. By one of those quirks of which history is so fond, it has died out in its homeland across the frontier.

I was able to visit some of these *mirandés* villages on my return journey. For little though there may be to see in Miranda, it took me more than the couple of hours that were all I could have allowed myself had I caught the last train back from Duas Igrejas at three in the afternoon. This time I had either to hitch-hike—or sleep by the roadside. It took me five lifts and five hours to cover the sixty miles to Torre de Moncorvo.

But at least I saw Sendim and Travanca, as the commercial traveller who had taken pity on me stopped to do business there. I noticed the same absence of younger men as everywhere else in Trás-os-Montes. I heard the same stories of large-scale emigration. And I remembered how the *pauliteiros*, whom I had been lucky enough to see dancing at a festival in Lisbon a month earlier, had mainly consisted of old men and boys.

My benefactor was proceeding to Alfândega da Fé, and dropped me off at Mogadouro. This is one of the remote towns always mentioned in accounts of the unwillingly-converted Jews, the 'new Christians', who were exiled to distant corners of the Beiras and Trás-os-Montes during the sixteenth century. In these secluded localities, away from the direct eye of the Inquisition, they were able to maintain a clandestine observance of their rites. Their communities are said to have appointed an officer whose secret and grim duty it was to suffocate the dying before the Christian priest had time to arrive with the detested last sacraments.

A quarter of a century ago a researcher (a Jewish friend assured me that it was the same man who rediscovered the synagogue at Tomar and made it a museum of Portuguese Jewry) found Jewish rites still being practised in remote areas by descendants of 'new Christians' who had lost all memory of their significance. I was, naturally, anxious to learn more of these fascinating survivals, and perhaps even to waylay some last 'new Christian' in his hidden lair. The reader may remember that the retired major who showed me round Pinhel (Chapter 6) believed he could identify several such. But he was an imaginative man. The answers I was given in the main café of Mogadouro were more down-to-earth.

The most I could learn was that there were various people '*de raça judaica'*. Two of these, a journalist and an officer, had publicly declared themselves as such. But there was no survival of rites of which anyone knew anything. An Israeli writer, evidently acting on the same reports as myself, had been in Mogadouro a year or two earlier, and had been unable to trace any such relics.

There was more Jewish blood, I was assured, in outlying hamlets such as Fornos, Lagoaça, and Vilarinho dos Galegos, than in Mogadouro itself. But my informants were vague, and I suspect that the *novos cristãos* of Vilarinho dos Galegos would fade into thin air once I got there. One man pointed out a garden wall in what seemed like a more recently-built corner of the little town.

'They used to say that that wall cut off the Jews from the Gentiles,' he said with a laugh, as if the phrase had always been more of a joke than a reality. And there I had to leave Gentiles and Jews alike on their windy upland, if I were ever to get a lift back to the *terras quentes* of Torre de Moncorvo, and the comfort of my motor caravan.

The Terra de Miranda is not the only area of Trás-os-Montes where the ancient Leonese speech has survived. A rather less pure variety still clings to life in the two small villages of Guadramil and Rio de Onor, right on the frontier fifteen miles north of Bragança. Rio de Onor, indeed, is quite literally on the frontier, for a third of its fifty-odd houses lie across the Rio de Onor stream, and over in Spain.

It was interesting to note that this 'Spanish village' had electric light to illuminate the muddy tracks between its houses, whereas the 'Portuguese village', though without this amenity, had well-paved streets. The national temperaments of the two neighbour lands are well reflected in this their order of priorities.

The street paving did not extend, however, to the track connecting the village with Bragança. The bus which was carrying our party therefore stopped at a hamlet short of our destination. After admiring a winepress whose corkscrew mechanism was carved in walnut, and the still universal wooden carts with solid wooden wheels on wooden axles—the screech of their movement is a characteristic sound of Trás-os-Montes and the remoter Minho—we covered the last six miles to Rio de Onor on foot.

I was lucky enough to be accompanying one of the noblest figures in the Portuguese academic world, Professor Lindley Cintra. His studies in dialectology had brought him here on earlier occasions, and the village was out in force to welcome him as a friend. Together villagers and visitors gathered in the church for a mass, taken by the young priest who had accompanied us out from Bragança. I was amused when he chided the inhabitants for 'not singing the hymn to Our Lady of Fátima with as much enthusiasm as the last time when this gentleman visited you'.

We had our picnic lunch beside the Rio de Onor river, stretched on the green *lameiros* (from *lama*, mud), the water meadows which are the village's richest pasture. These are held in common, and administered by two officers elected annually by everyone owning five or more head of cattle. This mild traditional co-operative was the nearest I could find anywhere to the 'communal farming' of Trás-os-Montes about which there is a lot of vague talk and writing. As with the secret Jewish rites, the reality is often less exciting than the legend.

We then repaired to the kitchen-cum-living-room of one of the few houses of any size, where a robust eighty-year-old had made himself available for an *inquérito dialectal*. I never ceased to marvel at the polite yet scientific way Professor Cintra conducted these inquiries. Chatting as man to man with often illiterate peasants and their womenfolk, he succeeded by gentle indirect questions in getting them to pronounce the word he wanted to hear, without ever uttering it himself.

'What is the thing by which the oxen are attached to the yoke?'

'And what other animals do you use to work the land besides the oxen?'

He was thus able to record, on tape, and on paper in those queer hieroglyphs employed by philologists, their exact pronunciation without their being tempted to imitate his own. This was all the more essential because we were dealing in nuances. Thus the Portuguese word for sheep is *ovelha*. The Spanish is *oveja*. The Leonese of Rio de Onor is some subtle compromise between the two.

Our veteran could distinguish all three perfectly. His pronunciation seemed unaffected by the eight years he had spent as a young man in Cuba and Argentine, before returning to Rio de Onor to marry a local girl and raise a family of ten. The artificiality of frontiers in such places was brought home to me by the fact that he had then sailed from Vigo, with a group organised at the Spanish town of Puebla de Sanabria.

But his mother tongue is probably doomed. For only two of his ten children have elected to remain in the village. And as we began our homeward walk he approached Professor Cintra, cap in hand, at the head of a little delegation.

'We wonder, Professor, if you would be good enough to speak to the authorities about the need to surface our road.'

For the road soon ends isolation, enabling local cultures to be swallowed by the admass. We had a good example of this the following day. Professor Cintra had several connexions with northern Trás-os-Montes. There he had carried out the research for his own doctoral thesis. There one of his English uncles (hence the 'Lindley' in his name) had crashed in the first aeroplane in the province, on his way to visit his private mine. But villages existed which even he had never yet managed to visit. After making some inquiries at Vinhais he got back into the bus with considerable excitement.

'There's a village right on the frontier which has only just had its road made up. My friends believe that with luck we may find all sorts of survivals there.'

We did. The village, cut off from the rest of Portugal by the Mount Coroa (4,300 feet), was called Moimenta. The frontier here was no longer with Leon, but with Galicia. It was *gallego* vocabulary which therefore influenced the local speech, and Galician customs which permeated the local folklore.

We began with the usual linguistic research which was our excuse for being there. Following a telephone call from Vinhais, the priest and schoolmaster had assembled in the village school a stalwart ancient and three toothless but highly entertained—and entertaining—old ladies. These squatted on the teacher's raised platform, fascinated by the tape-recorders, and by the interest being taken in the words they used to describe the time-honoured instruments of unmechanised agricultural and domestic life. Behind them stared down the out-of-date portraits of a youthful Salazar, and of President Carmona, who had died eighteen years before.

When this work was over we explored the village. Down beyond the primitive carts and cottages was a surprisingly grand little eighteenth-century church, with a couple of good carved wooden altars, and a valuable medieval saint in stone, kept by the priest under lock and key in the sacristy. In three of the cottages looms were at work, making cloth purely for local needs. To these the people owed the rugs for their beds, the material for their coats and jackets, the sacks for their grain, and all those bags and tapes required by pack animals (before the new road!).

But today the external market had arrived on their doorstep, for folkweave has a fascination for me. A long sack, striped in red, white and black, and woven in a hard-wearing mixture of linen, cotton and wool, supports my back as I write. Stuffed with particles of rubber foam, it serves equally as bolster or as rug-cum-mattress as I picnic or sunbathe, reminding me whether in Scotland or the Sahara of my visit to Moimenta.

My most abiding memory of that visit, however, may endure even longer than that closely-woven cloth. Professor Cintra had issued an appeal for anyone who knew local songs, dances or music to come forward; and a group of middle-aged and elderly people awaited us as we re-emerged on the large dusty space at the top of the village.

Pre-eminent amongst them was the only *gaita*-player left in the district. This instrument, a form of bagpipes still common in Galicia, reappears in the Terra de Miranda, where along with the *tamboril* it accompanies the *pauliteiros*. Presently he was joined by a woman with a *tamboril* or tambourine, made like the *gaita* entirely in the village and of local materials: well-seasoned wood, skilfully-carved horn, long-cured leather and tightly-stretched skin. To their accompaniment we heard a number of songs, and watched an ancient dance kindly performed for our benefit by a middle-aged couple.

But the song which provides my abiding memory was unaccompanied. Putting aside his bagpipes, the *gaiteiro* joined with a lean, archetypal farmworker in a haunting duet. It was called *O lavrador*, and this word, meaning 'the labourer', was repeated again and again both as refrain and theme. It seemed at once to be inspired by and to echo the bare brown hills a couple of miles away which surrounded us on three sides, forming the frontier with Spain. There is a word, *outeiro*, a poor upland pasture, exactly describing them, and often found as a place-name in Trás-os-Montes.

At first I felt that the song was infinitely sad, heavy with the sorrow of unending toil. But then I detected an even deeper note. For there are certain tasks which, once begun, can have no ending. It was in such marshlands as this that centuries even before *o rei lavrador*, King Dennis, simple labourers began the unending task of building Portugal.

Appendix 1

PLANNING A VISIT

Portugal's efficient and helpful State Tourist Office publishes each quarter a *Tourist Guide to Portugal* in English, French, German, Portuguese and Spanish, which is a *tour de force*. Its twenty-eight pages include a gazetteer, maps of the whole country and of the Lisbon region, plans of Lisbon and Oporto, details of coming events, opening times of museums, addresses of theatres, cinemas, banks, travel agencies, embassies, shipping lines, restaurants. There are even full details of postal charges, and a page and a half explaining how to 'say it in Portuguese'. Every three months the details are brought up to date, and the coloured pictures on the cover are changed. And it is free.

Though the Office issues several other publications, this is the essential tool for anyone planning a visit. Its headquarters are at Palácio Foz, Restauradores, Lisbon 2. But it has branches round the world: that in London is the Casa de Portugal, 20 Lower Regent Street, S.W.1.

In a generous spirit, this often has available information on package tours organised by private operators. And naturally it also has full details of the regular services:

1. By air to the three international airports of Oporto, Lisbon and Faro.
2. By sea. The various passenger services which call at Lisbon have recently been joined by two useful and inexpensive car ferry companies. Remember, too, that Spanish services to Galicia (such as the Compañia Trasatlantica Española from Southampton) offer a convenient route to northern Portugal.
3. By rail. Though tiring, and not cheap, this remains an experience in itself.

Although Portugal lies at the end of Europe, it is where the rest of the world begins, as the discoverers were aware. So if your holiday is of a month or more, or if you are planning a world tour, why not fit Portugal into your schedule? Few world capitals are better served than Lisbon by communications in all directions. And if your timetable is upset by one of those unforeseen contingencies which we are liable to meet anywhere, what a pleasant city to be delayed in!

Appendix 2
SLEEPING AND EATING

Both functions are easier to perform than in the *pais vizinho*. Portugal is a quieter country than Spain: perhaps *saudade* has something to do with it. But there is no melancholy about Portuguese cooking, although it is nearer to international norms of palatability than Spanish. If I had to compare it to some other cuisine, I would choose Belgian, allowance being made of course for less cows, plenty of olives, and the immense contribution of the sea.

Like France, Portugal is a country where it pays, in both cost and quality, to take the fixed price meal at a restaurant and the full pension rate at an hotel. In Italy, and nowadays all too often in Spain, the *pranzo prezzo fisso* or the *minuta turística* offered merely to conform to official regulations, consists of unattractive dishes in minimal quantities. Not in Portugal: if you do decide to forego the discount which goes with *pensão completa*, it will be because you find one main meal a day sufficient.

There *are* official regulations governing Portuguese hotels, and official prices, too, which I have never known exceeded. These can be found in the official pamphlet *Hotel Establishments in Portugal*, distributed by the State Tourist Office and its branches abroad. For convenience it is also available separately for the five zones of Lisbon and district; North; Centre; South; and Açores-Madeira.

This covers all hotels, *pousadas*, *estalagens*, and all except the very smallest pensions. All 'possess the essential amenities, and are capable of meeting—generally speaking and according to their category—the requirements of the guests for whom they are intended'. In other words, you get what you pay for.

And there I propose to leave the matter, without giving any prices, which can so soon be out of date. Still less do I intend to recommend individual hotels. Managements can change overnight, and tastes in hotels are as subjective as tastes in clothes or cars. What I can say from experience—for I have visited and eaten at hotels all over the country, though I rarely slept away from my motor caravan—is that the visitor is invariably sure of value for money.

I do not except from this statement the 3·1 per cent tourist tax he may find added to his bill. It is little fiscal devices of this kind which have balanced the budget, maintained the real value of the escudo, and given Portugal the order and stability which are amongst her greatest attractions.

Q

Appendix 3

SETTLING

❦

These attractions of order and stability are more important still for anyone thinking of joining the growing number of those in recent years
who have settled in Portugal. They are attractions likely to appeal most
to the middle-aged and the middle-class; and these are indeed the
predominant characteristics of British immigrants, who are often
deliberately seeking an alternative to the *discothèques* and fish-and-chips
of the Spanish *costas*.

In preferring Portugal these are generally accepting a rather higher
cost of living. It is possible, by eating local dishes, buying one's wine
straight from the *adega*, and finding a home off the beaten track, to
exist as cheaply in Portugal as anywhere in the world. But such
accessories of middle-class life as spirits, imported foods or toiletries,
and foreign magazines, are not cheap. And petrol is decidedly expensive.

Nor is middle-class housing in the bargain basement. This is because
government policy deliberately encourages quality development. None
of your £1,200 flats here! But as with everything in Portugal, the
purchaser can expect value for his money.

Some of the more far-sighted middle-class immigrants have calculated that the extra money they spend to live, and to buy their homes,
will be more than made up by the tax saving on their middle-class U.K.
incomes. Pronouncements on this subject are dangerous, and anyone
really contemplating a move should take specialist advice. But the
broad position is that Portugal, which like many other countries in
practice made little attempt to tax foreign nationals resident there,
recently signed a Double Taxation Agreement with the United Kingdom.

Although residents from the U.K. will now become liable to a pro-
gressive Portuguese tax called the *Imposta Complementar*, the overall
working of the Agreement seems likely to leave most of them sub-
stantially better off. U.K. dividends, formerly subject to full U.K.
income tax and surtax, will now pay only a round 15 per cent 'with-
holding tax' to the British Treasury. Only the 85 per cent balance will
be assessed for the *Imposta Complementar*. Considerable personal
allowances can be deducted before this becomes payable, for example:
60,000 escudos for a husband, 20,000 for a wife.

Even after these deductions, it is understood that under Article 22 (3) of the Agreement, the resident is allowed relief in terms of tax to the full extent of the doubly taxed income. As a result a married man with one child, and an unearned income of £3,000 from U.K. dividends, who in Britain would pay an effective rate of about 35 per cent, or some £1,050, will under the Agreement pay an effective rate of only 15 per cent, or about £450.

Appendix 4

MAPS

ᘒᘤᘣ

There is no point in looking beyond Michelin 37: Portugal 1/500,000, or 1 centimetre to 5 kilometres. This is available at 15 escudos all over Portugal, and can be acquired fractionally cheaper in France.

Appendix 5

O ESPAÇO PORTUGUÊS

ᘒᘤᘣ

Continental Portugal (88,829 square kilometres: 8½ million inhabitants) with the 'adjacent islands' of Madeira (Portuguese since 1419: 795 square kilometres: 300,000 inhabitants) and the Azores (Portuguese since 1445: 2,305 square kilometres: 340,000 inhabitants) is the centre of the only state on which the sun never sets. Its overseas provinces consist of:

Cabo Verde, an archipelago of ten islands off West Africa (Portuguese since 1460: 4,033 square kilometres: 200,000 inhabitants).

Guiné, a plain between Senegal and Guinea, with an offshore archipelago (Portuguese since 1446: 36,125 square kilometres: 520,000 inhabitants).

S. Tomé and Principe, islands in the Gulf of Guinea (Portuguese since 1470: 964 square kilometres: 65,000 inhabitants).

Angola, in south-west Africa (Portuguese since 1485: 1,246,700 square kilometres: 5 million inhabitants).

Moçambique, in south-east Africa (Portuguese since 1498: 783,000 square kilometres: 6¼ million inhabitants).

India, three pockets of territory on the west coast of the sub-continent, occupied by the Indian Republic since 1961 (Portuguese since 1509: 4,000 square kilometres; 625,000 inhabitants).

Macau, a peninsula and two islands off the coast of China (Portuguese since 1557: 15 square kilometres: 250,000 inhabitants).

Timor, the eastern half of an island in the south of the East Indies (Portuguese since the sixteenth century: 18,989 square kilometres: 520,000 inhabitants).

Appendix 6
REIGNS AND DATES

The very few books about the history of Portugal may not be easily available to the reader. And even they may not always give the names and dates of the kings and queens of Portugal, who although so little known abroad, played an even more preponderant role in their country's life than the monarchs of Spain or of England. So here they are, set against a few events mentioned in the text:

FIRST OR BURGUNDIAN DYNASTY

Henry of Burgundy, Count of Portugal (1095–1112).

Afonso I Henriques (1112–85), took over rule from his mother 1128, declared himself King of Portugal 1139, was recognised by Leon 1143, captured Lisbon 1147.

Sancho I (1185-1211), occupied but soon lost western Algarve (1189-91).

Afonso II (1211–23).

Sancho II (1223–48), deposed for not ruling strongly enough.

Afonso III (1248–1279), finally conquered Algarve 1249.

Dennis (1279–1325), married St. Isabel, consolidated frontier which has never changed since, built castles, founded Coimbra University. His reign was a golden age of medieval Portugal.

Afonso IV (1325–57).

Pedro I (1357–67), lover of Inés de Castro.

Fernando (1367–83), weak and under influence of his wife, Leonor Teles, who succeeded him as regent (1383–85) for their young daughter, married to the King of Castile to whom Leonor planned to hand the country over.

DYNASTY OF AVIS

John I (1385–1433), an illegitimate son of Pedro I, thwarted these plans, leading a popular uprising, defeating Castile at Aljubarrota in 1385, signing an alliance with England in 1386, and marrying Philippa of Lancaster in 1387. Their sons in 1415 captured Ceuta, first move in Portuguese overseas expansion and discoveries presided over by the third son, Prince Henry the Navigator until his death in 1460. Meanwhile there reigned

Edward (1433–38) his brother, and

Afonso V (1438–81) his nephew, who was more interested in campaigns in Morocco than in further discoveries, although these were now paying for themselves with the gold from Guinea. However,

John II (1481–95), a brilliant ruler, encouraged the explorers, with the result that his cousin

Manuel I, 'the Fortunate' (1495–1521), reaped the harvest which followed Vasco da Gama's opening of the sea route to India in 1498. This was the golden age of the second dynasty, symbolised by the elaborate late Gothic style called Manueline.

John III (1521–57) faced the severe problems of sudden empire by maintaining a prudent neutrality, but

Sebastian (1557–78), returning to the chimera of conquering Morocco, was killed there with most of his army.

Henry, the King-Cardinal (1578–80), his aged uncle, favoured as his successor Philip of Spain.

SPANISH DYNASTY

Philip I (II of Spain) (1580–98), had an excellent claim, and in any case the bereaved country was in no state to resist him. It remained a distinct kingdom, but was drawn into Spain's overseas wars. That with Holland was the most serious, leading to the loss of much of the overseas empire under

Philip II (III of Spain) (1598–1621) and

Philip III (IV of Spain) (1621–40).

DYNASTY OF BRAGANÇA

John IV (1640–56), head of the wealthiest family in the kingdom, was descended both from an illegitimate son of John I, and from a grand-daughter of Manuel I, and was the natural choice when Spanish attempts to raise taxes and reduce autonomy provoked a national rising. But the war of independence which continued until 1668 left Portugal bankrupt.

Afonso VI (1656–83) was mentally unstable, and

Pedro II (1683–1706) was *de facto* ruler from 1667. The disastrous economic situation only improved with the arrival of the first gold from Brazil in 1697, but it then improved very quickly, so that

John V (1706–50) presided over yet another, and literally golden age. His physical incapacity from 1742 led to a breakdown in government, which was repaired when

Joseph (1750–77) handed over executive power to the high-handed Marquis of Pombal. The gold of Brazil, still arriving in sufficient quantities to rebuild Lisbon after the 1755 earthquake, was diminishing before the end of the reign: this explains why Pombal encouraged cotton to take its place, why he left the treasury empty, and why the reign of

Maria I (whose consort was Pedro III) (1777–1816) proceeded less ostentatiously. Its most dramatic moments occurred after she had fallen victim to religious mania in 1792: the French invasion, the departure of the royal family and government to Rio de Janeiro in 1807, and the subsequent victories of Anglo-Portuguese arms right across the Peninsula and in France itself.

John VI (1816–26), who had been Regent ever since 1792, only returned from Rio in 1821. The U.D.I. by Brazil the following year dealt the economy a blow which was exaggerated by the effects of the civil war between

Pedro IV (who reigned briefly *in absentia* in 1826) and his brother

Miguel (1827–34), an absolutist supported by the old nobility, who unhappily were removed from political life with the triumph of liberalism represented by Pedro IV's daughter

Maria II (1834–53), whose accession was marked by the suppression of the religious orders.

Pedro V (1853–61), a Saxe-Coburg through his father, had at least as many qualities as Victoria's Prince Albert. His early death is still grieved at, for his brother

Luis (1861–89) had neither the training nor the enthusiasm for kingship, making no attempt to guide a parliamentary system which failed to represent large sections of the nation, and which carried out a superficial modernisation only by means of ruinous foreign loans.

Carlos (1889–1908) had to face the 1890 British ultimatum demanding evacuation of central African territories which might have linked Angola and Moçambique, and the subsequent rise of the Republican party. Unable to call on the alienated nobility, he showed more energy than his father, but in attempting to install a non-Parliamentary government provoked his own assassination.

Manuel II (1908–10) was unthroned by a revolt of part of the armed services, leading to the establishment of

THE REPUBLIC

Nineteenth-century habits of parliamentary ineffectiveness could not be unlearned overnight, and to all the other problems of the new régime were added those of participation in the First World War (in Africa throughout: in Europe from 1916). The unparliamentary but effective Sidónio Pais, had he not been assassinated a month after victory, might well have played the Cromwellian role which fell to Carmona in 1926. As President, this Marshal was happier in his search for civilian co-operators than the great Protector. Salazar, appointed Minister of Finance in 1928, at once balanced the budget, and a year after he became President of the Council (premier) in 1932 set up the constitutional machinery of the corporative New State. This has survived the strains set up by the Spanish Civil War, by the Second World War, by the death of Carmona in 1951, by the Indian aggression and African terrorism of 1961, and by the incapacitation of Salazar himself in 1968 which preceded his death in 1970. Under his successor, Marcello Caetano—the first legal brain in the country as Salazar was the first financial brain—government has become less austere and more accessible, whilst losing none of its efficiency.

BIBLIOGRAPHY

❦

As indicated under 'Foreword and Acknowledgements', there exists a considerable literature on Portugal in English: so considerable that I hesitated before daring to add to it. The following highly selective list limits itself mainly to those works actually mentioned in the text.

The invaluable *Guide Bleu, Portugal, Madère-Açores* (Hachette, 1968), with a hundred preliminary pages of informative essays on geography, history, art and so on, has an English edition.

The standby of 'The Selective Traveller in Portugal' has been the discerning and exhaustive book of that title by Ann Bridge and Susan Lowndes ever since its first publication by Chatto and Windus in 1949. It has been many times reprinted, and revised as recently as 1967.

The more recent writing partnership of David Wright and Patrick Swift has preferred to concentrate on specific regions. Their *Algarve* (Barrie and Rockliff, 1965) brings to life a province whose charm it is far from easy to pin down in words. They achieve this feat by focusing on it from their two distinct angles: that of a visiting poet reacting to an unfamiliar Portugal, and that of a resident artist who not only speaks the language and knows the people, but captures them and their background in exquisite line drawings which accompany the text. In *Minho and North Portugal* (Barrie and Rockliff, 1968) they apply the same technique to a wider region.

Sacheverell Sitwell's *Portugal and Madeira* (Batsford, 1954), although not the most successful of his travel books, gives insights into Portuguese art and architecture which only his immense experience and range of reference could have made available.

Franz Villier has given a brilliant but in some respects a biased portrait in *Portugal* (Vista Books, 1963). His personal bias is the more regrettable because the author knows the country and every aspect of its culture extremely well, and because his book has lost nothing of its readability in translation from the French.

The poet Roy Campbell offered in *Portugal* (Reinhardt, 1957) an

240

enthusiastic celebration of the land where he retired to farm, and where he died in a tragic motor accident.

Portugal, a Book of Folk Ways (C.U.P., 1936) by Rodney Gallop is rather awkwardly-arranged, but is a beautifully written survey of Portuguese folklore, the first work of its kind by a foreigner. He wrote it while attached to the British Embassy in Lisbon forty years ago, and was able to draw on living traditions still undisturbed by the internal combustion engine and emigration.

Besides *I gathered no moss* John Gibbons wrote *Afoot in Portuga* (George Newnes, 1931).

What he achieved for the upper Douro was done for *The hills of Alentejo* by Huldine Beamish (Bles, 1958), who also left in *Cavaliers of Portugal* (Bles, 1966) an account of Portuguese bull fighting.

For history, J. B. Trend's *Portugal* (Benn, 1957) is a brilliant, stimulating, but selective essay, with a fascinating chapter on the language such as we might expect from the former Professor of Spanish at Cambridge.

The more monotonous task of solidly covering the ground, century by century and reign by reign, has been most un-monotonously accomplished by Harold V. Livermore in *A New History of Portugal* (C.U.P., 1966), which takes the story up to 1961.

Rose Macaulay impressed history, humour, original research, and her rare gift for fine writing into the creation of *They Went to Portugal* (Jonathan Cape, 1946): studies of a kaleidoscope of British visitors from the crusaders, who helped take Lisbon, up to recent times.

INDEX

Baroque in Portugal, 35–6, 49,
63–4, 130–1, 133, 174, 183–4,
219 and *passim*, Plates 24, 25
Barrancos, 129
Barroso, Serra de, 216, 221–3
Batalha, 19, 71–4, Plates 12, 13
Beamish, Huldine, 111, 241
Beira Alta, 132, 137–44, 166
Beira Baixa, 132–7, 144–5, 216, 223
Beira, Cova da, 135, 216
Beira Litoral, 139, 161–7
Beja, 92, 102–3
Belém, 35, 44, 48–51, 84
Belém, tower of, 27, 50–1, 94,
Plate 2
Belmonte, 144–5
Berlenga Islets, 75, Plate 15
Bocage, poet, 97
Bom Jesus, sanctuary, 30, 196–7
Borba, 68, 108
Borges de Macedo, Professor, 15,
65, 67
Bouro, 198
Boytac, Manueline architect, 49,
97, 116–17, 138
Braga, 51, 192–9, 206
Braga, rite of, 195
Braga, Teófilo, 38, 159
Bragança, 34, 66, 79, 181, 219–20
227–8, Plate 32
Bragança, Dukes of, 47, 66–70,
83, 104, 177, 201–3, 219
Brandão, Raoul, 69
Bravães, 205, 209, Plate 29
Brazil and Portugal, 23, 32, 43,
66, 87, 144–9, 211, 214, 238
Brejoeira, 209
Briteiros, 199–200
British in Portugal, 42–3, 54, 55,
72, 81, 88–91, 92, 101, 124, 138,
142, 166–8, 175, 177, 187–9,
207, 241
broa, 182, 208
Buçaco, 54, 60, 115, 165–7
Bull fighting in Portugal, 88–9,
241

Cabo da Roca, 24, 57–8, 95

Cabora Bassa, 214
Cabo Verde Islands, 21, 145, 235
Cacilhas, 94
Caetano, Dr. Marcello, 98, 100–1,
159, 239
Caia, river, 108–10
Caldas da Rainha, 76–7
Caldeirão, Serra do, 120, 125
Calhariz, 95
Caminha, 208–10
Camoens (Luís de Camões), 17,
20, 40–1, 49, 51, 64, 72, 73, 84,
97, 146, 155, 161, 185, 211
Campo Maior, 109, 115
Caramulo, Serra do, 142–3
Carcavelos, 55, 90
Carlos I, King, 69–70, 238
Carmona, Marshal, 38, 230, 239
Cartaxo wines, 83, 88
Carvoeiro, 126
Cascais, 55–7, 90
Castelo Branco, 133
Castelo Branco, Camilo, 114, 141-
2, 197, 221
Castelo de Bode, 85, 135
Castelo de Vide, 111
Castelo Rodrigo, 140
Castilho, João de, 83, 84, 178
Castro Daire, 141–2
Castro de Avelãs, 219
Castro, Ferreira de, 221–2
Castro Marim, 122
Catherine of Bragança, 66–8, 88,
106
Cávado, river, 197–9, 203, 204,
222
Celorico da Beira, 139
Cete, 179
Ceuta, 72–3, 121, 173 fn, 237
Ceylon and Portugal, 21
Chantarène, Nicolas, 48, 60, 104,
105, 106, 154, 158, 162, 168, 194
Chaves, 183, 209, 218–19
Cintra, Professor Lindley, 15,
228–30
citânias, 49, 178–9, 199–200, 202,
204, 207
Côa, river, 139, 140